AMERICAN
SET DESIGN 2

AMERICAN SET DESIGN 2

Ronn Smith

Introduction by Ming Cho Lee

THEATRE COMMUNICATIONS GROUP

NEW YORK 1991

Copyright © 1991 by Ronn Smith
Introduction Copyright © 1991 by Ming Cho Lee

American Set Design 2 is published by Theatre Communications Group, Inc., 355 Lexington Ave., New York, NY 10017.

Design and composition by The Sarabande Press

TCG gratefully acknowledges public funds from the National Endowment for the Arts and the New York State Council on the Arts in addition to the generous support of the following foundations and corporations: Alcoa Foundation; Ameritech Foundation; ARCO Foundation; AT&T Foundation; Citibank; ConAgra Charitable Foundation; Consolidated Edison Company of New York; Nathan Cummings Foundation; Dayton Hudson Foundation; Exxon Corporation; Ford Foundation; James Irvine Foundation; Jerome Foundation; Andrew W. Mellon Foundation; Metropolitan Life Foundation; National Broadcasting Company; Pew Charitable Trusts; Philip Morris Companies; Scherman Foundation; Shell Oil Company Foundation; Shubert Foundation.

Front cover: Set for *Nixon in China* by Adrianne Lobel, photo copyright © 1991 by Henry Groskinsky.
Back cover: Model for *Sunday in the Park with George* by Tony Straiges.

Smith, Ronn.
American set design 2 / Ronn Smith; foreword by Ming Cho Lee.
Continues: American set design / Arnold Aronson.
ISBN 1-55936-017-8 (cloth) ISBN 1-55936-018-6 (pbk.)
1. Set designers—United States—Interviews. 2. Theaters—Stage-setting and scenery.
I. Title.
PN2096.A1S65   1991
792′.025′092273—dc20   91–4413
                                                              CIP

Manufactured in the United States of America
Second Printing, December 1995

The photographs in this book are reproduced by kind permission of the following: p. 12, 173 Joan Marcus; p. 13 George de Vincent; p. 14, 102 Richard Feldman; p. 16 Jay Thompson; p. 19, 48, 59, 68, 70, 118, 148, 157, 164 Martha Swope; p. 22, 54, 55 Carol Rosegg, Martha Swope Associates; p. 26, 76, 174, 175, 180, 181, 183, 184 T. Charles Erickson; p. 35 Eugene Cook; p. 40, 41 Bruce Siddons; p. 49, 52, 56 (color section, *Satyagraha* and *Gotterdammerung*) Ron Sherl; p. 51 Santa Fe Opera Company; p. 60 The Los Angeles Music Center Opera; p. 77 Kristin V. Rehder; p. 79, 83, 84, 86, 143, 144, 152, 155 Richard Anderson; p. 81 Chris Bennion; p. 94, 98 Lyric Opera of Chicago; p. 100 William B. Carter; p. 124, 125, 127, 129, 134 The Goodman Theatre; p. 128, Jennifer Girard; p. 136 Orion Pictures; p. 138 (bottom) Bridgitt Lacombe; p. 140 Roy Round; p. 147 Ney Tair Fraser; p. 158, 168 Michael Daniel; p. 167 Mark Sadan; p. 172 Joe Giannetti; p. 177 Yale Repertory Theatre; p. 189 Clive Barda. (Color section) *The Magic Flute*, Guy Gravett; *Mr. & Mrs. Bridge*, Miki Ansin.
All uncredited photographs courtesy of the individual designers.

FOR DAVID

CONTENTS

Acknowledgments   *ix*

Preface by Ronn Smith   *xi*

Introduction by Ming Cho Lee   *xv*

LOY ARCENAS   *3*

JOHN ARNONE   *17*

DAVID GROPMAN   *33*

ROBERT ISRAEL   *49*

HEIDI LANDESMAN   *63*

HUGH LANDWEHR   *77*

ADRIANNE LOBEL   *95*

CHARLES McCLENNAHAN   *111*

MICHAEL MERRITT   *125*

TONY STRAIGES   *141*

GEORGE TSYPIN   *159*

MICHAEL YEARGAN   *175*

Chronologies   *195*

ACKNOWLEDGMENTS

Fɪʀꜱᴛ and foremost, I want to thank all of the designers who so graciously found time in their busy schedules to be interviewed. This book would have been impossible without their generous cooperation and total collaboration. I also want to express my gratitude to Theatre Communications Group (for understanding that theatre is much more than a playwright's words, a director's eye, and an actor's performance), Ming Cho Lee (for kindly agreeing to write the introduction), M. Elizabeth Osborn (my fine, fine editor), Terence Nemeth (who ushered this book through production), the many photographers and public relations people across the country (who supplied the missing pieces), and Arnold Aronson (who agreed to allow me to write this "sequel"). Thanks, too, to the following friends: John Calhoun, Stacie Chaiken, Joan Duncan, Kim Konikow, Susan Lieberman, Claudia Luebbers, Pat MacKay and *Theatre Crafts* magazine, Gwen Parker, Carol Spector and Paula Vogel. And finally, my deep appreciation to David Savran, whose support never wavered.

PREFACE

THE TWELVE set designers profiled in the following pages exhibit a fascinating diversity of backgrounds, styles and approaches to design. Their work has appeared on theatre stages throughout the world; most also design opera, dance, film, television, music videos and commercials. Although all twelve are known primarily for designing sets, they sometimes design costumes and/or lighting. Some teach; others have no interest in teaching. As Ming Cho Lee points out in his introduction, it is an eclectic group.

Deciding who should be included in this book was difficult. I wanted to focus on designers who have produced a significant body of innovative, professional work in the last five to fifteen years. (This choice means that, in general, the designers are younger than those included in Arnold Aronson's *American Set Design*, published by Theatre Communications Group in 1985.) I also felt that the selection of designers should reflect a variety of artistic sensibilities and the diversity of the American theatre. Together with Betty Osborn, my editor at TCG, we reduced the original list of approximately forty-five names to thirteen. (One designer turned down my invitation to be included in this book.)

Except for George Tsypin, each designer was interviewed once, with interviews lasting anywhere from forty-five minutes to three hours (the average was about ninety minutes). Although I followed a general sequence of questions—covering background information, working procedures, an overview of the development of the designer's career, and the designer's personal opinions about contemporary theatre and design—I usually took my lead from the designers. The value of such an approach (as opposed to asking a predetermined set of questions) can be debated, I suppose, but I find that it allows interviewees more latitude with which to present themselves and their work, and to articulate their current concerns. As a result, these interviews, when read as a single document, present a provocative picture of the 1980s—of what it was like to be a set designer and what was happening in the rapidly changing American theatre during that decade.

The interviews were edited and cut, some more than others, to eliminate redundancy and reduce them to manageable length. Every designer was offered (and accepted) the opportunity to review his/her interview after an initial editing. Their suggestions for clarifying or elaborating certain points and deleting others were carefully considered and often—although not always—accepted. In all cases I tried to preserve a sense of the movement of the conversation and the dynamism of the designer's speaking voice.

My original intention was simply to allow each designer to speak for him- or herself. Brief introductions appear before each interview, however, to provide a context for readers who are unfamiliar with the designer's work.

In his Author's Note for *American Set Design*, Arnold Aronson wrote: "Tracking down illustrations for the text only reinforced my sense that design is undervalued by most people." Unfortunately, the situation hasn't changed much. Usually taken with an eye for newspaper publication, professional production photographs tend to be focused on cast members, not the surrounding environment. When full set shots are available, they appear to have been taken with the same lighting used for the production, which seldom provides the sharp image needed for this kind of publication.

Designers, too, are notoriously careless about documenting their work. While many designers admit to being pack rats when it comes to research materials, such compulsiveness does not extend to their own creations. Since finished renderings appear to be a thing of the past, the reader will find few of them in this book. Rough sketches and finished models are easier to come by, however, and I am pleased to be able to include examples of each for most of these artists.

Still, the reader may notice that visual documentation of some important productions (either in terms of theatre history or the development of the designer) does not appear in these pages. Photographs were not to be found.

If this book is to serve any purpose other than to document the exciting work of these twelve designers, I would hope that it will encourage an increased appreciation of the enormous contribution the design team makes to a production, and that, as a result, more consideration will be given to documenting these contributions. Designers—set, costume and lighting designers—are changing the face of the American theatre in radical and startling ways. The theatre of the future will owe this generation an incalculable debt.

Ronn Smith
December 1990
Lincoln, Rhode Island

INTRODUCTION by Ming Cho Lee

When I was approached to write the introduction to a forthcoming book on current American scene designers, I accepted without a moment of hesitation. After all, six of the twelve designers in the book were my students, and most of the others are friends whose work I admire. I am a natural for the job. This introduction would also establish my continuing presence in the world of design—an opportunity not to be missed. That was five months ago. Since then I have hardly had a moment of peace. This project hangs over my head like a mosquito droning in a summer night—forever present but elusive. I wanted to write something personal, something more than just a parade of generalities and cliches. I read the manuscript over and over again, as well as prefaces and introductions written by others, trying to find a shape, a theme, a key, anything to get the project started. I thought it would be a breeze. Wrong. The difficulties I have encountered so far in writing this article almost make designing scenery a piece of cake.

Twenty years ago, the great designer-teacher Donald Oenslager, on the occasion honoring his long history of teaching—some forty years—at the Yale Drama School, spoke of the bewilderment he experienced when faced with the new art of that time. He talked about the Pop and the Op in painting, the rock musical, the Happening in theatre, the mega-multimedia concerts, the emergence of soft sculpture reflecting the rising awareness of feminism, the fracturing and deconstruction of the linear narrative form in literature and drama. For him, the language, the landscape, the esthetics of the new art seemed strange and unfamiliar. The old rules, the old process, and the existing agendas seemed no longer valid. As much as Donald tried to keep in touch with the prevailing movements, he found himself on the outside looking in. Often he felt perplexed and somewhat left out. He thought that perhaps it was indeed the right time for him to step aside and leave the world for others to challenge. Then he paused and said, "Do I hear the bell? The class is over." Thus ended this remarkable address.

Today, as I look at the stage design of the last decade, I find myself feeling very much like Donald Oenslager during the summer of 1970—perplexed, bewildered, yet with an odd sense of exhilaration. Much of the territory seems unfamiliar to me, the ground slippery and unsafe. It is not a time for anyone to be complacent. The landscape of American theatre has indeed changed since Aronson's first volume of *American Set Design* six years ago, and it is still changing. I think this is all to the good, and reason enough to have another book about those designers whose work brought about those changes and whose sensibilities inform the American theatre of today.

What is it that separates today's design from that of the immediate past? After all, many of the conditions and concerns that plagued us then persist today. It is still a struggle to break free from the bondage of narrowly written, realistic theatre. There are still too few productions of the classics. The economy of the theatre and its near-poverty-level financial compensation still make it an enormous burden to make the choice to continue working in the theatre. (In 1990 at least one major New York theatre paid a designer $1700 for what is a minimum of ten weeks' work.) Despite the 100 percent increase in the number of women over Aronson's book, and the inclusion of one African-American and one designer from the Pacific Rim, set design remains the province of the white male. And designers' isolation from each other continues—I doubt if the designers in this book know each other well, or much of each other's work.

So what is different? I think there is far more true diversity. The work which was exemplified in Aronson's book was certainly seasoned by individual differences, but it was still basically stew from the same pot. The designers whose work is shown here come from much more diverse backgrounds, drawing their inspiration from a bewildering variety of sources, references, styles, approaches, roots; it is eclecticism in the best sense of the word.

The visual imagery here is stronger and bolder. It can be unashamedly pictorial or illusionistic and still not literally representational. These are images which seem to touch the recesses of the mind: the hidden emotion, the barely aware consciousness, the dream world. These designers tend to be less bound by logical rules of esthetic formalism, or by the actuality of the text and action. Shaped by the theatre of Peter Brook, Pina Bausch, Robert Wilson, Julie Taymor, the later work of John Conklin, etc., their worlds, much like those of Magritte and Friedrich, are freed from actuality, are suggested obliquely and ambiguously. These are layered landscapes that reflect both text and subtext, in which seemingly unrelated objects coexist, and interior and exterior are not mutually exclusive.

Finally, the interviews suggest that designers are no longer the ignored, unsung heroes—picture-makers who "get in the way of the action." There seems to be a new joy in designer-director relations. We are hearing of the designer as dramaturg—the recognition of the designer as a real collaborator in formulating the approach to a production.

However, I wish that there could be more events at which designers and directors could gather for the exchange of ideas outside of a production, and that there could be more financial help so that attending them is not a burden for independent artists. There should be more books like this one so we can be better informed about what other artists are doing. These publications are the norm in England and Europe— why not here? Why not publications that include the director and the costume and lighting designers—books that center on the productions, truly showing the process of collaboration? Theatre, after all, is a collaborative art.

I hope that American theatre will regain its vitality; that our work in whatever form will be truthful, infused with passion, laughter, tears; that it will challenge the mind and the senses. I hope that going to the theatre will be a national activity for all ages, one that we cannot live without. I hope that theatre and the arts will eventually take their rightful place in this country, like elections to preserve our freedom and education to nurture our minds. Art is our connection to our past and the heritage for our future. More than an act of beautification or glorification of a cliche, it provokes, it questions, it celebrates. In joy and outrage, it is the true expression of our time. A life without art is a life unexamined, a life without meaning. A society without art is a society without a soul.

I enjoyed reading these interviews. I am amazed by how articulate and truthful these designers are. Their lives are reflected in their design, and their design responds truthfully and personally to the work. I am glad that they have committed themselves to the theatre. It's a hard life but a meaningful one. I hope they stay with it and that they continue to grow.

I wish them the best of luck.

AMERICAN SET DESIGN 2

LOY
ARCENAS

LAST YEAR, 1990, was an exceptional year for Loy Arcenas. Off-Broadway productions of *Prelude to a Kiss* (Circle Repertory Company), *Once on This Island* (Playwrights Horizons) and *Spunk* (New York Shakespeare Festival) each garnered rave reviews, and two of the productions—*Prelude to a Kiss* and *Once on This Island*—were subsequently transferred to Broadway. Suddenly, Arcenas was the hot new designer on the block.

Arcenas, however, has been designing sets in New York since 1978, when he finished La Mama's Third World Theatre Arts Studies program and started working for various Off-Off Broadway theatres. In the early 1980s Arcenas met director Norman Rene, who asked him to design the set for a new play by the then unknown playwright Craig Lucas. The play was *Blue Window*, and it was the first of four plays Rene, Lucas and Arcenas would do together. With *Prelude to a Kiss*, the trio of artists landed on Broadway.

Although Arcenas discusses his sets in terms of their sculptural qualities, it is often a luxurious texture that gives them their distinctive character. Texture can

FACING PAGE, DETAIL OF THE PAINT
ELEVATION FOR THE PLAYWRIGHTS
HORIZONS PRODUCTION OF *ONCE ON
THIS ISLAND*, BOOK AND LYRICS
BY LYNN AHRENS, MUSIC BY
STEPHEN FLAHERTY. PRODUCTION
DIRECTED AND CHOREOGRAPHED BY
GRACIELA DANIELE.

result from the use of natural materials (i.e., the found doors and windows assembled for *Dimentos*, the wooden wall in *Spunk*) or the way in which a set is painted (the lush, tropical surround for *Once on This Island*), but it can also be supplied or enhanced through the lighting. It is no wonder, then, that Arcenas enjoys working with lighting designers. "Because my sets are so sculptural," he explains in this interview, "[lighting designers] have to come up with something interesting, or else [the sets] fall flat."

JUNE 4, 1990—
LOY ARCENAS'S APARTMENT,
NEW YORK CITY

I grew up in Cebu, which is in the middle of the Philippines. Cebu is small, so there wasn't much to see. My father is a doctor. I'm the eldest of five sons, and I was geared up to become a doctor. I went to the University of the Philippines in Manila as a premed student, in fact, just as the Marcos dictatorship was beginning. All of these avant-garde ideas were coming in from everywhere—when you are young you try to absorb everything—and it was at that time that I got interested in theatre and decided not to go into medicine. I was asked to direct musical productions in Manila, and for a while I thought of becoming a stage director.

What kinds of productions were you directing?

These huge extravaganzas. They were really stage pictures. We were working with a chorus, moving them around. I was involved with the Manila Symphony Society, which at that time did what we considered were gigantic productions of American musicals. Not entire musicals, but numbers from Broadway shows, because that was what people wanted to see. I was an assistant first, and then I directed. But eventually I realized that I wasn't going anywhere. Because I didn't have any formal education in theatre, everything I did was in relationship to what I saw. Other people would come up with very interesting interpretations of Sophocles, for instance, but I had no idea how they did it. If you don't have the technique, you eventually reach a dead end.

So what did you do?

My mother did a lot of traveling at the time, and she was in England when she decided she was going to look around to see what was available. She located a school in London, called the Drama Studio, that was willing to accept me without an interview. My mother did the interview, and they accepted me on the clippings she showed them.

They didn't ask to see a portfolio?

No. The Drama Studio—and I assume it's still the same—was a one-year course that accepted most of its students from the United States and Canada, plus some from continental Europe. I hated every minute of it because I knew I was not an actor. But I took the lessons because I knew that if I wanted to be in the theatre I had to have some experience of what it was like to be on the performing side. At the same time I was looking around to see what else might interest me, what I could do, how much I could learn.

I went to a show one day and saw in the program something mentioning the Design Course of the English National Opera. I thought it sounded interesting, so I talked with the director of the program, Margaret Harris, and was accepted even though I didn't have a design background. In fact, of the ten people in my class—it was an international class—only one had had any experience as a designer. The course was really for anybody with some experience in the theatre or the arts, but not necessarily in design. A lot of the students, in fact, came from dance or sculpture or painting. Each of us came with our own idea of what the course was going to be like, but all of us came without preconceived ideas about design. It was very interesting.

It was also very, very loosely structured—some of us never attended classes—but the whole point was to be in London at that time. If there was an art exhibit at one of the museums, a painter would recommend it. Or a dancer would recommend a dance program. The same with opera. The same with movies. Whether I understood them or not, I went to all of the German movies, all of the Italian movies, all of the Japanese movies that played at the Nottinghill Gate Cinema at midnight. When a theatre company from Japan or Africa came to London, I made a point of seeing them. We went to see everything and then we compared notes.

But it was what I had grown up doing.

My uncle had a subscription to *The New Yorker* and I would read it because I wanted to know what Pauline Kael said, or what Brendan Gill said. My grandparents did a lot of traveling long before it was the fashionable thing to do, and I remember my grandmother talking about how she could not breathe in Machu Pichu, or talking about Bolivia. I remember visiting Japan with my family and seeing Italian movies there. I had no idea what they were about because the subtitles were in Japanese, but I had to see them. That was my education.

At what point did you realize you wanted to be a designer?

There was really no one moment. Once I started designing, I felt very comfortable with it. My first project at the Design Course was to design a set for Edward Bond's *The Pope's Wedding*. I read the play and thought, oh my God, how am I going to do this? My first impulse was to decorate, which related to my experience of musical theatre, I guess. But Hayden Griffin, my instructor, would say, "No decoration, strip everything!" I also studied with Mircea Marsin, who is Rumanian. He came out of an Eastern European tradition that tends to be philosophically oriented—the opposite of Hayden. Somewhere in between those two extremes were all the shows I saw.

MODEL FOR THE SOUTH COAST REPERTORY PRODUCTION OF CRAIG LUCAS'S *THREE POSTCARDS*, DIRECTED BY NORMAN RENE.

How were the classes at the Design Course structured?

They didn't really have a structure. In fact, when I came out of the Design Course I was not very good at drafting, and my model-building skills were okay, but not great. The program took a more conceptual approach to design. I came out of the course being able to think for myself. You were faced with all these influences and had to say, okay, this is what I see, this is what I think.

But what was it about design that appealed to you?

I really don't know. Maybe it was that designing was the closest thing to directing that wasn't directing. What I liked about it was the talking process. The biggest high in designing for me is in the conceptualization process. That's where I fly. If the set is properly conceptualized, everything else falls into place.

When and why did you move to New York?

I moved to New York in 1978. I came specifically to work with the Third World Theatre Arts Studies program at La Mama. But La Mama was only one side of what I was doing. At the same time I wanted to see how far I could go as a designer, so I sent my resume all over. It

was very, very difficult because my techniques were not skilled.

Did you have a portfolio by this time?

Yes, but I couldn't even get work as an assistant because I wasn't in the union and my assisting techniques were not quite up to par. Eduardo Sicangco, a good friend of mine, said I could assist him and in exchange he would teach me drafting. So it was while working for Eduardo that I perfected my drafting and model-building skills. He was a very good teacher. Then I

MODEL FOR JO CARSON'S *DAYTRIPS*, DIRECTED BY MICHAEL ENGLER FOR HARTFORD STAGE COMPANY. NOT SHOWN IS THE PAINTED SCRIM THAT OCCASIONALLY MASKED THE AREA UPSTAGE OF THE DOOR.

went on to work with other designers, including Marjorie Kellogg and Santo Loquasto.

What happened after you finished the program at La Mama?

My first work after La Mama was with Soho Repertory Theatre. At that time they provided $100 for a budget and you had to make the set work as part of their rotating rep. They had one show at 7:00, and then you had to strike the set and put up the following show. That was really where I learned how to reduce the design to just what is needed. My designs became very, very stripped. What was the point of filling the stage with junk when all the show really needed was a chair? I would rather spend $100 on a chair than on a lot of junk.

Did you ever design costumes?

I did design costumes for a couple of productions in New York, including *Murder in the Cathedral*, but it nearly killed me. It's too time-consuming. When you do sets for an Off-Off Broadway production, it's impossible to spend several more hours on costumes. Now I wouldn't mind designing costumes in regional theatres.

When and where do you work out the technical problems in the process?

On paper, before I give anything to the shop. I usually come up with an idea first,

and then I develop the shape. By the time I present the shape to the director I usually have a fair idea of how to make it work. I hate presenting something and then not being able to make it work.

For the same reason, I hate over-designing. If I'm told I have $50,000, then I'll design for $50,000. I'd rather be told I have $50,000 and work within that budget than design a $100,000 set and hope I can get away with it. The conceptualization is always done with the budget in mind. I think my relationship with regional theatres is very good because I usually follow the budgets we agree on. The directors I've worked with usually respect budgets. If a budget proves to be too low, the administration is made aware of it right away. I'd rather not do a project than play budget games with people.

Let's talk about Once on This Island, Spunk *and* Prelude to a Kiss, *three productions that opened recently in New York to very good reviews. Let's start with* Once on This Island, *which was at Playwrights Horizons.*

Playwrights Horizons is a difficult space, although it helped that I had worked there twice before. I design with the mentality that this is the space and I have to make it work for this particular space. We were also helped in that Graciela Daniele, the director, had done a workshop production

of the show before we went into Playwrights. Judy Dearing, who designed the costumes, Allen Lee Hughes, the lighting designer, and I saw a workshop performance, which meant that we needed less time for the design process.

There were several givens about the design. Andre Bishop, Playwrights artistic director, believes that an audience thinks it is listening to canned music if they can't see the band. So the first given was that we would use a scrim in front of the band—the band was situated at the back of the stage—and then reveal them at the end of the show. The second was that I had to work within a tight budget. And third, I knew that the surround had to come alive.

Once on This Island is really about an obsession. The love affair between Ti Moune and Daniel is all in Ti Moune's mind, so how the affair is developed is very, very important. I sat down with Graciela after I saw the workshop performance and said, this is where I can add something. As far as I was concerned, the biggest numbers were the two love songs between Ti Moune and Daniel—"Forever Yours" and "The Ball"—and the last number, "Why We Tell the Story," which is where Ti Moune turns into a tree.

We needed to change the space for the first love song. I had seen an exhibition of Caribbean folk arts in Washington, D.C. last autumn, and was fascinated with the

idea that these people used whatever materials were available. Whatever they had, they used. So I thought, why not a patchwork quilt? We'll lower the quilt and put the chorus behind it so all of the focus will be on the two lovers downstage. We bought different white fabrics with different textures and pieced them together. So what we had was a beautiful white bedspread in the midst of this very lush painting.

Graciela wanted to fill up the space for the ball scene. Because we only had so many actors, we decided to emphasize the lighting—maybe have Allen use alternate lighting sources. Whatever came in had to come in with the dancers, I thought, so I designed pushcart candelabras that the dancers wheeled in. The designs come from various metal figures in Caribbean folk art, but they're similar to certain images in folk Americana as well. Graciela also suggested that we use the band for the ball since they were on stage. So lanterns were suspended over the band to help illuminate them and pull them into the scene.

The final problem was the tree. Ti Moune turns into a tree at the end of the show. In the workshop production the character climbed up a ladder, but I thought it was wrong. Someone suggested that we lower the tree, but I said trees grow up, they don't fall down. Then we thought that maybe Ti Moune could be lifted up at the same time something else was lowered to encase her. Graciela has a painting of a costume with an incredible headdress, and that's the concept we used. So we had this tree that looked like a headdress but was decorated like a fabulous Christmas tree, with all of this cheap stuff I bought on 14th Street. Why not? Given the space limitations of the theatre, we couldn't lower it in one piece. So we lowered it in sections, and once it's all together you have Ti Moune as this wonderful tree.

What was the biggest problem you faced in designing Once on This Island?

What the surround would look like. My assistant, Bill Kelly, and I went from one idea to another until we came up with the final painting. We considered Rousseau and Matisse and Gauguin and Haitian paintings, but nothing seemed to work. Then, over one weekend, I did a quick sketch. It was lush, but also very simple — the trees became brush strokes. Although it was based on three or four different sources, it was very skeletal.

When I saw Jo Carson's Daytrips at Hartford Stage, I was struck by the painterly quality of the set. Would it be fair to say that this quality is typical of your work?

Maybe, but I think of my work as more sculptural. I love working with lighting designers because they have to come up with something interesting or else the sets fall flat. Much of the painting in *Daytrips* is simple, but it was the different lighting textures that enhanced the painterly quality of the set.

What do you think makes a good design?

It helps if I can talk it out with a director. I'll come to a discussion with ideas, but I am very willing to throw them away if the director wants to go in another direction. If we're happy with something, then it's time to stop. But if I'm not happy — or the director isn't happy — I'll keep pushing. I like to be pushed.

The most exciting projects have been where I've been able to hit it off with the director. It's a very interesting process. You sort of feed off of each other, and the

THE BROADWAY PRODUCTION OF CRAIG LUCAS'S *PRELUDE TO A KISS*, DIRECTED BY NORMAN RENE.

PRELUDE TO A KISS, DIRECTED BY NORMAN RENE FOR SOUTH COAST REPERTORY.

because the model knows how to wear it. It looks stunning. When the dress goes to the buyer, however, it doesn't work. And you know why: the dress was designed for that particular model. The dress was alive because the dress and the individual enhanced each other. I think this is true in theatre as well. The design has to come alive in relationship to the stage action. Certain designs work well because they work well with the director. If the director does not get into the design, it's just a beautiful piece of scenery.

Would you say, therefore, that your work more closely relates to the director's work than to the script itself?

It's a combination of the two. It's what I think of the script and what I think the director thinks of the script. I can design something for a particular moment in the script, but if the director doesn't know how to stage that moment it isn't going to work.

Could you elaborate on this idea in terms of Spunk***?***

George wanted the set for *Spunk* to be a museum, or a gallery. He wanted to distill the images of each piece and then present them as museum pieces. A photograph of a 1938 revival meeting came to mind when I read the script. The slatted wall in the picture triggered an idea for the wood

more you do, the better the design. *Spunk* is a good example. A lot of *Spunk*, which was adapted from three tales by Zora Neale Hurston and directed by George C. Wolfe, is really off the wall. I've been very blessed with exciting directors this year. All of them—Graciela Daniele, George Wolfe, Norman Rene, Michael Engler, Tazewell Thompson—are headstrong personalities. I think the design of a show has got to fit the personality of the director.

Why?

Because in the end it's the director's personality that the audience sees on stage. The designer is there only to accentuate the relationship between the director and the actors, I think. It's a little like dressing up. A dress looks great in a fashion show collage sculpture that frames the cyc in *Spunk*. *Spunk* isn't about a revival meeting, but the photograph provided the germ of an idea.

George is also very much into folk art, so all of the pieces on the set suggest African folk art. We did *Spunk* originally at Crossroads, which has a pillar in the middle of the acting area, so the pillar was used as a Y-shaped tree. If I cannot get rid of something, I try to incorporate it into the design. George wanted to keep the tree for the production at the Public, so I had to design another one. It looked just like a beam at first. Then George suggested we add leaves. The leaf pattern evolved from an interesting shoelace pattern I came across in a book about folk art. Again, the shoelaces had nothing to do with the piece at all, but it triggered an idea.

In both Once on This Island *and* Spunk, *I was struck by the way you incorporated elements from various cultures into the design.*

There is no one culture. Everything can stand on its own if it is given a context. I think this is true with theatre as well. I was just in the Chiapas region of Mexico, where I went to a lot of churches. What was so beautiful about them was seeing the Indian interpretation of a Corinthian column, or a Baroque column. If you had just put a classical column there, it wouldn't have made any sense. But when it was reinterpreted, given a context, it became quite beautiful.

You have designed several productions of Craig Lucas's plays for Norman Rene. Which was the first production and how did it come about?

The first was *Blue Window*. Carey Perloff, now the artistic director of CSC, introduced me to Norman, and he asked if I would be interested in doing a show with him. We had no money for *Blue Window*, so we used both arches and a turntable left

MODEL FOR THE ARENA STAGE PRODUCTION OF TENNESSEE WILLIAMS'S *THE GLASS MENAGERIE*, DIRECTED BY TAZEWELL THOMPSON.

PRODUCTION PHOTOGRAPH FROM
THE GLASS MENAGERIE.

in the space by the previous show. Then we did *Three Postcards*, *Reckless* and four productions of *Prelude to a Kiss*.

Did the design for Prelude *change radically over the course of those four productions?*

I usually design for the particular space, so yes, the design has changed. If I design *Once on This Island* for another space, for instance, it won't look like the production at Playwrights Horizons. *Prelude to a Kiss* was first presented at South Coast Repertory, which is huge.

Prelude is written in twenty scenes during which Peter, the romantic hero, recounts his courtship of and subsequent marriage to Rita. The script was in three parts. The first part was the courtship and ended with the wedding, where a mysterious old man kisses Rita and magically switches souls with her. The second part was from the honeymoon up until Peter finds Rita as the old man in the bar. And the third part dealt with how Peter would get Rita's old self back. What we had was a triptych.

At South Coast Rep we used a rake and a turntable, and the design mirrored the triptych structure of the play. The first act was airy and spacious. For the second act we lowered a scrim. While the main action occurred downstage, the actors behind the scrim moved about almost

hypnotically, which stressed Peter's paranoia about what was happening. Then, for the third act, we flew in a solid wall with a sliver of a doorway to stress the doomed nature of the affair. In the end, however, when things were resolved, the wall flew out and you were back in the open space you saw at the beginning.

Each section contained a walk. I thought the first walk should be open and the second walk clouded. So the first walk was through an open landscape. It also had to be the most beautiful walk because that's where the two characters get to know each other. Norman is fixated on the idea of stars, so I used stars during the first walk. The second walk is on the beach, in Jamaica. It's clouded, so you don't see the stars, which again reinforces Peter's paranoia. The third walk is Peter with the old man, so we see the stars again.

Craig's plays are very cinematic. Because action flows continuously from scene to scene, the time and manner in which the scenery is changed is crucial to the success of the play. In many cases, the scene has to change while the stage business is happening, so the moving of scenery has to be fast, smooth and almost imperceptible.

I used two huge sliding panels, twenty feet wide. During Peter's monologues, the panels would glide across the stage with people running along behind them to change the scenery. You never knew what was going to happen. We wanted to do this when the play was first optioned for Broadway, in the spring of 1989, but it was too expensive and the producers backed out. We did the second production, which was rewritten for two acts, at Berkeley Repertory. The design was sort of between what we started with and what we have now.

Then Tanya Berezin, Circle Rep's artistic director, decided she wanted to do *Prelude*, so we had to make it work for that space. It was like moving from a Soho loft into a studio apartment. I thought we had to throw out everything and start from the beginning, which was what we did. The play had become much more of a fairy tale, so we threw out everything except the idea of the stars. I knew Norman wouldn't allow me to get rid of the stars. After throwing around several ideas, I suggested using the window again. We had a very large window in the production at South Coast, but I made it smaller and emphasized it by putting it in the middle of the stage. The surround at Circle Rep was designed as a walled garden to both stress the fairy-tale aspect of the play and mask the furniture and machinery. It also allowed the production to move as smoothly as it did at South Coast.

Prelude to a Kiss *is your first Broadway credit, isn't it? What was that experience like for you?*

There were so many things going on at the same time that I hardly had time to think about it. Because we couldn't make up our minds about which theatre we wanted to go into—and because we were trying to make the Tony cutoff date—I had only a few days to reconceptualize the show. The shop had to build the set in about a week. At the same time I was jumping from theatre to theatre, so I experienced Broadway almost as another regional theatre. I mean, I had to deal with the stage unions, which was a bit different, but after a while it wasn't. I didn't have any difficulties with

AUGUST WILSON'S *FENCES*, DIRECTED BY TAZEWELL THOMPSON FOR ARENA STAGE.

TOP, CALDERON'S *LIFE IS A DREAM*,
DIRECTED BY ANNE BOGART. BOTTOM,
SKETCH FOR DON DELILLO'S *THE DAY
ROOM*, DIRECTED BY MICHAEL BLOOM.
BOTH PLAYS WERE PRODUCED BY
AMERICAN REPERTORY THEATRE.

the union, but that might have been because *Prelude* was a proven quantity. The show had already received good reviews, so people knew what they were dealing with. Everybody was very, very supportive.

Are you typed as a particular kind of designer? Are there certain projects for which you would not be approached?

I think so, but that happens to every designer, which is unfortunate. I would love to do music videos or movies or operas, but no one has asked me.

Do you feel as if your career has been influenced by the fact that you are Filipino? Has this presented a problem in building your career?

If a career hasn't taken off it may be that the designer is not a proven quantity. I know a lot of very good designers who don't have a great deal of visibility. It doesn't mean that they are bad designers, it just means that the people hiring designers don't know them. People have to know you. I think this is what the system is about. People aren't willing to take risks. Norman Rene has always been a good director, but it's only recently that he has received such recognition.

You recently gained a lot of visibility in a very short period of time. Will this be a turning point for you?

It might be. I would love it to be a turning point, but we'll have to wait four or five years to see. It doesn't change the design process. Last year I was concerned because I had so little work. All I had was *Prelude to a Kiss* and *Once on This Island*. Interesting shows, but I was worried because there was nothing else. Then these other things came in: *Spunk*, then *Fences*, with Tazewell Thompson, and *Daytrips*, with Michael Engler. I accepted everything. They just happened to have happened at the same time.

Do you turn down projects?

Sometimes, but mostly because of scheduling conflicts. I'm not at a point where I can say no to many projects.

What would be an ideal project for you?

Right now, I would really like to do a big Broadway musical. I would like to do it like you've not seen it done on Broadway— not in terms of gargantuan machinery, but in terms of concepts. You can do massive productions, but it must all look so simple and smooth. I'd like to see what I could get away with.

JOHN ARNONE

JOHN ARNONE has no formal training as a set designer. Until he reached his mid-twenties, in fact, Arnone was heading toward a career as a character actor (he received a master's degree in acting from the University of Michigan). All that changed, however, in 1976 when the Lion Theatre Company produced a comedy about three Texas cheerleaders and credited Arnone, who was one of the founding members of the company, with the set design. *Vanities*, directed by Garland Wright, was a runaway success, and Arnone's career as a set designer was launched.

As he points out in this interview, Arnone's development as a designer can be charted through his work with Wright, Len Jenkin, JoAnne Akalaitis and Des McAnuff. Whether he is designing dark, unstable environments (*K: Impressions of Kafka's* The Trial), mysterious, miniature cities (*New Jerusalem*), or green neon beams that seem to float across the stage (*On the Verge*, whose set one New York critic described as "a semi-abstract demiparadise rapturously nuzzling the infinite"), Arnone's sets are highly provocative and extraordinarily theatrical.

In recent years Arnone has been trying to balance theatre work with production

FACING PAGE, THE MARK TAPER FORUM PRODUCTION OF ANTHONY MINGHELLA'S *MADE IN BANGKOK*, DIRECTED BY ROBERT EGAN.

design for both films and television. His film credits include *Dead End Kids*, produced by Mabou Mines; Mark Rappaport's *Chain Letters* (which was shown at the 1984 New York Film Festival); and *Penn and Teller Get Killed*, directed by Arthur Penn. Television credits include *The Days and Nights of Molly Dodd*, *Tales from the Darkside*, and *Hamlet* (with Kevin Kline).

FEBRUARY 10, 1989— JOHN ARNONE'S APARTMENT, NEW YORK CITY

I was born in 1949, in Dallas, Texas, where I went through the public school system, attended Jesuit high school, and then entered Southern Methodist University. So I was born, raised and educated in Dallas.

I never really had any sense of wanting to leave Dallas. I was born of Italian parents who came from families of ten to twelve children. Not all of them survived, but I had eight aunts and uncles on one side of the family and an equal number on the other, so if you multiply that by the number of children they had you can see I have an enormous number of cousins. It was a very patriarchal family unit, ruled by my mother's father. I have very joyful memories of going to my grandfather's farm in Irving, Texas, which is between Dallas and Ft. Worth, every Sunday . . .

whatever number of us on any particular day, out on the farm, having dinner, playing. Sometimes my grandfather would play his concertina and we would all dance. The day was always centered around him: great respect for the father figure. It was this sense of family that enabled me—maybe even conditioned me—to stay, not seek to leave the family unit.

I led a disciplined and highly educated life. You know the Jesuits. The personality that was forming was more interior—searching, introspective, quiet. Religion was an important part of the structure that informed my life as a child and as a teenager. In a way it worked out quite well. I always wonder what would have happened if I had left home, gone to San Francisco, and swept floors at ACT.

Did you go to SMU because you wanted to go into theatre?

Yes. I was an actor, or I was studying to be an actor. It was either that or being a dentist. My parents wanted me to be a dentist. I decided I wanted to be an actor. Even though SMU was less than a mile from where I lived, it was a very big step. The people I met there were the people who would shape my life and career.

Why did you want to be an actor?

I played Santa Claus when I was five years old? I don't know. I can't connect it with

any one experience. My parents never took me to the theatre. I do remember the first musical I ever saw—it was *Guys and Dolls*—but there was never any sense of "performance." I think it had more to do with the religious inclination, with the idea of the priesthood. The relationship is there: the religious life, the life of an artist. They each require both discipline and commitment, plus a sort of blind trust in the self and in the higher powers that the self is going to tap into.

For a long time I thought—as every good Catholic boy thinks—that the priesthood was something I should investigate. I got into high school and was sort of marked. The priests noticed something and said, oh, this boy is going to be a priest. It was one of those peak points in my life, not unlike what I faced at the end of my twenties, or what I seem to be going through right now, as I approach forty. I knew I was in the right area, but I didn't know what to sign as an occupation on the dotted line.

I began seeing productions at the Dallas Theater Center, which at that time was doing some very exciting work. They did an adaptation of William Faulkner's *As I Lay Dying* that was a total revelation to me. I hadn't read Faulkner, so I had no idea what to expect. It was a stripped-down production, very elemental—no scenery, simple costumes and straightforward acting. It was one thing to see a play like

Medea or *Oh Dad, Poor Dad* brought to life in an exciting way, but to see a novel deconstructed and then put back together in the form of a performance was the most immediate theatrical experience I ever had as a boy. I knew this was something I had to do. Interestingly enough, some of my best design work has been for novels adapted to the stage. It was a peek at what was to come, I guess, a hint at my destiny, which I firmly believe in. Destiny, not so much a strictly preordained series of events you can't escape, but destiny in the sense that there is a higher objective to which we are born, and which we seek as the way.

A lot of people have tried to snare me to come and teach, but I realize now as I'm talking about destiny that I've always had a certain distrust of literal education, especially the literal education of artists, which in school gets translated into set design or lighting design or costume design. It's identified as practical, concrete, something you can put credits behind. But then it becomes something very separate from the work of the play. You can see set design in schools as a thing on a piece of paper, or it's a rendering, or a model. It's an exercise, it's "how I please teacher" or "how I go to the top of the class." It has very little to do with the living soul of the play, which is what the artistic investigation is all about. That is, going into the deep inner recesses of the text, assimilating it in such a way that it echoes within your

MICHAEL HURSON'S *RED AND BLUE*, DIRECTED BY JOANNE AKALAITIS FOR THE NEW YORK SHAKESPEARE FESTIVAL. ARNONE DESIGNED BOTH THE SET AND THE LIGHTING.

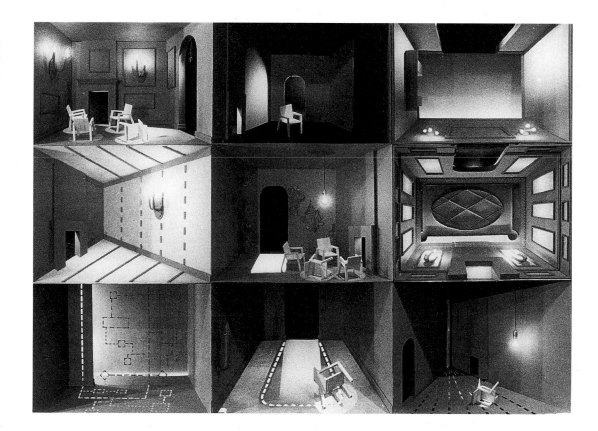

experience, and then bringing it back to life in a physical sort of way. That journey is a complex one, a scary one, a deep one . . . and it's a very psychological one. I suppose you could be guided, but ultimately you can't get it from someone else. You are the teacher and the student and the way.

So you wouldn't recommend going to school to study design?

That's always the question, isn't it: What do you recommend? People in this business are always saying, come to me and I'll show you. But what I remember is being five years old, sitting on my mother's knee, and learning how to embroider. I also remember the grand piano being wheeled into our home, and being fascinated by this object that had a science to it, that I could decode and then master. So I studied piano for a long time. I didn't have a great talent—I never had the key for turning it into an expression of art, which I regret—but I had some proficiency at it. The idea of music—rhythmics, structure, harmonics, composition—informs much of what I do as a designer.

Another part of designing is observation, just looking around. Ninety percent of this work is seeing. It's constant observation, every little thing. That's one reason why travel is so important. You learn so much just by observing. People talk less

because they read less; they lack verbal skills. That's just the way we have come to define ourselves, so pictures and images become even more important. In my case what is visual, concrete, out there, is the stuff on which I feed my imagination, from which I then compose. It's all raw material, distilled or purified into ideas, then personified in physical form. That's the alchemical process.

What kind of theatre work were you doing at SMU?

I have to admit that I was a character actor. I was the funny guy with a good sense of humor and playfulness. I did Restoration comedy, eighteenth century, Sheridan, Molière. I also studied directing and costume design. The classwork was very practical—there wasn't a lot of emphasis put on language, philosophy, history or science—but that was all right. I picked that up later.

Acting gave me a certain kind of gratification, which I'm not sure how to describe because it has become something else now. Directing, on the other hand, satisfied the need for something more tangible, more scientific. There was a certain way you had to approach a play. You had to take it apart and literally grasp its structure. You had to be able to picture it on stage. You had to block it. You had to understand how people occupy space,

how they move around, how they respond to each other. Directing is getting the actors to the same idea by the time you let the audience in. For some reason, as a student in college, I found the rules of directing set, very specific. Acting satisfied a certain psychological aspect; directing satisfied a certain intellectual aspect.

Where did you go after SMU?

I did a pit-stop in acting at the University of Michigan. Then, in order to get my Equity card, I went to San Diego to do a production of *The Taming of the Shrew* at the Old Globe. That was the summer of 1971, after which Robert Blackman, who was my mentor at SMU, got me a job as Ann Roth's assistant at ACT, in San Francisco.

Did you earn a degree from the University of Michigan?

Yes, but to what point? I was hiding. Michigan was so cold and so alien to me. I was terribly isolated in snowdrifts that were ten feet high. I was a little kid from Texas who had never been anywhere, never seen any of this. I did, however, discover Weight Watchers and went from 190 pounds down to about 130 pounds. It was great. That was probably the best thing that happened in Ann Arbor.

LEFT, THE ARENA STAGE PRODUCTION OF
THE TEMPEST. BOTTOM LEFT, THE ACTING
COMPANY'S PRODUCTION OF ERIC OVER-
MYER'S *ON THE VERGE OR THE GEOGRAPHY
OF YEARNING.* BOTTOM RIGHT, THE LA
JOLLA PLAYHOUSE PRODUCTION OF ANTON
CHEKHOV'S *THE SEAGULL.* ALL THREE
PRODUCTIONS WERE DIRECTED BY
GARLAND WRIGHT.

When did you move to New York?

After I decided I couldn't continue to buy shoes for ACT any longer. I decided to do the TCG auditions for the American Shakespeare Festival, in Stratford, Connecticut. Michael Kahn was the artistic director at that time, and Garland Wright was the associate artistic director. I got the job, moved to New York in February 1972 for rehearsals, and then moved to Stratford in April. It was sort of like *Candide*. It was great. I was young, excited, and so involved in what was happening that I just went with it.

Was it out of Stratford that the Lion Theatre Company was formed?

Yes. Stratford had The TV Room, where we did new plays and experimental work. You could sense that against the classical background of toga drama ran this current of renegades. The younger members in the company had their eyes set on what they were going to do after Stratford, after they returned to New York. It was out of that that the Lion Theatre Company was founded by Gene Nye, Garland Wright and about fifteen or twenty other people—people who were working at Stratford, friends of friends who were working at Stratford, and people who had worked at Stratford in the past.

And you were an actor with the Lion Theatre Company?

Oh yes, absolutely. Except none of us had any money and most of us were doing straight jobs. I had run out of unemployment and was working full time at Lord & Taylor, selling men's pajamas—I mean "men's furnishings"—so unfortunately I only had a minimal amount of time to devote to the company. Even though I acted in plays I was on the outside for much of the first year. It was only after I left Lord & Taylor that I was able to participate fully as an actor and, eventually, as a designer.

That first year we rented a studio on 19th Street and Eighth Avenue and did this bizarre repertory: *The Tempest*, *Gammer Gurton's Needle*. Playwrights Horizons, Circle Repertory and Manhattan Theatre Club were also relatively new companies at that time, and we all shared an incredible innocence. The nonprofit theatres weren't oriented—as they were in the 1980s or are now—towards commercial theatre. In the early and mid-1970s, commercial theatre was an accident. If you stumbled into it, fine. But there was a community then, and you went to see plays to support the community. It was social, it was cultural, it was innocent. And I believe, looking at where we are now, in a culture and in a society which no longer allows for that kind of theatre community, that we were extremely lucky to be at that particular place, at that particular time.

When and how did you start to design?

The Lion couldn't afford designers. Garland and I would sit down and figure out what he needed for a show, what we could afford. For *Casserole*, Jack Heifner's play, for instance, we used a giant quilted backdrop that was constructed in my apartment on Jack's sewing machine. We just put it together as we went along. I think Jack still has it. It was funny because there was never a design credit on the program, and people would ask who designed the sets.

Then one day, because there weren't enough women's roles, Jack wrote a play for three women. The Lion was a summer company. We would rent the old Playwrights Horizons space, now the Judith Anderson Theatre, on West 42nd Street, while they weren't in production. But the two theatres decided to coproduce this play, which was about three Texas cheerleaders, in the fall. I remember Garland doing some sketches and Jack reading this play he was working on, saying this role would be good for Kathy Bates, this would be good for Susan Merson, this would be good for Jane Galloway. Although the word "collaboration" wasn't used at the time, that's what we were doing. That's what we had always done, there just wasn't any need to identify it. We just did it. And in that sense it was an extension of our work at SMU. Playwrights Horizons offered us $100 for the director, $100 for the playwright, and $100 for the designer. There was very little money for the set or costumes, but here was $300 we could put into the production. Three hundred dollars was a lot of money back then, it would have bought *Les Misérables*, so we took it. Then Playwrights Horizons wanted to know who the designer was. Well, it was Jack's script and Garland was the director, so we told them the designer was John Arnone.

TOP, THE ARENA STAGE PRODUCTION OF BERTOLT BRECHT'S *HAPPY END*, DIRECTED BY GARLAND WRIGHT. BOTTOM, *FRANKENSTEIN: PLAYING WITH FIRE*, DIRECTED BY MICHAEL MAGGIO FOR THE GUTHRIE THEATER. THE SCRIPT WAS ADAPTED FROM THE MARY SHELLEY NOVEL BY BARBARA FIELD.

So you really just sort of stumbled into it?

Yes. And of course the play we're talking about is *Vanities*, which became a huge hit. It ran for more than five years, and it still holds the record for being the longest running nonmusical play Off Broadway. But there were also major productions all over the United States. We did it in Chicago, at the Mark Taper, in Washington, D.C. It was phenomenal. We went from a basement on 42nd Street, which had been a porno theatre, to major repertory theatres all over the country.

Did you have any idea that Vanities *would be such a large hit?*

No, none. We were rehearsing in the attic of a machine-parts shop, which is now a restaurant. It was winter, and everyone was all bundled up in blankets and coat . . . very *La Bohème*.

After doing *Vanities* all over the United States for a year, I got a call from Studio Arena, in Buffalo, New York, asking if I would like to design a production of *Sholom Aleichem*. And I thought, this is interesting, but what does it mean? I didn't have either the tools or the vocabulary to be a designer. I have to condense this part because it actually happened over a period of a year, but there are sev-

eral aspects to it. One, I took the job with Studio Arena. Two, I went to Garland, who was my best friend, mentor and cohort in crime, and I said, "Look, I consider you the greatest director I've ever known, the greatest friend I've ever had. I don't mean to put you on the spot, but I'm really at this crossroad in my life." This very nervous preamble lasted about thirty minutes before I was finally able to ask, "What should I be, an actor or a designer?" And without any hesitation Garland said, "Why, a designer, of course." I was stunned. I've often wondered since then what he thought of me as an actor, but I've never wanted to ask.

And no regrets about not being an actor?

No. I love actors, and they're why we do theatre. They're up there on stage every night, with no protection, just doing it. But my skills as an actor began to deteriorate as I got further away from acting. My ability to memorize lines and retain them went totally kaput. I also felt that my ability to respect the process of working with another actor on stage was a problem. No matter how good my performance was, I thought it could be ruined by someone else.

You indicated earlier that you studied costume design at SMU. Why do you not design costumes now?

I have a very healthy respect for actors, but actors feed on themselves. I mean, I feed on myself too, but I produce something tangible. You can stand on what I produce, you can look at it, you can light it. Actors produce themselves, which is a very complex process. It can lead to eccentricities that would seem like aberrations in any other society, that wouldn't be tolerated in a nine-to-five job at IBM. You have to respect those eccentricities because they're valuable to that actor, but I don't know how to respond when they get out of control—except to back off. I don't trust myself to remain objective about the costume design and remain objective about the person on whom I'm building the design. Costume designers have to work with actors more closely than set designers do, and although I will sometimes design costumes, I'd rather design lights.

Once the decision to be a scenic designer was made, what did you do?

I did what I had to do: I went to night school. I enrolled at Parsons and the Art Students League and Lester Polakov's studio. I took drafting and rendering and color theory, watercolor classes, modelbuilding . . . everything essential for establishing the vocabulary of a designer. I didn't take any design classes because I

THE HARTFORD STAGE COMPANY PRODUCTION
OF MOLIERE'S *THE MISER*, DIRECTED BY
MARK LAMOS.

was designing, and theatres were offering me productions.

But I concentrated on working with Studio Arena and Indiana Rep. They were producing modern plays and the classic repertory, everything from *Cold Storage* and *Talley's Folly* to *As You Like It*. It was an intense and rigorous process, and building a vocabulary was literally what it was about. I didn't try to decode what I did as an artist. I didn't even try to identify myself as an artist. I used my intuition, and I never questioned it. I never felt any need to turn what I was doing into a study.

It's strange what you begin to focus on, what becomes sacred, in this process. In *Parsifal*, for example, when Parsifal receives the magic sword, he is told that he can only use it once, and then it will break. But the sword can be renewed in the sacred waters of the sacred spring. For me, that sword is intuition. It's that which you only have once. You have this intuition about a play and then bang, it's broken, and you construct the set. Then you return that sword to the sacred waters of the psyche and it is renewed.

I'm curious about how you approach a project. You talk about intuition and instincts, but you also have to do your homework.

Oh yes. I always like to surround myself with an exhaustive amount of research. Then I pour over it. Part of the process is trying to get an intellectual framework for the play. I try to get every piece of information that might have had any influence on the formation of the play. This background material becomes the fabric on which I embroider the ideas for the design.

But there's another aspect to this too, which is that I think I'm buying time. This process, being ultimately mysterious, needs time. Specifically, it needs its own

time. We don't have a clear understanding of how time affects the creative process. You have to allow for it. The time it takes for the psyche to respond, to create, is very mysterious. In our temporal lives it could be no more than a second. So what I try to do to help it along is buy time. And while my active mind is absorbing research, I feel that some deep response from within the soul is also at work.

JoAnne Akalaitis and I were working on a piece based on *The Voyage of the Beagle* one summer, and she invited me to Nova Scotia for about a week. We worked in a little A-frame cabin in which we had plastered the walls with our research about Darwin. We would meet in the cabin every morning and work. Then we would go away. We would exercise or go running or play on the beach or take mud baths. And then we would come back and redirect ourselves towards the material. The process that had taken place between the morning and the afternoon sessions was remarkable. Possibilities that had eluded us in the morning were blindingly clear in the afternoon.

So time is a very important element in the design process. I can't give you what I know I can give you if I don't have time. That's the beginning of the process. From there you listen to the director listening to the play. The idea of talking, of two people coming together with all their similarities and differences, is very exciting. I like to

engage in dialogue which is focused on the play. When possible, the dialogue may also include the costume designer and the lighting designer. Having a dramaturg is very helpful. If I'm working with a director I've worked with before, the language, the vocabulary, is established and we speak in terms of ideas, in terms of visual responses.

Then it comes time to put up or shut up. With me it literally happens in a flash. I can't describe it, but I have a mental picture based on whatever internal process has been going on. I simply see it and I draw it. It's there and very malleable, so I move it around, play with it, punch it into shape. The first expression is hopefully accurate. Then I break it down into technical and practical requirements: how it fits into the theatre, entrances, exits, furniture, props. Then I start drafting, working on the model.

After that the designer is sort of babysitting, seeing the set through the shop and into the theatre. I try to work with painters or prop people or carpenters who are better at what they do than I am, so their interpretation of what I've done amplifies my intention—or the director's intention. The result, then, might be more successful than what I began with. This may be as simple as the way something is painted or the way a part of the set breaks apart, but I believe that if you can enable these craftspeople with a sense of the greatness of

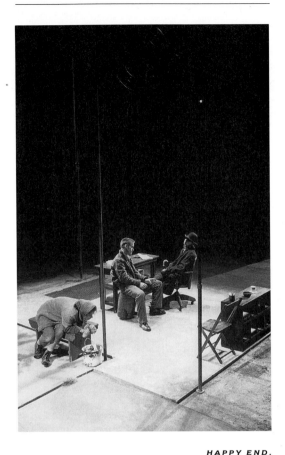

HAPPY END.

what they are doing, if you can somehow enable them with the occasion, the importance of their contribution, then the results are going to be magnificent. The Guthrie, Arena Stage and La Jolla Playhouse all have great craftspeople.

What kind of tools do you use to get that initial idea down on paper?

It varies according to how fast the idea has to come out. I'll usually do a rough sketch on a piece of paper, but I like to get to the model as soon as possible. It helps me, and it's more honest. You can modify a sketch. You can romanticize it, you can cheat, you can lie, you can do almost anything to a sketch to either sell it or not sell it. Sketches are a real tool, and certainly helpful given the situation, but I like to go right to a model.

Do you build the models yourself?

I do the rough drafting and a rough model. It's a way of getting familiar with what I produce. If I'm talking about the design to someone on the phone, I know the page of drafting and I know what they're talking about. What you produce comes about in a very practical way, but also in a very mysterious way. It's interesting to watch it as it's being built, to give yourself time to understand what the expression is really about. My associates, James Wolk and Jim

Youmans, usually complete the final drafting and model.

What have been your favorite designs?

Well, Len Jenkin's *New Jerusalem*, which we did at the Public in 1979, *K: Impressions of Kafka's* The Trial, and *Music-Hall Sidelights*. I also like the *Candide* we did—Len did the adaptation, Garland directed—at the Guthrie. Garland is the beginning and end of who I am as an artist. He very much affects and informs my thinking. You can clock my growth as a designer by the work I've done with Garland, Len, JoAnne and Des McAnuff.

Another favorite piece, which John Simon says was the nadir of my career, was *Red and Blue*, directed by JoAnne. It was a set consisting of nine rooms that were variations on one room. The rooms were 2' x 3' and stacked up on top of each other, so the entire set was about 15' high and 18' across. The audience came in and looked at a wall of cardboard boxes, with rooms that lit up. I also designed the lights. JoAnne and I were looking at a piece that was almost impossible to decode. We had a text and we had to make sense out of it in order to make something occur. Three actors with microphones sat behind the set. The audience heard their voices and saw different motifs, like fireplaces and windows and walls, lighting up. There were red and blue lightbulbs in the set, and the voices were lightbulbs. They were presences in the rooms, commenting on what was happening or what had happened—their relationship to each other. It was convoluted, but very interesting. It was the first thing I did for JoAnne.

And how did it come about?

I saw *Dressed like an Egg* shortly after I moved to New York, and it literally opened up my life as an artist. I had been thinking about these things on stage, but didn't know you could do them—or were allowed to. *Dressed like an Egg* was a magnificent piece of work. It provided the inspiration, or courage, to take a quantum leap into the theatre in terms of design. I wrote JoAnne a letter and told her I wanted to show her my work. We met, and several weeks later she asked me to do *Red and Blue*. People saw it and were transfixed. It didn't get good reviews, but many people thought it should have been reviewed by art critics.

I didn't see Red and Blue, *but I do remember* K: Impressions of Kafka's The Trial *and* New Jerusalem. *One of the many things that impressed me about those productions was how difficult it was to separate the design from the direction.*

It should be impossible. A great designer is a great director, and a great director is a great designer. They're actually the same person. They have to be or you end up with exactly what you end up with, which is scenery that is nothing more than a backdrop for the play—what I call "obscenery."

How many shows a year do you do?

It depends. In a year in which I do a film, I can do only three or four plays. Let's see, in 1988 I did the Penn and Teller movie, *Made in Bangkok*, *The School for Wives*, *American Notes*, *Frankenstein* and *Lulu*. I also did about eight episodes of a television series. So six plays, one major motion picture, and a television series. That's a lot of work, especially since the film took five months. That leaves seven months to do everything else.

My agent, Scott Hudson, and I are now working very closely to generate more television and film work. Demanding financial security of the theatre is problematic. It makes it about something other than the work. Not only that, but the more you design, the more familiar it becomes and the less dangerous it seems. I can support myself both financially and creatively with film and TV work. For one episode on a television series, which may take a week or ten days to do, I make what I would normally make doing one play at a major repertory theatre.

Theatre artists are very attractive to people in television and film. You have to be able to think quickly, you have to be good on your feet. Also, people in theatre are used to working with small budgets. Even though television and film budgets are larger, it's all relative. But because theatre designers know how to get more out of a budget, it adds to their attractiveness.

What do you think characterizes your work?

It has changed a lot. When I first started designing, people talked about my work in terms of miniatures. What characterizes one's work, however, is what is tangible about it. But what is tangible is also what constantly changes. Jerome Robbins asked me to design a piece he was doing with songs by Charles Ives. I love the songs, they're so beautiful, and I thought, here's a chance to work with the great Jerome Robbins. I cranked out about forty drawings over a period of two months. The design went from very realistic to something very expressionistic. And none of it satisfied Mr. Robbins. I was so frustrated that I finally had to say, "I think what you might want is no set, just a blank stage with black legs and borders." And he said, "That's perfect, that's exactly what I want."

The point of the story is that he had seen *On the Verge*, and he identified what I did with *On the Verge*. He defined it as a very

THREE PRODUCTION PHOTOGRAPHS FROM *K:
IMPRESSIONS OF KAFKA'S* THE TRIAL,
DIRECTED FOR THE LION THEATRE COMPANY
BY GARLAND WRIGHT.

structural, architectural, geometric look. How could I tell him that this design did not define my "style," that it was a very specific response to *On the Verge*? He thought that what he had seen in *On the Verge* could be applied to the Ives pieces, but I couldn't apply it to the Ives pieces any more than I could apply it to a Peewee Herman movie. What characterizes my work is an intellectual/artistic ability to form ideas. Garland says that great designers don't think in terms of sets, they think in terms of ideas. And I would agree. If we're going to characterize my work we need to talk about it on that level.

Where do you see theatre design going?

It's sort of frightening. We talk about the health of the theatre. I was lucky enough to be part of an Off-Off Broadway movement that was very conducive to unlimited and wild investigation. It wasn't that we didn't have problems to solve, but everything was viewed in terms of solutions.

The response was never, oh well, we don't have the money, we can't do that. The response was always, this is what we have and this is what we create with it. That's totally gone. It doesn't exist anymore.

What we've got now are producers who are obsessed with the idea of commercial theatre. They're obsessed with it because it's what audiences have come to expect. It's very shortsighted. The result is a tunnel view of what to nurture, what to develop. Producers are nurturing plays without serious content, that have no social interest or depth. And many of the young directors are only concerned with building careers—how fast can I make it, how fast can I get to the top. They spend more time in promotional meetings than with the process of theatre itself. This means you have directors—and I have had the good fortune to work with the one or two exceptions—who don't know how to move people around on stage, who don't know how to work with designers or playwrights.

And designers, where will they come from?

Well, now they're coming out of decaying schools, schools whose reputations are based on something that was established many years ago. It isn't there anymore, and it might not have been there to begin with.

Our culture, our community is so conflicted and diseased right now. And unless we discover what is missing—which is heart, the song of the heart, that inner voice within all of us—there'll be no more theatre. We are looking at a potential void after us, a dark place. It's very frightening. Where are the new designers, where are the new directors, where are the new playwrights? They're around, certainly, but they are inheriting or nurturing an infertile environment. They must seek and cultivate a new terrain: the inner terrain of soul and psyche. They must reinvent imagination. This is their quest, our destiny.

DAVID
GROPMAN

DAVID GROPMAN, who was raised in California and studied theatre design at Yale School of Drama with Ming Cho Lee, now works almost exclusively in film. This doesn't mean that he has abandoned theatre entirely. As he explains in this interview, he'll design the occasional theatre project when it is something he finds really interesting—and can be accommodated in his schedule.

Whether Gropman is designing for theatre or film, he believes that the goals are the same. That is, "to bring the script to life, to create a character or an environment." Consequently, his work demonstrates an acute eye for telling details. Although this is clearly apparent in his prop-packed sets for the Broadway productions of *The 1940s Radio Hour*, for which he recreated a complete period radio station, and *Come Back to the 5 and Dime, Jimmy Dean, Jimmy Dean*, for which two Texas dry-goods stores (the same store, actually, but from two very different decades) occupied the stage simultaneously, it is also true of the elegantly minimalistic set he designed for the Yale Repertory production of Edward Bond's *Bingo*.

FACING PAGE, MODEL FOR THE BROADWAY PRODUCTION OF ED GRACZYK'S *COME BACK TO THE 5 AND DIME, JIMMY DEAN, JIMMY DEAN*, DIRECTED BY ROBERT ALTMAN.

Gropman's film career began when *Jimmy Dean*'s director, Robert Altman, decided he wanted to rethink the production for the camera (rather than simply make a documentary of the stage production) and hired Gropman as his production designer. Since then Gropman's reputation has been built on expert handling of small budgets and intricate location work. Like his sets for the theatre, Gropman's film work—particularly as seen in *Slaves of New York* and the recently released *Mr. and Mrs. Bridge*—reveals a designer who is incredibly attentive to details.

FEBRUARY 13, 1989—
DAVID GROPMAN'S STUDIO,
NEW YORK CITY

I grew up in Los Angeles, California, just a heartbeat away from Hollywood. I wanted to be a movie star. I wanted to be on the Johnny Carson show. Not that any immediate members of my family were in theatre or television, but that was the environment I grew up in.

I had a very strong, very focused drama teacher in high school. Being on the fringe of Hollywood, the department was somewhat professionally motivated, so I began as an actor. But I also designed and directed productions and, at the same time, did a lot of graphic art. Although I grew up thinking I wanted to be in theatre, by the

time I left high school I had decided that theatre was not a responsible profession to be in—it took me years to realize that, in fact, this might be true—so I decided to pursue my interest in commercial art.

I went to San Francisco State College as an art major with an intention to transfer to the Academy of Art College after two years. But during my first year at San Francisco State, a friend from high school, who had already been there for a year, told me about a terrific teacher in set design and suggested that I take a class from him. The college wouldn't allow freshmen to take scene design classes, but I asked to audit it, just to sit in on it, to see what it was all about. And I was hooked. In my second year I was designing my first student production and earning my living by designing posters for the theatre arts department. So I was doing what I wanted to do. I was working as a graphic artist, supporting myself financially, and learning about scene design.

Who was the teacher?

Eric Sinkonnen. He was a true inspiration, and we've remained friends. He still teaches at San Francisco State.

What was it about scene design that appealed to you?

It was a way for me to do both theatre and graphic arts. I had this great major called

Interdisciplinary Creative Arts, which allowed me to pursue my education more as a career than as traditional studies. It was great. It made me feel very much like both an adult and a professional.

Did you do other theatre while you were at San Francisco State, or was what you were doing confined to campus?

I spent the summer of 1973 at the Pacific Conservatory of Performing Arts, in Santa Maria, California. I worked as an assistant to Robert Blackman. Bob was, at that time, one of the resident set designers at the American Conservatory Theatre in San Francisco. I loved the stuff he did at the Conservatory, so it was a thrill for me to assist him. I learned a great deal from him, including a lot of painting techniques, drafting, how to supervise construction, how to realize sets. That was my first professional job in the theatre.

Then in 1974, just by the skin of my teeth, I graduated from San Francisco State and it was time to look at graduate schools. I had decided that if I was going to go to graduate school in design, I wanted to go to one of the top schools. So I applied to Temple University, Carnegie-Mellon and Yale. My interview at Yale with Ming Cho Lee was horrible. We had two major arguments, one about an opera and one about Shakespeare. I thought, well, I'll

FOUR PRODUCTION PHOTOGRAPHS FROM
EDWARD BOND'S *BINGO*, DIRECTED BY RON
DANIELS FOR YALE REPERTORY THEATRE. TOP
LEFT AND RIGHT, SCENE 5. LEFT, SCENE 1.
ABOVE, SCENE 4.

never get into this school. So I went back to California and decided that if I was accepted at Yale, I would go, but if I wasn't accepted, I would move to New York City and see what happened. Then the letter came from Yale and I had been accepted. I couldn't believe it. I took the summer to work as a busboy at Lake Tahoe, and then went off to Yale.

Given what you have said about San Francisco State, was the transition to Yale a difficult one for you to make?

Yes, it was. I was going to say that I was a big fish in a small pond in San Francisco, but that wasn't it. San Francisco State, in the early 1970s, was a very mellow and apathetic place. The program at Yale was very demanding. In our first year we were turning out a project per week. We had to read a play in two or three hours—I used to take a week to read a play in California—come up with a concept, do renderings, and then present the project in class on Saturday. At the same time we were taking classes in theatre history and costume design and lighting. The structure was much more formal than I cared for, and the only way I could deal with it was by presenting myself as an *enfant terrible*.

I'd wait until Friday night to do my design. Somehow I got into the habit of designing on the back of shopping bags or pieces of scrap paper. I don't know what I was into, but, well . . . part of it was that I had never really had a formal education in drawing and I was intimidated by renderings. I was good at model-making, however, and much preferred using models to present my ideas. So I developed a philosophy about models being a much more honest way of portraying a design. I still think it's true. It's easy to cheat and romanticize what a set is going to look like in a rendering, but a model is very concrete. What you see is what you get. Except model-making wasn't offered in the first year at Yale, so I tried to render things in what I felt was a very improvisational and immediate manner—like working on found pieces of paper.

Which could also justify waiting until the night before the project is due.

Oh absolutely. You wouldn't want to bog yourself down; two days and it would already be labored. That was my technique. At the same time, I was very much into minimal design. Part of that was a result of having to design a project every week, of course, but I also saw designing as part of the process. I don't see design as a decorative art. I like design that is very much to the point. You read a play, see what it is about, and then figure out how to tell the story in as few visual moves as possible.

For example, we were asked to design a production of Anouilh's *The Lark* for an arena stage. My set consisted of a gymnasium floor, with a flag at one end and an upright piano at the other. Ming was furious with me. I must admit that my rendering looked like I had spent all of five minutes on it, but Ming thought I hadn't paid enough attention to the play. But I also think he was hard put to say that the play couldn't work in that kind of format. I mean, *The Lark* is a play of remarkably strong language and character. Given a strong director and good actors, the set would have been just fine.

Did your work change stylistically while you were at Yale?

I became much more efficient as a painter. My rendering technique improved continually during the three years I was at Yale. Although I did my last renderings within a year after leaving Yale, I do think it's essential for young designers to learn how to render. I've gotten by on a lot of fast talking and models, but rendering is a great way to get an idea across quickly.

After my first year at Yale, I spent the summer at the Santa Rosa Summer Theatre, in California, and designed three productions. I was totally broke at the end of the summer. I decided that there was no way I could go back to Yale and, what's more, I didn't know if I really wanted to be in that kind of educational environment. I went to Ming Cho Lee to say that I couldn't afford to stay at Yale, and his response was, that's too bad because we were going to have you design a production for Yale Repertory Theatre this year. At that time you didn't design for Yale Rep until your third year, if then. So not only were they asking a second-year student to do a production, but they were offering me some financial aid as well. I was kind of stuck. I was bought, I guess.

What was the play?

Edward Bond's *Bingo*, directed by Ron Daniels, an English director. It was right up my alley in that it called for—and the director wanted—a minimal approach to the design. So I was able to practice what I was preaching. So many times in class Ming would say to me, "How do you expect to get work in this business if you are always telling directors that they don't need any scenery. You're going to be talking yourself out of a job." I'm very proud of *Bingo*. In fact, it was strongly inspired by Ming's aesthetic, his way of capturing the beauty of a moment, which he does so exquisitely.

My original plan was to do a 20' x 20' platform with a 20' x 20' backdrop behind it. It was somewhat precious and contained. Ron looked at it and suggested that if I was going to do a sky, I should do the entire theatre as a sky, and that the sky

THE LINCOLN CENTER THEATER PRODUCTION OF *DEATH AND THE KING'S HORSEMAN*, WRITTEN AND DIRECTED BY WOLE SOYINKA.

should also be the floor. It's the same set essentially, and very, very simple scenically. Five scenes, all very much to the point. The first scene takes place in William Shakespeare's garden, so I had a wall of hedges with a gate in it and a bench. The second scene is Shakespeare walking down a road. He comes across the prostitute who visited him in his garden in the first scene, hanging from a gibbet. The stagehands rolled off the hedges and the gibbet rose up out of the floor with the prostitute hanging from it. It was very dramatic. The play then moves to a tavern, where Shakespeare has a discussion with Ben Jonson. That set consisted of nothing but a fireplace and a couple of tables and

chairs. After that there is a scene in which Shakespeare is walking in the snow. The snow was created by pulling a huge white sheet across the entire stage. But because it had air under it, when Shakespeare walked across it, it looked like his feet were going into the snow. Remarkably simple, but startling all the same. The last scene takes place in Shakespeare's bedroom, so a bed, a door, a chair. The door only because someone had to come through it. One of the nice things about Yale is that if you design for the Rep, you do have the chance of being noticed by people in New York and in some national publications. The production did, in fact, receive very good notices and definitely helped me in starting my career.

How do you approach a design project?

The first thing I usually do is sit in the theatre in which I'm going to work. I look for what is dynamically and emotionally there in the architecture of the space that might lend itself to the production. I start from the bare stage or empty space and imagine how the design can grow in as few brush strokes as possible. Even now, when I'm doing location work for a film, I'll begin the same way. It's different for a studio set, of course, but for location work, I'll sit in the space and figure out how this particular location can become the character or the environment that it

needs to be, again, in as few brush strokes as possible. Because there are many independent films being produced with small budgets, there are a lot of producers in search of designers who can deliver the most effect for the least amount of money. I have something of a reputation for this right now. It can be a trap, let me tell you, because it is very hard work, but it relates to how I have always approached design. It's also why, when people say that doing theatre design and doing film design is totally different, I have to say that it isn't, not at all. The goal is the same: to bring the script to life, to create a character or an environment, be it on a stage or up on a screen.

I read the script, and think it through until something clicks. Then I'll quickly put together a rough model and see what it looks like in three dimensions. I seldom do thumbnail sketches. One of the largest projects I ever designed for the stage was Leonard Bernstein's *A Quiet Place* and *Trouble in Tahiti*. I'm not going to say that it came to me in a dream, but in that case I listened to the music, read the libretto, tossed it back and forth in my head until I knew exactly what I wanted it to look like, and then built the model.

How much research do you do?

I like to make myself out as remarkably undisciplined and improvisational, but I do research. For something like *Trouble in Tahiti*, which takes place in suburban America in the 1950s, I didn't do a lot of research because I grew up in that kind of environment. For historical pieces, however, I'll do exhaustive research. I once did a play on Broadway that took place in a trailer home. I can't tell you how many miles of photocopies I did in researching trailer homes. But that's what the play was about—it was about a couple who live in a trailer home, not some abstract idea of what it is like. So I do research when I have to. On the other hand, the best part about starting a new project is the excuse to go out and buy lots of new books, even if I already have ten books on the subject.

What kind of interaction will you have with the director?

I feel very strongly that once you sign on to do a play, you have to trust the director. It's the director's vision that ends up on stage. You have to figure out what the director wants and how you're going to give it to him. The director may hang himself—and I certainly wouldn't suggest that you intentionally sell one down the river—but it is very important that the

FACING PAGE AND BELOW, BLUEPRINTS FOR THE THRONE IN HENRIK IBSEN'S *THE PRETENDERS* (TRANSLATED BY MICHAEL FEINGOLD), DIRECTED BY ALVIN EPSTEIN FOR THE GUTHRIE THEATER.

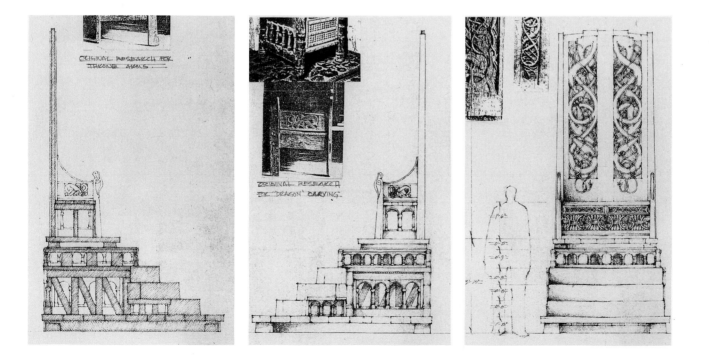

designer help the director realize his vision. If you don't want to do that, then direct yourself.

When did you move to New York?

Karen Schulz, my wife, and I went up to the Berkshire Theatre Festival the summer after we graduated from Yale. We each did two productions and made a lot of wonderful contacts. Then we came to New York and looked for the cheapest apartment we could find—a studio apartment on the Upper West Side. We're still in that apartment. Everything that is now in this working studio was in our apartment then. We had a bed, a dining-room table, which was the top of a drafting table, two other drafting tables, and work tables. Both Karen and I were working designers at the time and we often had two assistants working with us. There were at least five of us in that apartment at any one time, from sunup to sundown. And we lived like that for many years. The number of people in the apartment was never a problem, unless Karen or I was not working, then the one who was not working might get a little resentful about all of this activity in a place they wanted to call home. I must admit that I was a lot less patient in that situation than Karen. But anyway, we moved to New York and I had two shows at the Folger, in Washington, D.C.

How did those two shows come about?

The general manager at the Folger had been a management student at Yale when I was there. He convinced the theatre to hire me. The famous Yale web. They offered me two plays back to back: *Two*

FACING PAGE AND LEFT, THE YALE REPERTORY THEATRE PRODUCTION OF BERTOLT BRECHT'S *MISTER PUNTILA AND HIS CHAUFFEUR MATTI*, DIRECTED BY RON DANIELS.

Gentlemen of Verona and *Hamlet*. The first play wasn't scheduled until that winter, so for the first month I was in New York I worked as an assistant to David Mitchell. He was the first designer I assisted in New York, and I only assisted him for a month, but it was a wonderful education. *Annie* was a huge success and he was working on its first national tour, which I did some drafting for. He was also doing the first production of Studs Terkel's *Working*, written and directed by Stephen Schwartz, at the Goodman Theatre. Watching him work with a director and evolve a design was great. It was: Here's a bare stage, now what do we need? Okay, now how does it move from scene to scene?

Then, in the spring of 1979, I designed Henrik Ibsen's *The Pretenders* for Alvin Epstein at the Guthrie. I was very excited about it for a number of reasons. One, I would get to work in this wonderful theatre space. Two, it is a wonderful play, a sprawling, fifteenth-century drama about two rival kings of Norway. Three, I would be working with Alvin Epstein. And four, it was an opportunity to outrage the people at the theatre. I didn't think I was going to outrage them, but I did.

Because the play is about territory, I wanted as much space as possible, which meant covering the steps into the voms. Desmond Heeley was also there that season and he, in fact, supported what I wanted to do with the theatre. The

Guthrie has these wonderful workshops, and because I was doing fifteenth-century Norway on a bare stage, I put a lot of emphasis on the furniture. The technical director called me after I sent him the drawings to ask how I was thinking of doing them. I had been thinking vacuum-form pieces and bas-relief, but he suggested carving them out of pine. Well, yes, I said, carving would be good. So all of these beautiful pieces of furniture were hand-carved out of beautiful pine.

I think the first time I saw your work was in Buried Child, *at Theater for the New City.*

Buried Child went back to my days at San Francisco State and Robert Woodruff, who helped start the Magic Theatre. Bob had staged *Buried Child* in San Francisco, but he wanted me to redesign it for his production at Theater for the New City. It was my first production in New York. Theater for the New City did not have a lot of money, so basically there was me and one hippy carpenter. None of us knew it was going to be a Pulitzer Prize-winning play, but it was great fun and typical of my work. Here's the space, now how do I make it work for the play? By using the architecture of the theatre, of course. The theatre happened to have a balcony on stage, which I used to support a staircase. I did nothing more than that—except

build a back wall with a screened window in it. I used furniture that we found on the street and painted the whole thing, the theatre and the set, the same color. I think it had a certain majesty and strength to it. It certainly had a reality to it. The columns in the set were the real concrete columns in the theatre.

The costumes were done by another Yale graduate, Jess Goldstein. The entire production was very much improvised, which was the way Bob wanted to work. It went on to be this rough-and-ready hit. It was everything I believed design should be, and I was making a living doing it—not much of a living at Theater for the New City, but someone was paying me to do what I wanted to do.

That particular production was moved to the Theatre de Lys, which is now the Lucille Lortel Theatre, in Greenwich Village. They moved it without speaking to me, and the new producers thought they could just take the set from Theater for the New City and move it into the Theatre de Lys. Well, aside from the fact that the spaces have nothing to do with each other architecturally, there was nothing to take. There was just a flat with a screen in it. Even when they learned of their mistake, the budget wasn't adjusted. I finally just sold them my rights to the design. They're the same producers who closed the play the weekend before it received the Pulitzer Prize. The production was later remounted at Circle Repertory Theatre, and I designed it. I think I may like that version of the set the most.

How did it differ from the production at Theater for the New City?

It didn't have the rough-and-ready look of the original set. It was, in fact, a real set, with three walls. It was a chance for me to realize a real house with just enough abstraction to make it feel mythological, which is appropriate for Sam Shepard's work, I think.

This was also around the time you did The 1940s Radio Hour, wasn't it?

Yes, at Arena Stage, in Washington, D.C., and then on Broadway the following year. In the interim between the Washington and Broadway productions, during a sort of down period, I spent six weeks assisting Robin Wagner. Another great influence. When *The 1940s Radio Hour* was being moved to Broadway, the producers were very nervous about this young kid making his Broadway debut with a fairly large musical. They asked Robin about me, and Robin basically guaranteed me, saying that if there was any trouble, he would help with whatever they needed done. So I would say he was really responsible for me getting my first Broadway job. I don't know that I've ever done anything on Broadway that I am as proud of as that one.

It all takes place within a radio station in the 1940s, and it was as much a revue of the songs of that period as it was a play. It was important to me to actually realize a radio studio of that era on stage. So with *The 1940s Radio Hour* I went from doing bare stages to a stage that was absolutely filled with scenery. I'm willing to fill a radio station with equipment, or a dime store with junk, if that is what the play is about. Visually, details are as important as a bare stage.

When and how did you first start working in films?

Through Robert Altman. He had moved to New York and decided to direct a play called *Come Back to the 5 and Dime, Jimmy Dean, Jimmy Dean*, by Ed Graczyk. I had done several Broadway shows by this time, and I think his general manager gave him a list of New York designers that included my name. So I met with him. I don't think I even showed him my portfolio; I just talked. He called me back that same week and asked if I wanted to do it.

It was a difficult play to design because it takes place in the same dime store in two time periods, 1955 and 1975, outside Marfa, Texas. It seemed to want the trappings of a realistic dime store. At the same time it had to flipflop twenty years from one period to another. I think Bob said he wanted two sets, one of which would be a mirror image of the other. I went away thinking about the play in very realistic terms. In fact, the set I ultimately designed for the film version was what I had originally seen in my mind's eye for the play.

Then the play was cast. I was sitting in Bob's office one day and he was on the phone with Cher. He's going to cast Cher in one of the major roles of this play. So at that point he had Sandy Dennis, Karen Black and Cher. And I thought, I don't think these three women are going to survive a naturalistic setting. This isn't going to be a play, this is going to be an event. I saw something more akin to a three-ring circus.

My image of the set completely changed, from a naturalistic dime store to a large, elaborate, dazzling visual. It was, in fact, two dime stores back to back. The stage was divided in half on a diagonal, and behind the two sets I had a one-way mirror of stretched Mylar. It was about 40' long and 18' high. Beyond the mirror were rows and rows of shelves of dime-store merchandise. Sometimes you would get a mirror image of the actors, and sometimes that would bleed through and you would see shelves of merchandise. The characters would move upstage whenever they went back in time, and the audience saw a mirror image of them. The show curtain,

TWO MODELS FOR LEONARD BERNSTEIN'S
A QUIET PLACE, DIRECTED BY
STEPHEN WADSWORTH.

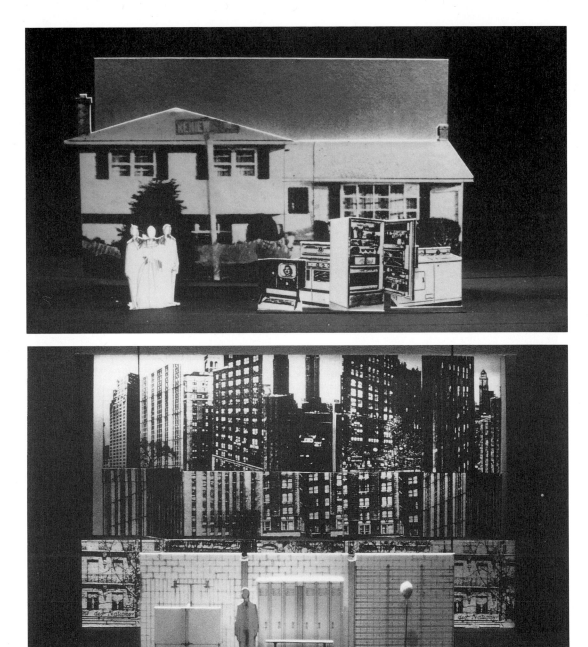

which consisted of two huge Woolworth signs, was also duplicated upstage in a mirror image. And then I had telephone poles, a light box, sky drops, and a 2′ x 4′ construction of the house from *Giant*. The set had a lot going on, but the director and actors had no problem filling it. It was a dazzling event, but a critical fiasco. Frank Rich called the set "prismatic confusion," which I don't think he meant as a compliment.

But the show ran for a number of months. At the end of the run, a young producer, Peter Newman, approached Altman about doing it as a movie for Showtime. Bob wasn't interested in doing just a film record of the stage show, however. He wanted to do a cinematic version. So when the play closed, Bob asked me if I wanted to do the film set. I said yes and that was my first movie. I did two other films for Bob before I started working for other directors.

You now work almost exclusively in film. Was this a practical decision?

A couple of things happened simultaneously. One, by the time I did *Jimmy Dean*, I was becoming more established, with a number of Broadway plays behind me. I was being asked to do Broadway productions, but the ones I was asked to do were closer to commercial packages. They were new plays, but very commercial—scripts I didn't necessarily respect.

The projects that interested me were the ones that were being done in the regional theatres. But it is very, very difficult to make a living doing just regional-

PRODUCTION PHOTOGRAPH FROM
A QUIET PLACE.

A QUIET PLACE.

theatre work. In fact, if one is going to become at all financially successful, which in New York means simply getting by, you have to have your one Broadway hit, like *A Chorus Line* or *42nd Street* or *Annie*. My one big commercial hit was *Lena Horne: The Lady and Her Music*. I earned royal-

ties off of it for years, but it was a concert evening. Maybe it was stupidity on my part, but I really felt that I couldn't design something well unless I really believed in it.

At the same time, the regional theatre scene was changing. The adventurous sort of theatre that I had cut my teeth on wasn't being done any longer. Basically, I was being asked to do a lot of box sets. I just don't think I had it in me.

So no serious regrets about leaving the theatre?

No, because I love doing film. It's a lot like the work I did in theatre. No matter how much you preplan a set, it all has to do with the moment. On *Jimmy Dean*, for example, I designed a fully realized set. But when Bob decided he needed to see into a little broom closet, I had to dress a broom closet with a history and personality. I had to improvise on the spot, pull things out of thin air. But I love that about film. No matter how thought out the design is, there is always something needed at the last minute. And that's very exciting.

I happen to be a production designer who likes to be on the set during the filming. It's not always possible, of course, but that's the way I like to work. For every shot that gets set up, something is going to get changed. It's going to get shifted this way or that, or a prop that hasn't been asked for will be needed immediately. And if you're not there to make those choices, someone else is going to make them. If you want that picture to have the visual impact and integrity you want it to have, you better be on that set. I also like the scale of film—the amount of work that has to be juggled and organized. I like having a staff that I am responsible for, but who are there to contribute and help realize my design.

Where do you see your career going from here?

I'll continue to do production design for films. The longer you are out of the theatre business, the fewer calls you seem to get. The other thing is that I'm a married man. Karen and I have a child and live in New York City. The last time I did theatre I did two plays back-to-back at Lincoln Center. It was several months of work, at theatre rates, for shows that didn't move into Broadway houses for extended runs. Financially, it almost killed me. I can't make a living doing theatre unless I accept a lot of projects, which would make me completely unavailable for film work, which pays very well. But I would also love to do theatre again, absolutely.

ROBERT ISRAEL

Rᴏʙᴇʀᴛ ɪꜱʀᴀᴇʟ, who lives in the Brentwood section of Los Angeles and teaches at UCLA, has designed both scenery and costumes for all but one production in a career comprised almost entirely of opera (Martha Clarke's work being the notable exception). His sets, which have appeared on opera stages throughout the United States and Europe, exhibit a romantic, sometimes lyrical appreciation of stage space.

Although Israel lived in New York during the late 1960s and early 1970s, he was not a part of the expanding Off-Broadway theatre movement that was occurring in the city at that time. Trained as a visual artist, Israel was instead interested in contemporary art. Issues of illusion and reality were of particular concern to Israel and his Soho neighbors and friends, including artists Jennifer Bartlett, Chuck Close, Elizabeth Murray and Joel Shapiro. "[The dialogue] had great bearing on theatre," Israel explains, "but it was all brought to focus in terms of painting and sculpture. So it was relevant [to what I do in theatre], it just wasn't direct."

Israel's set designs, which continue to display a keen regard for questions about

FACING PAGE, MARTHA CLARKE'S *MIRACOLO D'AMORE*.

illusion and reality, have been exhibited in major museums and art galleries across the country. His set and costume designs are also included in the permanent collection of the Museum of Modern Art (15 drawings for *Satyagraha*), the Levi Collection (15 costume drawings for *The Yellow Sound*) and Robert Tolin's theatre design collection (37 drawings for *Akhnaten*). Israel, a committed teacher, has taught at the Minnesota School of Art, The School of Visual Arts (NYC), Cooper Union and the University of California/San Diego.

MARCH 9, 1990—
ROBERT ISRAEL'S HOUSE,
LOS ANGELES, CALIFORNIA

I grew up in Detroit, where I lived until I was seventeen. My father was a doctor and I had been accepted in premed at the University of Michigan, but I wasn't sure that was what I wanted to do. I had also been accepted at Pratt Institute, so I moved to New York. After four years at Pratt I still wasn't sure what I wanted to do, but I decided to go to the University of Michigan and get an MFA in painting.

I think, in the long run, going to the University of Michigan was a good choice. I was able to take courses in anthropology, archaeology and art history, and just mix with people who were more involved with the humanities. It liberated my curiosity. I suppose if there was anyone who really affected me more than anyone else in school, it was Oleg Grabar, a professor who later taught at Harvard. I took his course in early Islamic architecture. Both the subject and Grabar's thinking about the subject were extraordinary.

How did Grabar approach the subject?

He was both an art historian and a philologist, so he had ways of getting into the subject that had to do with culture and language. It really made the art seem inevitable in terms of its evolution. It was a wonderful class. When I finished at Michigan I moved to Minneapolis, where I taught painting at what was then called the Minneapolis School of Art. While I was there, the Walker Art Center, which is physically connected to the Tyrone Guthrie Theater, sponsored opera at the Guthrie. The company was called the Center Opera, and Martin Freeman, who was the director of the Walker, and John Ludwig, who headed Center Opera, asked me to design an opera.

Had they seen your work somewhere, or did you approach them?

I had a show of drawings at the Walker which intrigued them, I guess. From there, one thing led to another. I became more and more a designer and less and less a painter. After four years in Minneapolis I moved back to New York, still painting, and . . . well, I was very hesitant about whether I wanted to be a designer.

Why?

Because I loved painting more. Because I felt uneasy about the collaborative process. But as I did more theatre, it became clearer that this was what I needed to do. And I didn't want to be a Sunday painter. So I stopped painting. It was a long process, with intermediate steps related to performance.

Performance?

Yes. None of my friends in New York were in the theatre; they were all in painting or sculpture—Jennifer Bartlett, Joel Shapiro, Elizabeth Murray, Chuck Close. Jennifer and I read some things at the Paula Cooper Gallery once, but there were a number of other situations like that.

Were these friends from Pratt?

No. I lived in Soho, and they were my neighbors. I don't know how it happens, but you end up being attracted to certain

people. They were the people I was attracted to. They were the people I had a dialogue with. Even though I was moving away from the kind of work they were doing, I found the dialogue with them much more meaningful than the theatrical dialogue. I think it gave me a perspective on what I do that I might not have had otherwise.

What was that dialogue about?

It was an unabashed, primary argument that had to do with illusion and reality. Chuck Close, for example, was interested in perception and marks and how they are perceived. Joe Zucker, another friend, was interested in the surface of the canvas. With Jennifer it had to do with indiscrimi-

THE SANTA FE OPERA PRODUCTION OF BENJAMIN BRITTEN'S *THE TURN OF THE SCREW*, DIRECTED BY DAVID ALDEN.

THE SEATTLE OPERA PRODUCTION OF
RICHARD WAGNER'S *SIEGFRIED*, DIRECTED BY
FRANCOIS ROCHAX.

nate information. The dialogue seemed to be intellectualized, but it was very exciting. It had great bearing on theatre, but it was all brought to focus in terms of painting and sculpture. So it was relevant, it just wasn't direct.

Several designers interviewed for this book started in painting, but then switched to theatre. You seem to have a much broader, more extensive background in painting.

It's bizarre to think this way because I know it's not true—I'm a theatre designer, this is what I do—but I still perceive myself as an outsider.

Did you go to the theatre while you were living in New York?

I would go to the final dress rehearsals at the Met. I would take a pad of paper and go to the stage door. The first couple of times I told them I was sketching for *Opera News*. It was a ridiculous thing to say, but I loved music and wanted to see the productions. After a few times they recognized me and just let me in. I didn't draw a thing.

Were you aware of the Off-Broadway theatre movement that was happening at that time?

Not really, because I was very involved in painting and sculpture.

At what point did you realize that theatre was something you wanted to do?

I guess that happened about three years after I returned to New York. I was teaching at Cooper Union and working in Europe. I had enough work in Holland to support me, so I decided to move to AmThat was when I figured out my commitment to theatre.

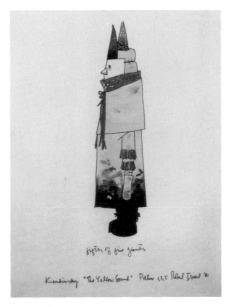

COSTUME SKETCHES FOR *THE YELLOW SOUND*,
DIRECTED BY IAN STRASSVOGEL.

How did the work in Holland come about?

The general director of the Netherlands Opera had seen my work in the United States. They gave me four operas in one-and-a-half years, and because the pay was better than what I was earning in the States, I had enough to move. I lived there for a total of four years. My first opera in Amsterdam was *The Good Soldier Schweik*. The last opera I did while I was living there was the premiere of *Satyagraha*.

What was it about the theatre experience in Europe that appealed to you as an artist?

A couple of things, I think. One, I really loved Amsterdam. Two—and I don't know whether it was true or not, but it was my perception—I liked the way the designer in Europe, as opposed to the designer in America, was treated. And three, from the pictures I had seen, European design looked different. It was much more interesting to me than American design.

In what way?

That's a very good question. This gets involved in a lot of political stuff. I think there was a great freeze that happened in the United States right after the Second World War—the Red scare, McCarthy, that stuff—that affected the arts. It enabled certain things to flourish and caused certain things to wither. All of the social painting of the 1930s, the WPA paintings, went away out of necessity. It was replaced by the great American paintings which, to me, exhibit this incredible, almost macho virulence. They were extraordinary, but they also lacked a kind of specificity in subject matter that the Social Realists' paintings possessed. Theatre faced the same problems, except it couldn't move into the realm of abstraction. Words tend to be a hell of a lot more specific than images, or at least we attend to them in a more specific way.

THE MUSIC-THEATER GROUP PRODUCTION OF
MARTHA CLARKE'S *THE HUNGER ARTIST.*,

American theatre moved into the living room and into the mind—into psychology, into interpersonal relationships. The heroism one associates with romantic theatre retreated. American theatre became incredibly domestic, and domesticity is not very interesting visually. Look at Europe during this same period, at Wolfgang Wagner's famous production of the *Ring* cycle at Bayreuth, for instance. In retrospect one can say that it, too, was designed out of a political necessity—the necessity to break away from that association between Wagner and Hitler. It was a very liberating production, and still very romantic. I think this production was pivotal in terms of European theatre. It is one of the great productions of the twentieth century. That kind of theatre didn't exist in the United States.

Will American theatre ever recover from this?

I don't think it's a matter of recovering. It's reacting. If you want to put it that way, painting has never recovered, but who wants it to recover? It's doing fine. Theatre design may evolve and revolve in other ways, but that period of time created an attitude toward the relationship of the designer and director, and the kinds of plays that were politically proper to do.

This is interesting in light of what is now happening with the National Endowment for the Arts, isn't it?

The need for substantial funding of the arts is very clear. There are very few areas in which we are allowed to deal with sub-

jectivity and ambivalence, which is really what life is about. One very good way of mirroring life is in the arts. Our society is incredibly brittle in dealing with these issues. We're not dealing with them wisely, and we're not funding the arts. Our society has this kind of self-perpetuating

THE HUNGER ARTIST.

THE SEATTLE OPERA PRODUCTION OF
RICHARD WAGNER'S *DAS RHEINGOLD*,
DIRECTED BY FRANCOIS ROCHAX.

death wish: the more brittle we get, the less we really want to deal with these issues because they are threatening. It's a terrible situation.

I'd like to return to something you said earlier about collaboration, about your reluctance to commit to the collaborative process. Is this still true for you?

No, it isn't. I think it was just a reticence on my part to take part in group activities. I think that's also why it took me so long to commit to theatre—and because I was skeptical of theatre as a high art. As someone who grew up in the sixties and was involved in the closing of schools, I had—and to a certain extent still have—a very idealistic and romantic view of what I approve of. Sometimes it's a little impractical. I can be too critical. I didn't want to collaborate and I didn't want to interpret. I wanted to be a primary mover. I don't feel that anymore. If I now have any misgivings about theatre, they don't have to do with collaboration.

What we do in collaboration is work together to make the project a theatrical experience. I have to laugh when critics say you come out whistling the set. What a ridiculous thing to say. The set should be as good as it can possibly be. Certain areas become more dominant at certain times, but to say that you're whistling the set must indicate that the other areas are weak . . . or the critic isn't being very clear about what he means. I like to work with people who want me to do my best. I like to work with people who will challenge me in terms of both what they want from themselves and what they want from me. One is involved in a project as a designer because one has something to offer that the director doesn't, which means there is a dialogue in which both people are exposed to each other. It is not my job to be a service-station attendant. It is my job to be involved visually in articulating a world on the stage.

For example?

The last thing Martha Clarke and I did, *Miracolo d'Amore*, for example. I gave her a set that wasn't easy to work on, that presented idiosyncratic sightlines. It had rooms off the back and side of the stage that were available—and only to a certain extent—to certain members of the audience. It was a very quirky, difficult set, but it gave her the possibility of doing things that she wouldn't have been able to do, obviously, with a living room and a couch. Whether the show or the design was successful doesn't matter at this point. We contended with ideas and found a way to make them work—because we have a relationship that allows for that problematic aspect to be nurtured.

Is your working relationship with Philip Glass similar?

Yes and no. Phil is very open, and he is very easy to work with. We're good friends, too, so we have a friendly, easy working relationship. When I did *Satyagraha*, I worked with both Constance DeJong and Phil in setting the piece, actually setting the libretto. The set for *Satyagraha* was designed before the director was hired, which was very difficult. I don't ever want to do that again. I think we had a very idiosyncratic working relationship with that particular opera. That wouldn't

be the same if I worked on another opera with Phil and another director.

Unlike all but one of the other designers in this book, you have spent much of your career teaching. Why?

I think arts education is very problematic right now, but I really like teaching. And I don't like being on the road a lot. It's a simple combination of these two things. I didn't teach while I was in Holland, but I taught for eleven or twelve years at the University of California at San Diego/La Jolla. And now this is my first year at UCLA.

Does teaching feed into your work?

It does if I have good students. If I don't have good students, it doesn't.

I'd like to talk about how you approach a project. Let's talk about The Flying Dutchman, *which you are currently designing for a production in Munich. What was the first thing you did?*

I went out and bought a new CD. Then I realized something that I probably knew underneath, and this was that I really love mid-nineteenth-century German theatre.

Was The Flying Dutchman *an opera you were familiar with?*

Yes, although it wasn't a piece I had thought about doing. There are some pieces you think about doing and then some pieces you don't, but when they present themselves you think, oh, this is just perfect. So I quickly got very excited about designing it.

I was doing *Don Giovanni* in Florence at the time Nicholas Lehnhoff called to ask if I would be interested in doing *The Flying Dutchman*. We figured out that I could fly to Munich and we could talk there. The talk went very well. We hit it off beautifully. I liked the way he addressed the subject in an unabashedly romantic way. His ideas were open-ended; they conjured up all kinds of images in my mind. I know that something is happening when images begin to resonate with one another. It's not just one image, but something happens there and then something else happens over there and they dovetail. That was happening in my mind during our conversation.

Then I left. We said we wouldn't talk or think about the opera anymore, but of course you think about it—although I didn't think about it that much. I did listen to the recording, however. Then we met again for about a day and a half, just a few weeks ago, and it just kind of exploded at that point. We knew what we wanted to do. I didn't know specifically what things were going to look like, but the egg had been fertilized.

What was it about that second conversation that, as you say, fertilized the egg?

A kind of ability on Nicholas's part to explain personalities in a way that allowed me to extrapolate environments. I guess that's the way it should work, but it doesn't always.

I prefer this to having someone say, "I need a table here, a window there, an extrance here, an exit there." If a director has specified that much before you meet, you're not going to be designing, you're going to be decorating. I don't like situations like that. I do not like decorating. I like collaborating.

I think of your work as environmental. There's almost always the sense of a complete environment on stage.

It's a three-dimensional space, but I'm not sure that it's sculptural space.

At what point do you start putting something down on paper?

Sometimes it happens with incredible ease; sometimes it's like grunting and groaning. It doesn't have to do with the director as much as with the work. In this case, it happened from our conversation. In *The Flying Dutchman* there are two ships and two real personalities who ex-hibit very different points of view in the first act. If one can imagine this merchant sailor—and that's all he can possibly be—in this bizarre setting, where all these women are spinning, we might extrapolate some sort of sweatshop or mill situation. We also have this spectral figure, who wants more than anything else to be at peace. The question I asked was: Are these things compatible with one another? Not that they should be, but then what does it mean if they are not compatible? I don't think they are directly compatible, but they don't clash with each other either.

Then we have Senta, Daland's daughter, who has perhaps the opposite vision. The Dutchman's vision may be identified as one of bourgeois rest; Senta's vision is one of a romantic hero. So you have all these things that weigh against each other and which create a very rich atmosphere when you bring them into contact with each other.

I was wandering through the Rizzoli bookstore in Milan, and I asked if they had any nautical books. And sure enough, they had these two books of incredible technical drawings of the Lusitania and Aquatania. Incredible, really spectacular. They resonated perfectly in terms of what Nicholas had spoken about. I also felt I wanted the Dutchman's environment, which is something unreal, to intrude in some way, to break in on that first scene. I didn't want to be tethered by technical problems, how it would happen, so I just let that go. What I came up with was a very simple platform that looks suspiciously like the steps at the Parthenon. Then I placed industrial columns with Corinthian capitals around the steps and put these huge turbines and an extrapolation of a steering wheel in the middle. It became a kind of industrial temple.

For the second scene I took a cue from Nicholas's idea that the Dutchman was an image of bourgeois rest. Well, what was the most bourgeois-restful thing I could think of? I thought of an Edwardian drawing room with a big fireplace. So I'm using wood paneling for the walls, which are very detailed, but they're out of scale, too big. The doors are too big, which makes a person look very small. Then, extending from the back wall, tipped on its side, is the large hull of a ship. It's a gigantic presence, but simplified—a huge whale-like shape. Over the fireplace is one of those insipid sea paintings in which there is no ship. And then just an easy chair for the Dutchman to sit in.

The industrial temple—with the columns, those turbines, and the wheel—sinks down and the scene-two set moves forward. It looks so bizarre, but I'm very excited about it. I think what excites me the most is how it intrudes on the commonplace. It's a common room, but with this gigantic, intruding presence. There's

MARTHA CLARKE'S *ENDANGERED SPECIES*, A MUSIC-THEATER GROUP/BROOKLYN ACADEMY OF MUSIC PRODUCTION.

something so wonderful about intruding on the common with something fantastical.

How much sketching do you do?

Very little. I am mistrustful of sketching because I can't work out the proportions exactly. It's one thing to draw a figure and another to draw a space. You can't tell how far this boat is from this wall in this sketch, for instance. I have an easy time visualizing things and changing them over and over again in my mind, so when I get an idea—and this may be tedious—I go to the model right away. It may be very, very rough, very crude, but the closer I can approximate the stage, the better I like it.

PROKOFIEV'S *THE FIERY ANGEL*, DIRECTED BY
ANDREI SERBAN FOR THE LOS ANGELES
MUSIC CENTER OPERA.

This is not what you're taught to do, but I don't care. What I think is important is what process works for you, which is why I don't like imposing processes on people. In fact, I think it's dangerous.

Do you follow the same process when designing costumes?

One doesn't manipulate space in the same way with costumes. And yet one can be more specific about the sets in terms of the mechanical drawings. A right angle is a right angle. The lack of specificity in costumes is a far more empathetic discipline. I'm pretty specific in drawing costumes, but at the same time it doesn't happen until you pick the fabrics, until you pick the colors, until you have the fittings.

You almost always do both sets and costumes. Why?

It means fewer meetings. No, that's not totally accurate. I think I've done only one production for which I did not do both sets and costumes. It gives me a sense of control over both the color and the content. I don't want to make this room and then leave it to someone else to come up with costumes. That figure is the Flying Dutchman, and it has to do with this room. People inhabit rooms who are supposed to inhabit rooms. When you're deal-ing with metaphors that butt up against each other, you want to make sure they're the right metaphors.

But you don't design lighting.

No, but I'm there all the time with the lighting designer. There's only so much I can do without having a nervous break-down. I also think that the lighting designer, to a certain extent, is at a disadvantage in that his work happens in the theatre. He has got to think on his feet. This also means that the set and costume designers are able to have greater input because they're there when the lighting designer is thinking.

Which productions are you most pleased with?

I guess I'm never completely pleased, and I look back fondly on certain productions not because of the design but because of who I was working with. If I have to pick a few pieces, they would have to be *Satyagraha* with Phil, *Vienna: Lusthaus* and *The Hunger Artist* with Martha Clarke, and the *Ring* cycle, which I did in Seattle. One more: *The Kaiser of Atlantis*, which was seen in Holland. It was really wonderful. It was a world premiere of an opera written during World War II in a German concentration camp.

What do you think characterizes your work?

I hope this doesn't sound evasive, but I think it shows a certain aggressiveness about space. I think there is a focus and, at the same time, within that focus, a certain anxiety. What this creates is a space with which one is both comfortable and uncomfortable. A space in which things come into contact with each other, and in which things seem to have a good sense of clarity and proportion in relationship to each other—except something is wrong. It sets up a kind of vibration that, I guess, is the thing I'm most proud of.

I'm very finicky when it comes to details. And I do not like stage painting. If the set is going to include that kind of painting, it has to be reduced in some way. In *Siegfried*, for example, the forest was all very tight paintings of forest trees, but on flats that were leaning against other flats, some painted and some not, like a jerry-rigged forest. When Siegfried entered, the flats fell as he walked across the stage.

I'm also always straining with the idea of sightlines, even when there are very good sightlines in the theatre. The idea of a sightline is an intolerable tyranny that we inflict on ourselves and the audience. Sightlines are also a part of that dialogue which has to do with illusion and reality, which concerns me as a designer.

What would be an ideal project for you?

What I'm doing. I can think of things I would like to design, but I am very happy with what I'm doing now. I just wish there was a little more breathing room. The ideal project would be to build a theatre in the backyard and do it here. That's what I really want. This is a very strange part of the world, and it doesn't respond well to theatre for a number of reasons. Hopefully this will change, but I don't know that it will. I've only done two things in southern California, *The Fiery Angel* and *Mahagonny*—and I've been here for twelve or thirteen years. But that's okay. I like living here. My wife and son are here. I'm always rushing back here because I like being here. I like to be able to flop down on my own bed or come into this room and work.

What do you think it is about Los Angeles that doesn't support theatre?

That's a simple question to answer. Los Angeles' most prominent feature is the film industry. And it's not an art form, it's an industry. The fact that it utilizes some people who might be in theatre makes it very confusing. A lot of the people who do theatre here are doing it to be showcased, which means that few people are concerned about the plays. Everyone knows that actors are at the center of the theatre, but as Shakespeare says, the play's the thing. But it gets fragmented here. People go back to theatre, they say, to be stretched. That seems like a bunch of bullshit to me. Does that mean that when you go away from theatre to do film, you are flabby? If that is the analogy, then the question is, how can you be any good in theatre if you're not practicing all the time? One should always be in shape. It's a combination of things that produces an insidious underbelly to the art form. There are people here who want to make theatre happen, but it's a bigger struggle here than in a lot of places that have far less resources.

Where do you draw your inspiration from?

I read. I talk to friends. I talk to my wife and son. I work in the theatre. And I love going to art museums. I love going into the Uffizi and looking at those Botticellis.

HEIDI
LANDESMAN

Heidi Landesman, following the example of designers like Oliver Smith, is also a producer. As she explains in this interview, producing and designing the same production makes sense for a number of practical reasons, but "finding an exciting project and then putting it together is thrilling. It makes you feel a lot less powerless, more in control of your own destiny, than when you're just a designer for hire."

Although Landesman, who was raised in California and received her training as a set designer at Yale, admires the abstract theatre work of European and Russian designers more than much of the work being done by her American contemporaries, the work for which she is best known is anything but abstract. The bucolic landscape of trees and flowers assembled for the Central Park production of *A Midsummer Night's Dream*; the oppressive, seemingly airless interior for Marsha Norman's *'night, Mother*; and the affectionate, almost poetic interior for Tina Howe's *Painting Churches* reveal a designer skilled at handling realistic environments. This is not to imply that Landesman's abstract sets are less successful,

FACING PAGE, ANTON CHEKHOV'S *THE CHERRY ORCHARD*, DIRECTED BY TOM MOORE FOR LA JOLLA PLAYHOUSE.

however. Her sets, whether realistic or abstract, almost always exhibit an unmannered theatricality that illuminates the script, and provide an all-encompassing single environment in which the play can take place.

FEBRUARY 24, 1989—
HEIDI LANDESMAN'S STUDIO,
BROOKLYN, NEW YORK

I grew up in California, near San Francisco. Although I don't remember anything about the design, the first show I remember seeing was *Othello*. And I saw *The Nutcracker*. Nobody in my family was involved in theatre, nor were they particularly interested in it. I became interested in theatre in high school and got involved in all aspects of it—acting, directing and designing—when I went to boarding school, in Connecticut.

What was the name of the school?

Miss Porter's. I'm a preppie, I admit it. But coming from California and being in the repressive atmosphere of an Eastern boarding school, I think it was natural for me to get involved in theatre. I went back to California after Miss Porter's and attended Occidental College, in Los Angeles. I double-majored in art and theatre, which meant I could do a lot of painting and sculpture plus act, direct, write plays and design. It was an extremely unstructured education, which I highly recommend. It's a good way to become a better designer.

Were you interested in art as a child?

I had always drawn. Most designers will probably say that they don't have the self-discipline to paint on their own. I need to be forced to do it; I need to work with schedules and under deadlines. Maybe I'm just lazy, but I could never be a studio artist. I just don't have the temperament for it. Also, I genuinely enjoy the collaborative process. At some point I realized that theatre design was a good way to combine both loves. Then I went to Yale, where I got my master's and was able to do a little bit of acting.

What kinds of roles did you do?

I acted only occasionally, but I did new plays—little things here and there, one by Albert Innaurato. At the time, Yale didn't like students crossing over into different areas. They were fairly rigid about it, in fact, which I still think is a mistake. I don't think it's a good way to run a drama school. It generates a sort of defensiveness, a sense of obsessive protectiveness, in the people in each area.

Why did you decide to go to Yale?

Partly because of Ming Cho Lee, who also went to Occidental and knew one of my professors. The professor suggested I apply to Yale, and at that time the alternatives were not appealing. UCLA had a big program, but it was enormous, mechanical and cinema-oriented. And there was NYU, which wasn't particularly good. All the other schools seemed so technically oriented, less interested in the entire theatre experience. Even now I notice that students coming out of, say, Carnegie seem to be focused only on their area of interest. In general, they don't have a broad base of educational interest.

Did you ever consider going into film?

No. I've never designed a film, so I speak from a certain mythology of what it must be like, but film appears to be much more realistic than theatre. Unless you're doing futuristic movies, you're interior decorating most of the time . . . or just recreating something from a different period in a slightly different color. I'm interested in doing work that is much more abstract.

What kind of influence, if any, did Ming Cho Lee have on you at Yale?

I always fought away from Ming. We would fight a lot, in fact, but in a friendly way. I think he enjoyed the fact that our sensibilities were so totally different. I could never imitate Ming. A lot of the students, even now, go through a period of trying to please Ming before they find their own style. I didn't have that problem. My aesthetic was so different that I didn't have to struggle to discover what it was.

How would you describe your aesthetic at that time?

It was very theatrical and very anti-architectural. I took an extremely conceptual approach to design. Whenever I found out what the traditional approach was, I tried the opposite—even if it was completely inappropriate. Ming, on the other hand, was very involved in using bits of architecture, which never interested me.

When did you graduate from Yale?

1976. Then I lived in New Haven for another year because Rocco, my future husband, was teaching at Yale.

Were you designing at the time?

Yes, I did some regional-theatre stuff. I did a couple of shows in St. Louis, I taught, I did something at Playwrights Horizons.

How did you get those jobs?

I knew some people in St. Louis. I took my portfolio around. The connections I made at Yale didn't really help until later, until after they had established themselves as well. I was in a wonderful class, but it wasn't that someone wrote a play that immediately went to Broadway. Nor did Yale Repertory serve the same function that it does now, in terms of moving productions into New York City.

THE CHERRY ORCHARD, ACT 3.

THE CHERRY ORCHARD, ACT 2.

was having a conversation with a friend recently about the correlation between water and creative thinking. She was saying that she gets her best ideas in the shower. Some people say they get their best ideas while they're brushing their teeth. The point is, I avoid sitting down at the drafting table and thinking of ideas. I find it creates a block. I also avoid problem solving or doing a ground plan too soon. I hope to come up with some imagery that can stay in my mind long enough that it can be translated eventually into solving the problems of the show.

Do you do research?

Yeah, yeah. In fact, I usually do a lot of research first. I look at material and then put it away. I find images in the research that kind of just sit there, and then they become appealing to me. I tend not to do much reading, so the research is usually visual. But it's very specific to the play.

What kind of interaction do you have with the director?

It depends on the director. Some directors want to sit down and look at all of the research, others don't. I prefer not to go through the research with the director until I've had an opportunity to edit it. Then I'll bring in images that I'm responding to.

I did a series of shows at the Public Theater after I moved into the city. The Dodger Theatre Company was started by some of my friends from Yale, and while working for them I met directors like Des McAnuff. Then Des did some work at the Public, so I worked there again with him. That led to other work. James Lapine, who was also from Yale, directed some things, and I worked for him, which then led to other productions.

How do you approach a project?

I try to read the script a couple of times. And then I ignore it—I'll go swimming. I

You've worked with some very different directors, from Des McAnuff to Richard Foreman. How would you compare the two?

Richard is very specific; he knows exactly what he wants. I think he does fascinating work, but working with him wasn't a satisfying experience. Des, on the other hand, tends to be very open-minded. When we did *Romeo and Juliet*, for instance, he said he wanted something architectural and in bad shape, almost like a ruin. That was it. I came up with something based on that. For *Big River* I brought him rough sketches, which he liked, and we refined it from there.

Unless the director has something specific in mind, I generally like to bring a specific, strong image to the director first. I do the initial rough sketches in pencil, making them as grubby as possible because I assume we'll draw on top of them. When I come up with an idea for the whole image, the color usually comes with it. I suppose it's like dreaming in color as opposed to black-and-white.

At what point do you start solving design problems?

After the director looks at the roughs and says he likes the general idea. Then I'll go to a rough model. I'll use the rough model to play with volume and dimension and sometimes color. I think white models are confusing, deceptive. The purity of a white model has such a presence that the director is always surprised when that pure, sculptural space receives whatever treatment it's going to receive. Very few directors can leap from what the white space looks like to what it will look like in color. I'll do a white model for myself—I'll cut out things, move them around—but I've found that it's not very helpful for the director to go through that part of the process with me. I will, however, mock up a ½″ model later when we start working out the details.

THE CHERRY ORCHARD, ACT 4.

Have you ever gotten into the middle of a project and then decided that the design is all wrong?

Sometimes. It usually occurs when the design gets compromised. That happened with *Urban Blight*, at the Manhattan Theatre Club. The show had two directors who didn't agree on anything. And the producer had a fairly strong opinion as well. The set became neutral so as not to offend any of the three. It just died in the process. But I realized that I couldn't find myself in that kind of situation again. There is just no solution, no way to please three very different aesthetics. I've never quit a job, but at the end of a bad situation I always think, I knew this was coming, I should have walked away.

Is design more easily compromised on Broadway?

Because of economics?

Yes.

No, I don't think so. On the contrary, Off Broadway you find yourself in very, very tight-budget situations. And because the financial stakes are so much lower, the producers are less willing to spend large amounts of money on the scenery. On Broadway, where everybody has now decided that the scenery is part of the spectacle that the audience is paying fifty dollars to see, most producers realize that it is part of the expense. I think you are in much more danger of compromising Off Broadway.

Does this mean that you are less willing to do Off-Broadway work?

It's much more difficult. Doing an Off-Broadway show, as opposed to doing a resident-theatre or a regular Broadway show, is the most work of all because there is no staff. You end up doing everything

THE NEW YORK SKAKESPEARE FESTIVAL (DELECORTE THEATER) PRODUCTION OF A MIDSUMMER NIGHT'S DREAM, DIRECTED BY JAMES LAPINE.

yourself. Off Broadway is almost always underbudgeted. So unless the project is something you're dying to do, it's a lot of time and a lot of labor and very little money. And there's not a lot of satisfaction because the work gets compromised.

Which of your designs are you most pleased with?

I really like the *Midsummer Night's Dream* in Central Park. I liked the landscape. It was really fun, although it was a real battle getting it done that way.

A battle with the director or with the producer?

Joseph Papp was fine, actually. He thought the design was terrific and had no problem with it. I think the staff at the Delacorte thought it would create enormous problems. It certainly did create a lot of problems, but anything you try that hasn't been done before will do that. The process was fascinating, and it seemed to be a good solution to designing in that very difficult space. Plus I learned a lot about gardening and landscape architecture.

How was the idea for that design developed?

It was one of those things that was so obvious that it never had to be developed. I remember James Lapine suggesting we do *Midsummer Night's Dream* in the park. I said, "Gee, wouldn't it be fun if we did it with real trees and flowers." Jim said, "That's what I was thinking, too." And that's what we did. Nobody racked their brains. I worked out the topography with a landscape architect because it wasn't something I knew anything about. We selected trees from nurseries all over the country. Jim and I worked out what he needed and then we worked out a couple of tricks the set did.

You have done two shows with Marsha Norman, 'night, Mother and Traveler in the Dark. What input does the playwright have on your work?

'Night, Mother was another design that was very easy to come up with once I understood the intention of the play. It's so clear and direct, and what was required was crystal clear to me. It wasn't hard to translate the image into scenery—how to make the space oppressive without being depressing. The color, too, fell into place. Everything had the same intensity, but nothing was too dark or too light. We charted it all so that it had this blandness to it. It was amazing how many people came to us after seeing the show and said they had an uncle who killed himself in an apartment exactly like that. I didn't do any research for *'night, Mother* at all. I've spent almost no time in the Midwest or South, and I knew nothing about what those places looked like. But many people told us that they lived in Kentucky or Missouri, and that their mother lived in a place that looked exactly like the set, down to the carpet. It was really spooky.

How would you explain that?

I don't know. I think some sort of instinct took over during the design process because I really tried to work from the characters in the play. They were very clear, and their taste was very clear. I never wanted to make fun of the characters' taste, because that would have been wrong, but I wanted to find a way to express the tragedy of their taste within their environment. The set struck a lot of chords that people recognized.

When Marsha and I did *Traveler in the Dark* at ART, however, I didn't know how to design the play because it was much less clear. Marsha said she knew there were problems with the script when she saw the trouble I was having designing it. The script was unclear, and I couldn't find a style for it. Because the play lay between two stylistically different poles, it was hard to find the right way to express it visually. Marsha was helpful about specific elements—and some of the elements worked well individually—but I couldn't come up with a notion that pulled it all

together. Although the set got good reviews, it never really worked for me.

And the director couldn't help?

I think he was confused, too. He tried to be helpful, but we were unable to pin down the script, which was also unresolved.

Has your design aesthetic changed over the years?

It goes through different phases. It even goes through different phases of color. I don't think it was ever decorative. Nor was it ever particularly detailed, or based on accumulated detail. It still isn't. I went to the Soviet Union in the fall of 1987. There design tends to be extremely bold and abstract, and the trip reinforced my tendency to move in that direction. I guess I realized what I do well as opposed to what I don't do well, and I learned to avoid shows I'm not going to do well. I'm not going to do realistic interiors well, nor do I want to spend my time doing them—they just don't interest me.

Does this mean you turn down projects?

Yes. I have two small children and my time is really precious, so I can design only a few shows each year. They have to be shows that I have a real desire to do. It's

not possible for me to do ten shows a year. I did a show in Los Angeles and found it really too difficult. I can't spend that much time away from home. It may limit the kinds of projects I can accept, but I think that's healthy. I've become very specific about what interests me, what projects I want to do.

How many shows a year do you do?

About three or four.

You both design and produce. How did that come about? What is the relationship between the two?

Traditionally there have been a lot of producers/designers. Oliver Smith is the

FACING PAGE, TINA HOWE'S *PAINTING CHURCHES*, DIRECTED BY CAROLE ROTHMAN. ABOVE, MODEL FOR *PAINTING CHURCHES*.

MODEL FOR THE BROADWAY PRODUCTION OF
BIG RIVER, DIRECTED BY DES MCANUFF.
FACING PAGE, MODEL FOR THE MARK TAPER
FORUM PRODUCTION OF JON ROBIN BAITZ'S
DUTCH LANDSCAPE, DIRECTED BY
GORDON DAVIDSON.

people are in every field, so they're usually able to put together a good creative staff.

I also think this has happened because of the shortage of wonderful projects to work on. The material may be wonderful but the director isn't interesting, or the director is great and the material isn't. There's always some flaw. Finding an exciting project and then putting it together is thrilling. It makes you feel a lot less powerless, more in control of your own destiny, than when you're just a designer for hire.

But as both producer and designer, how do you interact with the director? Isn't that problematic?

I think most directors need someone who can function as an editor. Very few directors are capable of editing down material without being prodded to do so. A lot of directors also ask for everything they think they can get, which is sort of the nature of directors. They need an authoritative figure who can say, you don't need this, this is unnecessary, or this is confusing the issue. There are very few producers who can do that anymore, which is a problem. In a good collaboration, a good producer performs that function early enough in the process so that it doesn't have to happen during previews, when everyone is hysterical.

most obvious one. It actually makes a lot of sense. Because designers tend to be slightly removed from the process, they're able to both analyze it and remain somewhat objective. Designers tend not to have the ego problems that a lot of the playwrights or directors have. And I think many designers frequently have a better overall vision of a show than the director. The designer certainly knows how the show is put together, in terms of the practicalities. Designers, because they've worked with them, also know who the best

If the designer also produces the show, he knows what's going on at every moment. The nondesigner producer is rarely in that position. It's easy for a project to get out of the producer's control. Producers are always considered the money people, the outside people, even when they may have originated the project. When the producer is not a part of the creative team, he has less influence over the direction the project is taking.

Will there come a time when you move completely into producing and no longer design?

Oh no, I don't think so. I really enjoy designing. And producing alone is a pretty thankless task.

Do you teach?

No. I taught at both the School for Visual Arts and at FIT for a year, but I'm not interested in teaching. There are too many other things I want to do.

What do you see happening now in design?

The Yale kids tend to be rather conservative, but I think that's reflecting the nature of the school right now. It's also a reflection of the times we're living in. I don't see much European influence, which I regret. American design is twenty years behind European design . . . at least twenty years. It may have something to do with directors and with the material they're being given, but American design, in general, tends to be conservative.

Who are the designers you admire?

Some of the Russian designers we saw in 1987 are wonderful. The designers who work in the Berlin theatre. Sally Jacobson. I think Maria Björnson does some fascinating work. And I think the Japanese designer who did *M. Butterfly* is quite wonderful. I fine those abstract designers very appealing. American designers? Not many.

Why?

Because the work of American designers tends to be rather traditional, not particularly startling. But I don't blame them. I think they're victims of the directors and the direction that American theatre is taking now, which isn't very interesting.

Do you think this will change?

Yes, I think it will. I think the British design we are seeing on Broadway is a healthy influence. I hope that as a result, American design will become less decorative, less realistic.

But British design is often criticized for being too spectacular. A number of people question whether it is a healthy direction for American design.

If "spectacular" means extremely theatrical, then it's all for the good. On the other hand, if it means just a lot of scenery decorated to within an inch of its life, then I don't find "the spectacle" particularly appealing. But the design for *Les Misérables* was brilliant. It wasn't spectacular in the American sense of the word, but it was spectacular in that it created a truly theatrical event, an event that couldn't be reproduced in any other media. When the spectacle contributes to the theatricality, which can occur only in the theatre, I think it's fine, it's exciting, and I think it's doing the theatre a service. If it's spectacle just for the sake of excess, like in *Legs Diamond* . . . that was just a lot of scenery, and who knows to what end. There have been periods of theatre history in which the sense of spectacle has been integral to the theatrical experience. Fine. This is not an unusual period we're going through. Minimalism gets boring, too.

What would be an ideal project for you?

I love doing Shakespeare. No matter how bad the production might be, I never feel as if I'm wasting my time. With Shakespeare, you always learn something. I'd really like to do *King Lear* or *Macbeth* or *Hamlet*. But women get typed into the romances and men get to do *King Lear*. I think it's a sexist thing.

Which brings up my next question. Has being a woman in this profession been difficult? Is it easier for women designers now than it was?

Oh, it's a lot better now, sure. I was the first woman designer to graduate from Yale, and I was the first to win a Tony. But I say that and then think, gee, if it's so much better, where are the rest of the women? If it is better, there should be a lot more of them visible and working. A number of women call me and I'll look at their portfolios, they'll work with me, they'll assist me. But they don't seem to be emerging in the same way as the young male designers. And I don't know why.

Have you lost projects because you are a woman?

Oh yes, I think so. But I'm also sure men lost projects to me because I'm a woman.

Certain projects, I think, are perceived as being either feminine or masculine. I probably get more offers to do plays written by women than many men because I am perceived as being more sensitive to the needs of those plays. Women designers are not given technically complicated shows because they are perceived as not being mechanically inclined. Although I know a lot of male designers who know nothing about mechanics, the perception isn't applied to them.

I also think that the decision is an economic one, that the biggest chunk of the budget for a Broadway show goes to the physical production. Both male and female producers are nervous about trusting that much money to a woman. But it's the same for women architects. For generations and generations there were no women architects because the perception was that they were unable to handle steel and wood and hard materials.

Would you like to do opera or film?

Not really. Opera doesn't interest me. In fact, I try to avoid opera whenever I can. I know this is heretical, but having to sit through an opera is almost unbearable for me. I feel the same way about ballet and modern dance. I find them both extremely boring. If it's not something I can respond to, it's not a good project for me to do.

HUGH LANDWEHR

H<small>UGH</small> <small>LANDWEHR</small> may be the quintessential regional theatre designer. Although Landwehr lives on the Upper West Side of Manhattan and maintains a studio on lower Broadway, his busy schedule, which may include as many as fourteen productions a year, takes him to regional theatres all across the country, from Williamstown Theatre Festival, Long Wharf and Center Stage, in the East, to the Old Globe and Seattle Repertory, on the West Coast.

Landwehr is not what one would identify as a "concept designer." That is, his sets, which can be visually complex and full of telling detail, do not illustrate a script in such a way that the audience, on first seeing the set, immediately knows what the play or the production is about. Rather, Landwehr talks about developing a "strategy" for the set, which he feels creates a more interesting kind of tension for the audience. While this approach to set design is evident in much of Landwehr's work, it is best illustrated by the Williamstown Theatre Festival production of *Holiday*, which Landwehr discusses in detail in this interview.

Having recently decided that he would like to contribute to the continuance of

FACING PAGE, THE WILLIAMSTOWN THEATRE FESTIVAL PRODUCTION OF TENNESSEE WILLIAMS'S *THE ROSE TATTOO*, DIRECTED BY IRENE LEWIS.

"this handmade activity which we call theatre design," Landwehr has started teaching at the University of Wisconsin, in Madison. And while he admits to not having mastered the juggling of an academic schedule with his professional commitments, he is quick to point out the benefits of teaching: "It has made me articulate ideas and issues in design that concern me. Not unexpectedly, I'm probably learning more than my students, and the moments when we both step forward are very rewarding."

FEBRUARY 23, 1989—
HUGH LANDWEHR'S STUDIO,
NEW YORK CITY

I was born in what was known at the turn of the century as the vaudeville capital of the world: Trenton, New Jersey. My father's family was in the restaurant business. My grandfather was from Germany via Switzerland, and was trained to be a chef when he was a boy. My father became a part of that business, and my grandparents and he ran a very successful restaurant not too far from Washington's Crossing, in New Jersey, for about forty years. My mother's family was in the fruit and produce business in Trenton.

There were stifled visual artistic ambitions on my father's side of the family all the way back to my grandfather, and ama-teur and professional musicians on my mother's side. How those strains ended up in me I'm not precisely sure, but I think they have something to do with what I'm doing now.

I went to public schools in Trenton until I reached ninth grade, when I went to a private school called Lawrenceville. I graduated in 1972 from Yale College with a B.A. in art history. During the summers, from the time I was seventeen, I did summer stock. In some ways I had an old-fashioned apprenticeship in practical theatre, but at college it was an extracurricular activity because there was no formal drama major at Yale at that time. I enjoyed art history and it exercised a part of me that, as it turns out, has been very useful in my work.

Were you involved in theatre in any way while you were growing up?

Oh, I did a lot of theatre in junior high school and secondary school. I acted and I designed scenery, although back then I had no idea about how it all fit together, or how to serve the play. We just kind of did it. I seem to remember it turning out okay.

Did your parents take you to the theatre?

My mother took us to musicals in New York when I was a kid. I can remember seeing *The Sound of Music* and *My Fair Lady* and *Ben Franklin in Paris*, plus more obscure stuff. *The Sound of Music* was particularly impressive. I don't remember who did the design, but it was at the Lunt-Fontanne, and I remember a whole hill emerging from backstage for the first number. As an eight- or nine-year-old, I was really wowed by that. Straight theatre? Not really. I only became interested in plays when I was twelve or thirteen, I guess, when I got two of the Gassner anthologies. I read them from cover to cover, retaining very little, but excited by the idea of all these different plays. Occasionally I would also come across a book in which I could find a picture of the scenery for a play I was reading, and that excited me.

It sounds as if you were most excited by the physical aspect of the theatre.

Yes, I think so, probably because I had a number of abilities—interpretive, manual and visual skills—that I could put together and do what is close to what a set designer does. I had always drawn, even as a very young child, so that means of expressing myself was available to me right from the start. I was very interested in music. And I acted, which I think is everybody's entry into the profession.

THE CENTER STAGE PRODUCTION OF SAM
SHEPARD'S *BURIED CHILD*, DIRECTED BY
MICHAEL ENGLER.

A lot of designers once acted.

It makes a lot of sense. Acting is the core of
the onion. All of the other layers you can
peel away.

*What was it about the design process
itself that attracted you?*

I loved collaborating with people. I also
think that a lot of people in theatre are
easily bored—I'm probably one of those

people—but I never seemed to be while I
was doing theatre. Also, my interests are
radial, they fan out, and I'm able to pay
attention to—and take in—lots of different influences. The theatre is that kind
of activity par excellence, I think. There
was a point at which I thought about being
a fine artist, an easel artist, and I did some
painting in school, but I couldn't imagine
what to do after about three weeks of sitting in front of an easel. I would do well for
short periods of time, but then I would

feel intensely nutsy and lonely. I think it's
a very, very hard job, which I'm not tem-
peramentally suited to do.

How did you choose to go to Yale?

They chose me. I had a very strange series
of college choices as I recall. I applied to
Yale, to Carnegie Tech as an undergraduate design candidate, and to Tulane, which
was known at that time for having a good
drama department. But I went to Yale.

ABOVE, SKETCH FOR *MEASURE FOR MEASURE*, DIRECTED BY DOUGLAS HUGHES FOR SEATTLE REPERTORY THEATRE. FACING PAGE, PRODUCTION PHOTOGRAPH.

There was some pressure from my parents about getting a complete background, and I think I share that view. I don't think professional, undergraduate training for designers, or for other theatre people, is such a good idea. Knowing a little something about biology or French literature or archeology is actually very helpful. Narrowing down is not something you want to do too soon, maybe not even ever. In college I would work in three-week stints. I'd do art history for three weeks, and then I'd go off and do theatre for three weeks. I was quite content going back and forth between the two.

I'd like to return to your summer stock experience.

The first summer after I graduated from Lawrenceville I went to the New London Barn Players, in New London, New Hampshire. It was, and is, a small, non-Equity company in a barn. Everyone lived on the property. No one had a car, so you could only walk about a mile in any direction. It was one-week stock for eleven weeks. We did nine musicals and two straight plays. The musicals were *Desert Song, Pal Joey, Camelot, Half a Sixpence, Wonderful Town* . . . big shows. The stage was something like 14' deep and 24' wide. You couldn't cross backstage. You had to cross on a porch behind the stage, and if it was raining you had to watch that you didn't slip and fall.

As I recall, there were eight male apprentices and eight female apprentices. We all lived in one house, we all built the scenery, we all cleaned the toilets, we all acted in the plays. I remember in *Desert Song*, for instance, there were so few in the cast that the guys playing the Arabs also had to play the French Legionnaires. Very tricky. We weren't worrying about character so much as where the rifle was we were supposed to be carrying in that scene. It was the epitome of "summer stock." It was the normal, exploitative sort of relationship that apprentices in the theatre experience. But it was very useful.

Where did you learn the technical aspects of designing?

I learned it while doing it at Yale, really. When I was a freshman, I saw a notice for *The Hostage*, being produced by the Yale Dramatic Association. They were looking for a set designer. So I thought, oh, that sounds interesting, I bet I could do that. So I set up an interview with the director, and I did twelve or thirteen little sketches for him, one right after the other. He liked the sketches and decided that I should do the play. Okay, great. So I built this little model and did some more sketches. And then they asked for the draftings, and I thought, oh no. I had never done draftings before. So very coyly I said, "Do you have some old draftings I could look at. I'd like to know how much information you need." They said, "No, they all get destroyed in the course of the production."

So I sat down with a scale rule, which I had never used before, and thought, I guess this is how it works. I did it by being under pressure to do it. I found out that one of the most important things in designing is that, once you have decided what something should look like, you have to be confident about your own decisions. What I needed to do was be very careful

about how I got from the sketch to the drafting to the finished piece, which really describes the technical process of designing. If you can't be confident about your own initial decisions, you should be doing something else. The real core of this work is confidence in your own instincts.

Did being dropped in the deep end, so to speak, influence the look of your work in any way?

I think I was dumb enough not to let it influence my work. I knew what I wanted

for the set, and no one was there to ask why I wanted it green with sticks at the top of the wall, or why I wanted crummy plaster here and there. I had thrashed all of that out with the director in those original sketches. It was the first time I was designing something that was entirely my own. I recall it being a good set, but I was flying almost entirely blind. I was lucky in that the guys building the scenery were much more experienced than I was. They were respectful of both me and the design.

What happened after Yale?

The question was whether or not I wanted to go to the drama school at Yale. I had been in New Haven for four years, and I wasn't keen on staying there. Donald Oenslager had retired two years before and Ming Cho Lee was just coming in. I was approached about applying, but I eventually decided not to. A friend of mine, an assistant designer at Hartford Stage Company, decided to go back to drama school and suggested that I apply for her job.

I went up to talk with Paul Weidner—I didn't even have a resume, that was how ignorant I was—and he very kindly listened and wrote out my resume as I talked. I got the job, and that's what I did for the next five years. I had the great good fortune to be working at a theatre where John Conklin, Santo Loquasto, David Jen-

kins and Marjorie Kellogg were designing. I was the assistant designer, so I was their representative when they weren't in Hartford. I also had certain prop duties and I painted the shows. So, in fact, it was a drama school. They were fabulous people to learn from. I can't imagine where I would have gotten better or more varied teaching.

How would you describe their sensibilities, particularly John Conklin's and Santo Loquasto's?

I always think of John as being the Mozart of design and Santo as being the Beethoven. John is a painter, he presents the audience with flat surfaces that are painted or textured, and Santo is a maker of spaces, frequently hollowing out a space and then filling it or not. The ease with which John works is astounding. He makes himself the conduit for the work that is going to happen. It's evident in his scenery, which is not encumbered in the least. It's just out there.

Santo investigates everything. He worries and goes back over things, he invests things, builds. His concern with detail is amazing. He is also a person who is supremely in the moment. He's right there as it is happening. I don't think there is anyone more comfortable in a theatre than Santo. John will sometimes listen to Mozart on his Walkman while he's watch-

ing a tech rehearsal, but Santo is right there, going up on stage, complaining, thrashing around, fiddling.

Their sensibilities and individual processes are much more complex, of course, and each can do what I think the other is known for, but that's how I would characterize their work. It was extraordinarily lucky for me that I was exposed to both of them early in my career.

Were you designing for other theatres while you were at Hartford?

Not really, except during the summers I worked at Williamstown.

Did you work with Nikos Psacharopoulos?

I had worked with Nikos at Yale. He directed my last show there, which was Gorky's *Enemies*. He was a great soul. He was full of contradictions, and the lessons he had to teach were many and various. His energies will be missed in many ways.

What did you learn from Nikos?

During *Enemies* I learned a kind of additive design that I had not been exposed to up until that point. By this I mean that Nikos showed me how to create the life of the characters—which is to say, the life of the play—on stage, bit by bit. He taught

me about the geographical location of the scenery, its architectural logic . . . stuff I was sensitive to but hadn't put together yet. He taught me how to show that something had happened before the scene started, as with the cucumbers that litter the table at the beginning of the second act of *Enemies*. As we continued to work together over the next fifteen years, he sensitized me to the difference between concept and strategy. I think many drama schools try to teach students how to de-

THE CENTER STAGE PRODUCTION OF G.B. SHAW'S *MAJOR BARBARA*, DIRECTED BY STANLEY WOJEWODSKI, JR.

GRACE MCKEANEY'S *WHO THEY ARE AND HOW IT IS WITH THEM*, DIRECTED BY JACKSON PHIPPIN FOR CENTER STAGE.

velop a concept for a play. A play needs a certain amount of artistic apparatus to support it, but it also needs a strategy to make it a full production and not just an idea.

Could you give me an illustration?

Yes. I learned this lesson when Nikos and I were working on *Holiday*, the Philip Barry play. I had recently done the show at Hartford and I had certain preconceived notions. I said, "Nikos, I've done this show, let me show you what I did. If you don't like it, we'll do something else." For some reason we looked at the second act first, and he said, "Very nice." Then I showed him the first act, and he said, "No no, it's too heavy, too dull. I know Barry says a big, heavy room, but we shouldn't do that." I found that in first meetings with Nikos you had to probe for a kernel of meaning, and he would eventually say one thing that was usually the solution to the design. I didn't get that kernel in our first conversation for *Holiday*. I didn't get it after three conversations. I would bring back different ideas and he would say they were too heavy, too dreary, too dull. Then he finally said, "It's got to be fun to be rich." That was it! We shouldn't have told the whole story when the curtain opens. We shouldn't say that the family is going to come down hard on Linda, the second daughter, and it's going to be her struggle

to get out of this place. If we did, the whole evening would be decided the minute the lights come up. Instead, what we ended up doing was this rather shallow room with a glass wall behind it, big drapes, and a staircase seen through the glass wall. It was all in gold. The curtain went up and the audience—this is the usual Williamstown reaction—the audience gasped. People knew immediately that it was fabulous to be a part of this family. So what's Linda's problem? Now there's some tension. That's what I mean by the "strategy" of a design. I think it mandates a more flexible approach to a play. By comparison, with a "concept," you might have designed a sarcophagus of a room in which all of Linda's hopes and youthful spirit are imprisoned, which is in its way appropriate to the playwright's intentions, but which doesn't go anywhere.

It also doesn't give the director and cast anything to work with.

Oh, absolutely. When Irene Lewis and I did *Born Yesterday* at Hartford, we decided to make the hotel room "pink." We thought that some people in the audience might consider it a very beautiful room, but that for us it really would be a bit tasteless. It was intended to be a subtle joke. I remember Irene saying to the cast at the first readthrough, "The set will be pink, with a rose-colored carpet and lots of

marble, so I don't want you to be too funny. Don't push it. Play against the environment."

When did your association with Long Wharf begin?

All of the time I had been living in Hartford, I was writing to Long Wharf and saying, I want to work at your theatre. But I never got much of a response. Then, out of the blue, they called me after I moved to New York, in 1979, and we've had a pleasant and fruitful association ever since.

Was the move to New York difficult?

It was, although I didn't admit it to myself at the time. I remember my last day in Hartford. There was no furniture in the apartment, only the phone. It rang and it was Stan Wojewodski, from Center Stage in Baltimore, offering me a show. That job, a show at the Hartman, and three shows at Hartford Stage were enough to keep me going my first year. I was extremely lucky.

Around that time I was also considering whether I should go back to drama school. I thought about going to drama school in London—I actually went to England to scope it out the year before I moved to New York—but decided that if I was really going to design, I should do it in the

WHO THEY ARE AND HOW IT IS WITH THEM.

United States. Then I moved. It does give one a certain credibility, I suppose, to be out on a limb without a weekly paycheck.

I'd like to talk about how you approach a script. Where do you start?

The first thing I do, of course, is read the script. I think what Howard Bay says in his book is true, that's the precious moment. The instinctual things that float through your mind in the course of that reading are very important. You have to latch onto them, not desert them, if you feel strongly about them. Of course, no script is a completely unknown quantity; you always arrive at the first reading with some pre-

conceptions. Sometimes, when I'm asked to redo a play I've done before, I'll already have an impression of what I want to do. That happened in Albany, when I designed *Glengarry Glen Ross*, with Gordon Edelstein. I knew the play well enough to know that what I wanted to do would work. I had to see if it would fit into the space, and I had to design the proportions and so forth, but the instinct to design this long, serpentine banquette that wound out from backstage was what came to mind. I saw this Chinese red banquette in a black space with a gold column. It came to me as a complete picture, which sometimes happens. For other plays, I have to slog through more images because they won't yield themselves up as easily, or there is more problem solving to be done. So what I do is reread the script. Then I try—and I just realized this in the last couple of years—then I try not to put anything down on paper until the last possible moment, because that's a kind of commitment that immediately shoves other possibilities aside. It's usually better if things can float through my mind as long as possible.

Will you have a conversation with the director before you start putting ideas down on paper?

Yes, but it depends on the director. With Stan, for instance, a lot of the work seems to happen in conversation. The conversations vary according to the play and the people I'm working with. I tend not to do fancy presentations. I like to do tiny little scrawly sketches, two inches by two inches, which give light and atmosphere in an instant. Also, there's nothing invested in that tiny piece of paper. If I do big color renderings at all, they're usually done as a final step. But I very rarely do them.

I feel most secure when I've worked out the ground plan of a play. With an interior set, that's the first thing one has to do, of course. If you haven't made a clear decision about where the actors are going to move, or even where the furniture will be placed, you've really solved nothing. Take a play like *You Can't Take It with You*, for example. If it's not clear where Penny's nook is and where the kitchen is and where the upstairs is, if there aren't good comedy connections between those places, the evening is going to be a mess. No matter how beautiful the set looks—the nice wallpaper, the pretty colors—the production will be a mess.

In terms of finding solutions, my predilection is for the spatial. Although this has changed a bit in the past five years. When I did *The Normal Heart* at Center Stage, I didn't have a spatial impression first. My ideas were all about color. The colors I saw were intended to be both postmodern chic and the colors of organs on an anatomical chart. They were livid browns becoming reds, purples, blues. That was my first instinct, and it developed from there. But the play allowed for that because its form is episodic, fragmented. It requires less realistic detail. I did very detailed interiors for a long time at Hartford—and I think a lot of people think that that's what I do—but most of the work I have done for Center Stage, for instance, is not that at all. It's an epic, sculptural space, and unless one responds to it in that way, the result is not going to be successful scenery.

THE OLD GLOBE PRODUCTION OF ANTON CHEKHOV'S *UNCLE VANYA*, DIRECTED BY JACK O'BRIEN.

Very different from Long Wharf.

Or the old Hartford, both of which are— or were—intimate thrusts. The old Hartford Stage was a fabulous place to design a room in because it was a room. For example, there was no need to do self-conscious ceilings because the ceiling was right there. One had to be careful about sightlines in that space, but that's the story of designing for a thrust theatre in any case. The backstage was quirky, but it was fun to figure out show by show. And there was an air-conditioning duct that was always in the way. Santo would say, "Some you win and some the duct wins." When I begin working in a new theatre, I have got to see the space. I get drawings, but I feel very insecure until I actually see the space. It doesn't take very long—it can take less than an hour and I'm on the plane again—but I have to be able to anchor the design spatially. Then it develops from there.

Do you do a lot of research?

It depends on the play. I have an enormous number of American/European architecture and art books at home. I try to pull ideas from them. But for other plays one finds oneself working from nonspecific images and memory. For instance, we did a play in Hartford called *Past Tense*. I think it was the second play in the new building. It's about a husband and wife who are getting a divorce and moving out of their house at the same time. The set was empty of furniture. The source I used for the three rooms was a memory of the second house my parents lived in. I filled in the detail from my own life because I have very clear memories of that house, even of the wallpaper.

On the other hand, when I did *"Master Harold" . . . and the boys* in Charleston, I went to the Picture Collection and got pictures of Port Elizabeth. It was important to me that the cafe not be some ersatz idea about South Africa. For all that, I think initial realistic research has become less important to me. I used to come armed with pictures and notions and sketches, but I find that I don't do that so much anymore. I have specific details in mind, but it doesn't get in the way. I'll show things to the director when he asks, did they really have that kind of window or chair? Design decisions should not be movie decisions. That is, they should not be about naturalistically reproducing a real space. They should be theatrical decisions—what emotionally makes us choose this window as opposed to that one. It's never the full answer to say this is what it was in the research. The answer is in the play.

FACING PAGE, JACK ZEMAN'S *PAST TENSE*, DIRECTED BY PAUL WEIDNER FOR HARTFORD STAGE COMPANY.

SKETCH FOR DAVID MAMET'S *GLENGARRY GLEN ROSS*, DIRECTED BY GORDON EDELSTEIN FOR CAPITAL REPERTORY COMPANY.

Is this also about being confident in your own ability?

I'm sure it is, absolutely. Young designers have to feel as if they are covering all of the bases, they also feel as if they shouldn't make any mistakes. But there are so many choices to be made that the designer better have some sense of what's appropriate to the texts, not just the period, location, etc.

Is the designer's personal taste ever a factor in design?

Yes, inevitably, but I don't think personal taste should ever be an issue. The most horrible point in a design meeting is when a director says, I don't like beige, or I don't like sconces. You have to say, okay, you don't like them, but why doesn't the play like them? Why are they wrong for the set of this particular play we're doing? Explain that to me and we'll take the sconces out. I know Nikos trusted me with prop decisions because he thought I had good taste. Designers have to be tasteful, but taste is somewhere down the line from the emotional core of the evening. I think that ultimately, if the larger framework of the design is correct—and the details should be correct, too, of course—then the evening can be a success.

Do you have a preference for a certain kind of stage?

No, not really. Most of my work is done in the regional theatres, and many of them have thrust stages. I must say that I'm a little weary of them. I was talking with Eric Overmyer several years ago when we were doing *On the Verge* at the Guthrie. Eric said that he felt the prevalence of the thrust stage had to do with television, that people liked being three feet away from an actor, seeing the actor breathing and sweating. It gives them the illusion of a television closeup. The palpability of the thrust has, in many places, replaced the special world of the proscenium, which is where I would love to do more work. The proscenium says: This is the play and you are the audience. There's an equity between the stage and the audience that is never quite present in a thrust. The thrust stage, for instance, is terrible for comedy. Half the audience laughs, half doesn't. I suppose the sculptural presence of an actor out on a thrust can have a tragic quality—and certainly movement on a thrust can be exciting—but for me it's ultimately not very flexible. Some thrust theatres are better designed than others, of course.

Which ones are the good ones?

A good thrust? Maybe "good" isn't the right word. There are some thrusts that are fully committed to being thrusts, like the Long Wharf, which is a three-quarter thrust, and Hartford Stage. Then there are thrusts like StageWest, which is dreadful because the audience is aimed in the wrong direction in relation to the shape of the stage. Theatres like Center Stage combine a semi-thrust with a proscenium. There's this invisible line below which you have to design as if you're on a thrust and above which you design as if you're in a proscenium

—all the furniture ends up positioned around that line.

In the regional theatres though, space is not the whole story. I like regional theatres because they are places that allow me to do my work. The staff is helpful, they're good colleagues, I get to do good plays. But I'm drawn to theatres for a lot of different reasons. The collaborator is the most important element, first of all. When Gordon Edelstein asked me to do *Glengarry Glen Ross*, I had done the play before. I like the piece, it's worth designing, but if Pat Collins hadn't done the lights and David Murin hadn't done the costumes and Gordon wasn't directing, I wouldn't have been too thrilled about being involved in the production. Those collaborators—and Gordon's willingness to see the play in a non-slice-of-life fashion—made for a very exciting end product.

Have you ever had to design a show you really didn't like?

No. For practical and emotional reasons, I have to find something that engages my interest. Even if it's just finding fabulous furniture for a show, or knowing that the fabrics will say something special. It's a practical approach because designers are offered projects that they really have to take. Maybe other designers turn down plays, but I don't. I don't do a lot of industrials, I haven't done films, and I haven't

done television. I prefer doing theatre because it's what I'm interested in, so I accept a lot of offers in order to maintain a cash flow. But when I get a show or a director who is not all that interesting, I need to find a sustaining point of interest somewhere in the project.

How many shows a year do you do?

Between ten and fourteen, but the average is probably close to eleven.

Is the choice not to do film or television a conscious choice?

Not really, although it might be in the case of television. I assisted David Jenkins on several *Theatre in America* projects for WNET when I was in Hartford. That was very good television, but I found the pace very strange. It was either rush rush rush, or nothing. I don't seem to have those gears. Television is very well-paid work, so perhaps it would be smart of me to do more of it, but most of the television I see doesn't interest me. I just don't think I have the capacity to do it—no matter how well-paid it is, no matter how nice my brownstone on the East Side would be.

What about films?

I'd like to do films. Film seems to be about organization and covering the bases. It's

about filling in the entire frame so that no matter where the shot is taken from, you've done the job of creating a world— which is what I do in theatre.

Film requires a lot of time, and it doesn't allow for much theatre.

The only guy I know who really manages to do both is Santo Loquasto, and that's because he has the energy of five people. I have great stamina, but the level of energy you need to do both is extraordinary.

What would be an ideal project for you at this point in your career?

Opera.

Have you done opera?

I did one at Juilliard: *Manon.* It was not successful, and I pulled out in the middle of it because there were enormous problems with the budget. It was not a happy experience. But I'm desperate to do opera. I would also be thrilled to do any big, classical play: any Molière, any Shaw, any Ibsen, any O'Neill. Any Shakespeare, of course.

Why these playwrights in particular?

Because first of all, the classics are the plays against which you can measure the evolution of your work. Secondly, I think people think of me as a designer who excels at detail. I enjoy designing rooms full of things, but I'd like to do work that is freed from so many specifics. I've been trying to get to a simplicity and directness that is less impeded by "things." Many younger designers are doing what I identify as "the simple look," but when I've been pleased with my own recent efforts to reduce a design to its essence, it's because, I think, there was a lot of richness and detail there to begin with. In other words, I don't want to abandon my love of complexity—I probably couldn't, anyway —but I do want to become more selective in my choices. I want to see if the emotions of a play can become the scenery's detail, the way music supplies much of the detail in the experience of watching an opera.

Has design changed since you started? Are there fashions in set design?

Oh yes, I think so, fashion always threatens the personal in a job like theatre design, where art and craft so perilously mix. The New York theatre as a point of dissemination for design ideas is less crucial and potent now than in the past. The sculptural part of Boris Aronson's aesthetic was very influential when I first became aware of set design. In the seventies, Josef Svoboda's approach to design seemed very powerful, which was unfortunate for those who only grasped the architectural and not the theatrical message of his work. It's difficult to say if there is a "look" that's "in" right now. It's probably good that the question is hard to answer.

Robert Wilson's work has been important to me, also some of the West and East German and Russian design that I've seen in exhibitions and in reproduction. The other arts are very fleet-footed compared to theatre, perhaps because of the layers of collaboration through which people in the theatre have to move. New visual ideas don't enter our mainstream quickly. It's one thing to see students designing Ming Cho Lee's sets from 1968; it's another to see them recreating Lee Simonson's from 1933. The point is that every designer should be designing his or her own work at this moment in their life.

ADRIANNE LOBEL

BOTH OF Adrianne Lobel's parents were artists who made their living by illustrating—and in her father's case, writing—books for children. "It may sound horrible," Lobel says in this interview, "but it's almost as if I was trained from a seed to be what I am. . . . I sometimes feel as if I really had no choice but to be an artist, and almost specifically to be an artist in the theatre."

Lobel, who was born and raised in Brooklyn, received her training in set design from Ming Cho Lee, after working in Hollywood's film studios for two years. Since graduation, and almost always as a result of a connection made at Yale, Lobel has designed for theatre, opera, dance, movies, music videos (including Michael Jackson's *Bad*, directed by Martin Scorsese) and the occasional commercial. Her work exhibits a hip, slightly ironic, thoroughly contemporary sensibility that often is in keeping with the people she most enjoys working with, people like director Peter Sellars, choreographer Mark Morris and playwright Harry Kondoleon.

While Lobel has worked for a variety of directors in the United States and Europe, some of her boldest, most remarkable design work has been seen in the

FACING PAGE, THE CHICAGO LYRIC OPERA
PRODUCTION OF GILBERT AND SULLIVAN'S
THE MIKADO, DIRECTED BY PETER SELLARS.

95

innovative productions of both classical and contemporary operas staged by Peter Sellars. Among the most notable are *Così fan tutte*, set in a roadside diner; *Nixon in China*, in which a full-size replica of the presidential jet landed on stage (see cover); *The Marriage of Figaro*, set in a Trump Tower-like penthouse; and the Glyndebourne Opera production of *The Magic Flute*, which used a series of projections inspired by slightly garish postcards of southern California.

MAY 25, 1989—
ADRIANNE LOBEL'S APARTMENT,
BROOKLYN, NEW YORK

I grew up in the Park Slope section of Brooklyn. Both of my parents were artists. They illustrated—and my father also wrote—children's books. So it was a house in which everyone freelanced and worked at home.

Did your parents actively encourage you to become an artist?

Yes, they did. When they were working and didn't want to be disturbed they would give me drawing materials and say, go over there and play. They also exposed me to a lot of culture. My mother is European, and when I was nine she insisted that the family go to Europe. It was very unusual in those days, in the early 1960s, for an American family to travel, but we made a grand tour of Europe: Paris, London, Amsterdam, Copenhagen, Stockholm. I just loved it. I cried the first time I saw Paris. And I loved looking at paintings for hours. It was probably the happiest, most stimulating time of my childhood. It was also the period during which I got along best with my parents. We were traveling together as equals because we were all experiencing new things at the same time.

Were your parents involved in the theatre?

Not professionally, no, but they loved it. It may sound horrible, but it's almost as if I was trained from a seed to be what I am. Some people grow up and they have no choice but to be a doctor or a lawyer. I sometimes feel as if I really had no choice but to be an artist, and almost specifically to be an artist in the theatre.

Because they did children's books, my parents led isolated lives, which I know was frustrating for them. They worked with editors, of course, but the emphasis was always on "children." It wasn't very satisfying socially. So I figured out as I was growing up and watching them work that I didn't want to be as isolated as they were. I wanted to work in a field that involved other people—and specifically, other people who were adults.

What are your earliest memories of the theatre?

Oh, I have some very strong ones. We went to Drottningholm when I was nine years old and saw *La clemenza di Tito*. It was amazing. I remember my brother rustling candy wrappers through the entire performance, but I also remember the fire on stage and what the theatre looked like. And I remember wondering how someone could stand in one place and sing for such a long time. We also saw *Aida*, in an outdoor amphitheatre in Rome, but all I remember about that production were the palm trees falling over in the wind. They weren't designed to fall over, but it was really exciting.

When and how did the interest in design come about?

Well, that period is like the dark ages of my life. It gets very black in there, but I'll try to remember the chronology. First I went to Art and Design High School, in Manhattan. I hated it. It was like being in jail. It was a special public school in which you had all the academic classes, but then you also had three extra hours for so-called "art training." Except it wasn't very sophisticated art training. The school was steeped in something from the advertising world of the 1940s—you learned to letter, for instance, things like that. I tried to introduce a life-drawing class, but the teachers wouldn't approve it. I ended up majoring in sculpture because it was the only class that was in any way related to the fine arts.

I was also taking evening classes at the Brooklyn Museum School. They had some very good teachers, like David Levine, Bruce North and Harvey Dinnerstein. They were old-fashioned, academic teachers, but that was a good way to begin. I was quite serious about painting, and I did a lot of it. I wanted to be an Impressionist; I wanted to be Degas. But I still had a feeling that I should be doing something more social and more collaborative.

Then I went to this little college, called Marlboro, in Vermont, for a year. Another dreadful experience. The problem was that I was always very clear about what I wanted to do, and being in school at that time was painful because most students didn't know what they wanted. I'm sure I was very obnoxious about it, but I was also very ambitious. I just wanted to do and make and be and prove myself. So in order to get away from everybody—Marlboro had a very small theatre department—I'd go to the basement and build sets and make costumes for the productions.

The summer following my first year at Marlboro I got a scholarship to work as a costume assistant at a summer stock theatre in the Berkshires. I wasn't very useful. The poor woman who ran the costume shop just didn't know what to do with me. I finally ended up doing all the props and scenery because no one else was doing them. The woman suggested that I go to the Lester Polakov Studio in New York. So I quit college, moved back home, and started taking classes at Lester's. That was really the beginning.

How old were you at this time?

I was seventeen. Along with Lester's design class, I took a wonderful mask-making class from Fred Nihda and a

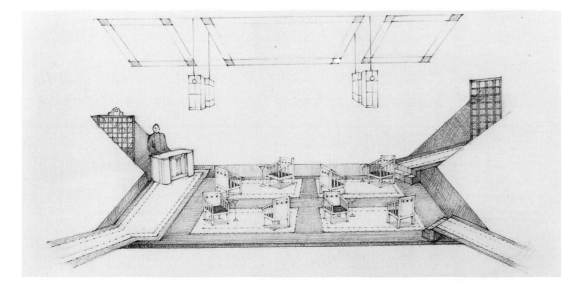

SKETCH FOR ARTHUR SCHNITZLER'S *UNDISCOVERED COUNTRY* (ADAPTED BY TOM STOPPARD), DIRECTED BY GARLAND WRIGHT FOR ARENA STAGE.

THE CHICAGO LYRIC OPERA PRODUCTION OF *THE MIKADO*, DIRECTED BY PETER SELLARS.

model-making class from Paul Zalon. He's no longer a set designer, but at that time he was right out of Yale Drama School. He was working at the Public Theater and Juilliard, and I assisted him for a while. I was an okay assistant, but I wanted to be a designer. He suggested that I apply to Yale and then arranged an interview with Ming Cho Lee for me. It was December, so it was already late in the season, but I did the interview and was accepted on the spot.

So then you went to Yale?

No, then I met a man who was leaving New York and moving to California. I decided that I wasn't quite ready for Yale, that what I really wanted to do was go to California. So at the age of eighteen I drove across country with this man, and we set up a house in Los Angeles. I thought I might get work in California, and after a couple of months I did. It was difficult, but it was also very interesting. I had car payments and rent to pay. I was being a real person, an adult . . . except I wasn't old enough to be served drinks in the bars.

When was this?

Around 1975, 1976. It was a very busy time in Hollywood. The movie studios, where I got work, were doing gigantic productions. They were shooting movies like *King Kong* and *New York, New York* . . . a lot of built productions. I loathed living in Los Angeles, but I loved working at the studios. It was just like what you imagine Hollywood should look like. I was hugely impressed by the scale of that world.

There was one shop at the Burbank Studios that only made rubber molding. The shop was four stories high, with huge windows, and it was covered in plaster. As the sun set, the whole place would turn into this pavilion of pink icing. They could build anything you would design. I got very spoiled. I was shocked when I finally got back to Yale and all of the molding came out of Dyke's molding catalogue.

Did you do any theatre work in California?

No. I was a "set designer," which is really a draftsman, and I built some models. But it was wonderful training because the drafting done at the studios was incredible. And the people who were working in Hollywood at that time were mostly old men who had grown up with the industry, who had been trained in the architecture schools of the 1920s.

Who did you work with?

I worked with Robert Boyle, who did a lot of work for Alfred Hitchcock, including *The Birds* and *North by Northwest* . . . some of the greatest movies ever, some of the greatest production design ever. I also worked with Richard McDonald, an insane English production designer who did the two *Exorcist* movies, and Eugene Lourié, a fantastic, little, ancient man who worked with Renoir and designed both *Rules of the Game* and *Grand Illusion*.

But you did eventually attend Yale.

Yes. There was always the August telephone call to Ming. It didn't seem all that urgent at the time because I was so young, but each year I would call and tell him that I was staying in California for another year. And Ming would say, okay, whenever you're ready. I think I did that twice because I was in California for two-and-a-half years. Then my good friend Andy Jackness, who I had met at Lester Polakov's, applied to Yale. He was accepted and we decided it would be fun to go to Yale together.

I'm a victim of my environment. The thing that is going on around me at the time is the thing I want to do. I knew I could stay in Hollywood and gradually work my way up to being a production designer, but at the same time I knew I wasn't really designing. I needed time to be a kid again—that is, to be a student, to be in school—and I needed time to figure out what I did as a designer: how I thought, how my aesthetic worked, what my aesthetic was. I remember talking to Eugene Louri about this, and he said, well, you have to decide whether you want to design *Hamlet* or *King Kong II*. I really didn't know.

Since Andy was in New York he took care of all the logistics, like finding the apartment we shared our first year, and I worked in California up until the day before classes started. It was a very difficult transition. On my first day I was told to paint the back wall of the student theatre black. I know I thought this was beneath me, but there was also this great snobbery at Yale about Hollywood. It appalled me. In Hollywood you could design anything you wanted, but at Yale they thought you had "sold out" if you had worked there.

Ming, however, is a wonderful teacher, and the training I got in Hollywood was very useful. I don't think Yale teaches the nuts and bolts, like drafting, terribly well. The students who have more professional experience get a lot more out of the program. What Ming is so good at is teaching a process. He can teach you how to develop ideas. You have to be very strong to study with Ming, and it's hard, rigorous work, but it's also a lot of fun. It was the end of the Robert Brustein era—he left when I graduated, in 1979—so it was a superlative time to be there.

Lots of people think that designers coming out of Yale design like Ming, but I really don't think that's true. I don't think I design like Ming. My work has an ironic edge that you won't find in Ming's work.

Ming's work is not funny. But the great thing about Ming is that he gives you a wall to hit. He can be so impossible at times, so tactless. He'd make me so angry that I had to prove to him what I saw—and that what I saw could work. That's where Ming is a real genius. If you didn't have anything strong to say, then it was easy to succumb to his influence.

Did you make professional contacts at Yale?

Well, yes. I can trace almost everything I've done since then to someone I met at Yale.

Including Peter Sellars?

Yes. Peter was a senior at Harvard the year Brustein established the American Repertory Theatre in Cambridge. I think Bob saw Peter's puppet *Ring* cycle and then invited him to direct a professional show. Bob knew my work, of course, and he thought we should meet, which we did. And then Peter and I did *The Inspector General.*

Was that your first professional show out of Yale?

No. My first professional show was *The Cocktail Party*, directed by Paul Weidner at Hartford Stage. I did both the sets and costumes. *The Inspector General* was my second show.

You've done a lot of work with Peter, including Così fan tutte, The Marriage of Figaro, The Mikado, Nixon in China and, most recently, The Magic Flute. I'd like to hear more about that working relationship.

There is no one like Peter, which is a terrible thing in a way. It can get pretty close to guru worship. And then sometimes you just hate him so much that you never want to see him again. When I first met him I thought, who is this little aberration? But he's so funny, and his ideas make so much sense to me. He takes my work so much farther than I could. He has taught me so much. But I think I've taught him a lot, too. He didn't know how to work with a designer when we met. He didn't know what a model was. We've been through so much—so many huge successes and terrible traumas.

Are you referring to My One and Only?

Yes. It was our second project together. I was twenty-six and he was twenty-four.

We were so dumb. We like to think of it as our three-million-dollar education.

How did My One and Only come about?

Peter got a call from a producer asking if he would do a musical with Tommy Tune. Peter had always wanted to do a Gershwin musical, so he met with Tommy, hired Tim Mayer to write the book, and then called me. It all started benignly enough, except the producer hadn't raised any of the money. So Peter and I decided we would raise the money ourselves. We did about eighty presentations, and with the help of Lewis Allen did manage to raise it. It took about two years. Then, even before we had teched in Boston, Peter was out.

For what reason?

Panic, I would say. Tommy and Peter were not getting along, which was the big problem. And Peter was a huge risk. People now understand Peter's working process, but they didn't understand it then. We now know that everything is in a huge mess one week before previews, and that even during previews the show may still look like a mess. But there are so many ideas going on, and the performances get better and better and better. Peter's work is always alive. It's not a dead, packaged thing that is set before the audience comes in. I can see that a big star like Tommy

Tune might have been very scared. But as I've said, we didn't even have the opportunity to tech the show. I must admit that Peter was being difficult, too. When Peter gets scared, he gets very stubborn—sometimes he's right, sometimes he's wrong.

Once Peter left, my heart was out of it, and I did not have a very good attitude. Then the "doctors" started to arrive. The show opened in Boston to very bad reviews, except for the scenery, which got good reviews. I don't think that was liked very much. When things go wrong it's like a war, and I was associated with the side that had lost. I was willing to alter things, but there was no communication. I wanted to know how the book was changing so that I could think about changes in the set. But no one ever told me. It was kept from me, which was a way of pushing me out.

I have very clear memories of the set, with its huge expanses of color. How much of it was your work?

A lot, about eighty percent. But it didn't really move the way I had planned for it to move. It also didn't have the rigor. The set was used as decoration rather than as an integral part of a book with songs. I had designed something with a lot more exposed machinery, much of which got softened. Instead of a Russian Constructivist

painting, which was what I had been looking at, it was turned into something Deco.

How do you approach a project?

In different ways, but mostly with panic. I'll draw on tracing paper for three or four days, usually before I conduct research because I don't know what I'm researching yet. I'll just sketch and sketch and sketch, and hope that something interesting will eventually show up. They'll be very messy sketches in which you can't tell what is going on, but every now and then I'll hit on something that feels right. Then I'll draw on top of that and something else will appear. Generally I don't spend more than two or three minutes on a sketch. Just when I get to the point where I think, this is leading nowhere, I'll start another sketch. It's really thinking with a pencil. Then I'll do a lot of research—I don't like to get too creative too quickly—because everything must come from somewhere. The more information I can absorb, the more interesting the combinations of these elements will be—even if some are eventually rejected.

Then I'll start working on a really rough model—little pieces of masking tape and Bristol board stuck together. You can't be afraid of doing something ugly. I'll go back and forth between the sketches and the rough model. Every design begins to form its own logic. One idea will give birth to a

SKETCH FOR ACT 3 OF W.A. MOZART'S
THE MARRIAGE OF FIGARO, DIRECTED BY
PETER SELLARS. FACING PAGE,
PRODUCTION PHOTOGRAPH.

lot of little ideas, but you must have the overall structure first.

What I find satisfying after spending so much time on the unknown is to draw several mechanical plans of the set. With each revision the set becomes more definite. In order for this to work here, that has to go there. It's then that I feel I have come up with something inevitable—the result of all the information I absorbed. By "information" I mean, what the director has said, everything I looked at, the requirements of the piece, and—the most important part—my personal point of view.

Another important element is the relationship between the human figure and the space around him. How does the individual relate to his environment? Is he overwhelmed by it? Is it claustrophobic? Is there a lot of air, a lot of space? Is he tiny in his world, or is he giant? In *Nixon in China*, for instance, I knew I wanted the space to be as enormous as I could make it. The show was designed for touring so it had to be kept simple, but I wanted the background to be air, winter, cold, gigantic. As it turned out, everything in *Nixon* is life-size, but on stage you get the sense of tiny people standing next to very large elements in a very large space. For *The Magic Flute* I just did, it's exactly the opposite. The Glyndebourne space is already quite small and I tried to make it even smaller—the characters fill the space like giant marionettes in front of miniature backdrops.

What kind of information does Peter give you at the beginning of a project?

None and too much . . . both. He gives a lot of conflicting information, all of which eventually becomes useful. The difficulty is in finding what relates specifically to the set, what relates to the staging, what relates to the lights. But Peter also gives you a great deal of freedom. Sometimes he doesn't know what he wants until he sees it. At other times, you have the feeling that he knows exactly what he wants, but he guides you to discover it for yourself.

Although Peter and I always set our pro-

ductions in the present, all of our choices are influenced by the past. I did as much historical research for the Mozart productions as I would have done for a production set in the eighteenth century. For *The Marriage of Figaro*, for example, we knew we wanted the characters to be rich New Yorkers. But we also went back to the original play by Beaumarchais and realized that we had to have real rooms, that the set had to make sense architecturally. Only with a firm background of historical material could we draw parallels between life then and life now.

Besides opera and theatre, you've also done movies, commercials and music videos. I'd like to hear you discuss the different forms. Is one more satisfying than another?

I've tried everything, yes. I think all set designers have a love/hate relationship with the theatre. You have one really bad experience, and you say, that's enough, I can't do this anymore, I'm not being paid enough. I've gone through phases where I just want to let it drop, but you have to be able to see the whole picture. You have to be able to stop and do something else once in a while. So about three years ago I started looking for movie work. I've been fairly lucky, I guess, because whenever I've felt the need to make a change, a change usually occurs. In this case I had

worked with John Patrick Shanley on a play called *Savage in Limbo*. He had just written his first screenplay, *Five Corners*, and when it was sold he recommended me for the position of production designer. So I interviewed with Tony Bill, the director, and got the job. It was an interesting experience. You don't have the control in film you have in theatre. You have to fight so much harder to get so much less on the screen.

Would you want to do more movies?

Yes, I do. In fact, I did another one, called *Ask Me Again*, for American Playhouse last summer. It had a smaller budget, but I had a more cooperative crew, and in the end I think I got more on the screen.

How do you choose projects?

Some projects are inevitable, and there are no questions about doing them. Those are the things I like to fill up my time with. There's no question, for instance, that I'll design a *Magic Flute* for Peter Sellars. There's also no question about working with Mark Morris or designing a new play by Harry Kondoleon. You have to find other things to fill in around those projects. I'll read a play and have an idea for it, or I like the director and am anxious to work with him again. Or I'll want to continue a relationship with a particular theatre.

How many projects a year do you do?

Not so many. Operas take so much time. Last year I did a lot of different things: a movie, two operas, a giant dance piece, two commercials, two children's television shows, two new plays. You can do a play and throw in a commercial, or a video, if you have an extra week or two. That sort of thing comes up at the last minute anyway, so you can decide on the spur of the moment. But as for major projects, maybe two or three a year.

What characterizes your work?

Logic. I think my designs have a strong logic, even if it's abstract. I might not remember the logic a year after I've designed a production, but while I'm designing it I have to understand why everything is the way it is. I also think my work is very clean and modern. I'm not big on texture. I prefer color and line to texture, which can be a problem because my sets require very good, neat, solid construction. I go through agonies during tech week over every bump and wrinkle.

What about the general state of theatre design right now?

It's a larger problem than the state of design. There's just not much of interest

going on right now. It's just not a very fun time in the arts. It seems to be a vital time in dance, and new operas are being written, which is good, but experimental theatre is at an all-time low. It seems as if everyone has lost interest. Regional theatre just hasn't been as exciting as most people had hoped it would be. It's all subscription, and they all do the same plays. I did regional theatre for a number of years—it was my bread and butter for a long time—but I'm not pursuing it much right now.

You don't teach, do you?

No. It's not something I want to do, not yet. I don't know that I'm passionate

W.A. MOZART'S *COSI FAN TUTTE*, DIRECTED BY PETER SELLARS.

THE PLAYWRIGHTS HORIZONS' PRODUCTION
OF HARRY KONDOLEON'S *ANTEROOM*,
DIRECTED BY GARLAND WRIGHT.

enough about the world of theatre to instill that passion in someone else. I'm passionate enough about my own projects, and I'm happy to be doing what I do, but in a way I think theatre design is a silly thing to pursue and a little bit immoral to teach. And that's not a good attitude for a teacher.

So if a young designer comes to you for advice . . .

Oh, I'm always happy to give advice. When I was in school the code was to accept anything that came along. You couldn't turn anything down. But the money isn't so good that you have to do something you hate or something you think will sully you or something that will make you terribly unhappy. Part of the responsibility of building a career in the theatre is what you choose to do—not what

LEFT AND BELOW, ADRIANNE LOBEL'S SETS FOR THE GLYNDEBOURNE OPERA FESTIVAL PRODUCTION OF W.A. MOZART'S *THE MAGIC FLUTE*, DIRECTED BY PETER SELLARS.

FACING PAGE AND ABOVE, GEORGE TSYPIN'S MODELS FOR *DEATH IN VENICE*, DIRECTED BY GRAY VEREDON FOR OPERA COMPANY OF PHILADELPHIA. LEFT TOP, HUGH LANDWEHR'S SET FOR THE CENTER STAGE PRODUCTION OF MOLIERE'S *THE MISER*, DIRECTED BY STAN WOJEWODSKI, JR. LEFT BOTTOM, JOHN ARNONE'S SET FOR FRANK WEDEKIND'S *LULU* (TRANSLATED AND ADAPTED BY ROGER DOWNEY), DIRECTED BY SHARON OTT FOR LA JOLLA PLAYHOUSE.

ABOVE, MICHAEL YEARGAN'S SET FOR THE
YALE REPERTORY THEATRE PRODUCTION OF
EUGENE O'NEILL'S *AH, WILDERNESS!*, DI-
RECTED BY ARVIN BROWN. RIGHT, ROBERT
ISRAEL'S SET FOR PHILIP GLASS'S *SATYA-
GRAHA* (LIBRETTO BY CONSTANCE DEJONG),
DIRECTED BY DAVID POUNTNEY. FACING
PAGE, ISRAEL'S SET FOR THE SEATTLE OPERA
PRODUCTION OF *GOTTERDAMMERUNG*, DI-
RECTED BY FRANCOIS ROCHAX.

LEFT AND BELOW, TWO STILLS FROM THE
MOVIE *MR. & MRS. BRIDGE*, DIRECTED BY
JAMES IVORY; DAVID GROPMAN, PRODUCTION
DESIGNER.

LEFT, CHARLES MCCLENNAHAN'S SET FOR MICHAEL WELLER'S *MOONCHILDREN*, DIRECTED BY MARY B. ROBINSON FOR THE SECOND STAGE. BELOW LEFT, LOY ARCENAS'S SET FOR THE ARENA STAGE PRODUCTION OF TENNESSEE WILLIAMS'S *THE GLASS MENAGERIE*, DIRECTED BY TAZEWELL THOMPSON. BELOW RIGHT, TONY STRAIGES'S MODEL FOR *INTO THE WOODS* (BOOK BY JAMES LAPINE, MUSIC AND LYRICS BY STEPHEN SONDHEIM), DIRECTED BY JAMES LAPINE.

RIGHT, MICHAEL MERRITT'S SET FOR THE
GOODMAN THEATRE PRODUCTION OF DAVID
MAMET'S *AMERICAN BUFFALO*, DIRECTED BY
GREGORY MOSHER. BOTTOM, HEIDI LANDES-
MAN'S SET FOR *THE SECRET GARDEN* (BOOK
AND LYRICS BY MARSHA NORMAN), DIRECTED
BY R.J. CUTLER FOR VIRGINIA STAGE
COMPANY.

you do with a terrible play, but that you chose to design a good play. That's part of the design process. So my advice to young designers is that you don't have to do a project unless you feel something for it, unless you have a very good reason for doing it.

Do you think studying design in school is a good idea?

Oh, I do. I think you need that time. It would be a mistake to work as an assistant thinking that someday you'll design because you've assisted.

I'd like to ask you about being a woman in theatre.

It's a question that's asked of me a lot, yet I must admit that it is not a great part of my consciousness. I suppose feminists would all get up in arms, but I haven't found it to be a problem. In fact, being a woman has its advantages. No one would think twice about hiring a woman for the projects I'm interested in doing. And the projects which wouldn't hire me because I'm a woman are projects I probably wouldn't want to do anyway.

And you don't think you've been passed over on projects because you're a woman?

Maybe, but I've had enough interesting projects to do that I haven't been sitting around thinking, oh, I didn't get that project because I'm a woman. I know that some of the older designers did have a much harder time. They really had to clear the path, and it must have been very aggravating, but I don't think that bitterness at this point is very helpful. I don't find that I'm sitting here waiting for the phone to ring. As long as I have work that I'm interested in and people I love working with, it doesn't matter what sex I am.

THE GOODMAN THEATRE PRODUCTION OF MUSTAPHA MATURA'S *PLAY MAS*, DIRECTED BY DEREK WALCOTT.

CHARLES
McCLENNAHAN

Cᴴᴀʀʟᴇs McCʟᴇɴɴᴀʜᴀɴ, who was born and raised in North Carolina, has an undergraduate degree from the North Carolina School of the Arts and a master's degree in set design from Yale. Since 1983, when he designed his first professional production (the Yale Repertory Theatre/Broadway production of August Wilson's *Ma Rainey's Black Bottom*, directed by Lloyd Richards), McClennahan has designed, with equal skill, both heavily detailed and starkly minimal sets for many theatres throughout the country. He admits, however, that his favorite sets have been the simple, inexpensive ones he has designed for the small black theatres in New York.

McClennahan has also worked in film and video, and is particularly concerned about the scarcity of minorities in the technical areas of all three fields. "There are a lot of us out there, but we work up to a certain level and then we start to trickle down. I'm not sure why . . . but it has nothing to do with design." In order to address this complex issue, McClennahan established the Minority Designers and Technicians Network (MINDTEK). As the name suggests, its primary function is

FACING PAGE, AUGUST WILSON'S
MA RAINEY'S BLACK BOTTOM, DIRECTED BY
LLOYD RICHARDS.

the networking of information, either recommending designers and technicians to producers and theatres or helping individuals locate additional career opportunities. Like most young designers, McClennahan has had to learn how to balance theatre and nontheatre employment. So this, too, has become a part of MINDTEK's mission: to assist designers and technicians in combining theatre and nontheatre opportunities so that they can continue to work in the theatre as they gain experience and expand their professional skills.

FEBRUARY 12, 1989—
CHARLES McCLENNAHAN'S APARTMENT,
BROOKLYN, NEW YORK

I was born in North Carolina, in Laurinburg, which is about forty-five miles southwest of Fayetteville. My mother worked as a maid, and my father worked as an orderly at a local hospital. I also remember watching my mother touch up photographs people would bring to the house. I think that's where I picked up my interest in artistic expression.

I went through the public-school system in Laurinburg, had good grades and was really into drawing and painting. By the time I got to high school I had won most of the local art awards. The drama teacher came into my art class in high school one day looking for someone to paint a huge backdrop for the school's production of *Oklahoma*. I was asked if I wanted to paint it, and said "Sure." We then went to the theatre so that I could look at the drop, which covered the entire back wall of the theatre, and it was, like, whoa! I had no idea it would be that big. She told me what *Oklahoma* was about and what she was looking for. At the time I didn't know what a set designer did, but I showed her a drawing of what I thought the drop should look like. She liked the drawing and agreed to use it.

I had three students help me paint the drop, which we painted on stage. Because we were painting on a vertical surface, I decided not to use brushes. We used large cotton balls, tightened or flattened according to the detail I was trying to get. The entire drop was painted with cotton balls. Seeing my work on such a large scale opened up a whole new world for me. It got me out of a lot of classes, but it was also really exciting. I realized that this was something I really enjoyed doing, and wanted to continue doing.

I was in the drama teacher's office one day, talking to her about this, and noticed a leaflet on her counter from the North Carolina School of the Arts. They were touring a show throughout North Carolina advertising their program, and I think they came to my school the following week. They put up what I thought was a fantastic set, which included tracking lights and letters that flashed on and off—like Broadway marquees.

It was that excitement, that falling in love with "entertainment," that convinced me I should go into theatre. I decided I had to go to the North Carolina School of the Arts. I didn't have a lot of work to show them—all I had was what I had done for *Oklahoma*—but because they were a state-supported institution interested in enrolling students from the state, they accepted me.

North Carolina School of the Arts was, for me, a kind of reckoning of whether or not I wanted to work in this business. It was very frightening, but I learned a valuable lesson about the exciting versus the unexciting realities of this business.

What kinds of productions did you do?

Mostly classical, like Molière and Shakespeare. The school encouraged us to do as wide a variety of productions as possible, so besides plays I also did ballet and opera. It was a BFA program and they wanted students to receive a well-rounded training in theatre. They didn't want us to specialize. I also got experience designing lights and costumes. I can't imagine what would have happened if I had only taken set design, because in order to be articulate in this business now you have to be able to understand every aspect.

How did Yale come about?

While in college I did the local beauty pageant that is associated with the Miss Black Universe pageant. People from New York saw it, liked the set, and asked me to design the New York pageant, which was presented at the Westchester County Center. One of the old stagehands, when he heard I was the set designer, asked me what I was doing in North Carolina. He thought I should be going to Yale.

What year was this?

1981. I went back to North Carolina and applied to Yale, which surprised people at my school, I think. I mean, people came down from New York for the training.

I'm curious about why you went to Yale. Did you go because a stagehand told you about the program, or because there were people at Yale with whom you wanted to study?

I had read design books on Ming Cho Lee and Donald Oenslager. In fact, my undergraduate thesis was on Jo Mielziner, so I knew a lot about him too. But I couldn't connect these people with Yale—or with any other university—because I didn't know who was teaching where. They only became real to me after I received Yale's catalog.

I was very isolated in North Carolina. I knew nothing about theatre outside of the North Carolina School of the Arts. The instructors at Yale were like icons to me, like statues you might see in a museum. Going up to New England was like entering a new world. I graduated from a college that had four hundred students, where individuals got a lot of attention, and suddenly I was on a campus of thousands.

I remember my first meeting with Ming

THREE COSTUME SKETCHES FOR ATHOL FUGARD'S *BOESMAN AND LENA*, DIRECTED BY ZAKES MOKAE FOR CENTER STAGE.

Cho Lee. I went to his office with my portfolio. It was nice work—the drawings were pretty and the paintings were well crafted—but it lacked guts. Ming zeroed right in on that. That's what is so wonderful about him. His genuine reaction is what counts, and his reaction to my work was: It's very pretty, but where are you?

Yale was both frightening and very exciting. It was good for me in that it stripped down all those layers, all that unsureness toward my work that I had developed at the North Carolina School of the Arts. I didn't regret for one minute feeling emotionally or psychologically embarrassed about my work at Yale. The classes were really hard, but you felt good after a class.

Some people complain that Ming's students end up designing like him. Do you think this is true?

A lot of people told me after I graduated from Yale that my work looked like Ming's—and that may have been true. But it's part of the process for a student to emulate his teacher. Besides, people like Ming's work, so emulating Ming wasn't always a bad thing.

But out of my emulation of Ming came a sense of discovery. Once the sketching and drafting techniques are enhanced, then the enlightenment comes by way of using what you have learned. I don't think Ming wants anyone to design like he does. I mean, he has already done it, why would anyone else want to repeat it? But it's part of the process: Now do what I do, but don't always do what I do . . . go out there and find yourself.

Who else did you study with at Yale?

Michael Yeargan, William Warfel, Jane Greenwood, Dunya Ramicova, Jennifer Tipton . . . and then there were the pro-

SKETCH FOR LONNE ELDER III'S *CEREMONIES IN DARK OLD MEN*, DIRECTED BY DOUGLAS TURNER WARD FOR THE NEGRO ENSEMBLE COMPANY.

fessors who would come and go. It was the cream of the crop. I couldn't believe that I, coming from North Carolina, was studying with these people. These were the designers I read about in books.

Did you go to Yale with a specific interest in designing sets?

Yes.

Did you ever consider designing lights or costumes?

No, not really. I did costumes at Yale because it was required, but I never saw myself doing costumes or lighting professionally. I think you need to focus. As horrible as it sounds, you need to be put into a slot because that's how people get to know you. You have to focus on one thing and be good at it. Spreading yourself too thin can weaken both your style and your influence. I suppose that someone who is established in one area can decide to branch out into another, but I don't think it's possible to do two areas when you're trying to build a career. It confuses people.

But a number of set designers like to do their own lighting or costumes because it gives them more control over the look of the production.

Yes, except what's exciting about this business is working with other people. I'm always discovering new things, and that's because I'm working with others. If I put a window on a set, of course I'm thinking about a shaft of light across the floor. But working in theatre is also about trust, about collaborating. So if I put a window on the set, I trust that the lighting designer will use the window in his or her design.

I also understand that hiring decisions get made for financial reasons. I've been asked to do both sets and lighting because a theatre's budget won't allow for a full staff. But I prefer to share thoughts. You never know when the other person is going to come up with an idea that is better than your own.

What is it about the process of set design that appeals to you?

There's more passion for me in designing sets than in designing costumes or lighting. I can't see lighting until it hits something. I can see what lighting does in a set, but a lighting designer sometimes has to know what he wants before the set is completed. My early training was in painting. I remember doing a series of charcoal studies about light in high school, and in one of them I had light coming through a stained-glass window. But for me the picture was about the window, not about the

light coming through it. It's that tangible element that I enjoy, the manipulation of the architectural world. Only the set designer can have that sort of creativity with an environment.

I love clothes, and I like designing costumes, but again, the element involved in designing costumes is not as tangible as in sets. You have fabrics, which are tangible, but what you do with them isn't. Another reason I decided not to go into costume design was because I didn't like dealing with people's attitudes about what they would or would not wear. Someone comes in pissed about something at home, so they decide they're not going to wear this two-thousand-dollar costume. The costume designer has to be able to put up with that. There's a certain mentality needed to work in costume design, and I don't have it. But I deeply respect the people who do.

How do you approach designing a show?

It's always different. Every director is different, so my process differs accordingly. If I get a call from a director I've worked with before, it makes it easier and I'll jump right into the project. I'll read the script, do research, and then do some quick sketching. What bothers me is working with a director I haven't worked with before who doesn't know what he

SKETCH FOR AUGUST WILSON'S
MA RAINEY'S BLACK BOTTOM.

design. I don't think it's fair to anyone, including yourself, to stay with a production in which you are constantly fighting with the director. It sabotages both the relationship and the working experience. If this is the case, let it go. I'm lucky not to have had many experiences like this.

Will you turn down a project when you have reason to believe that it won't be a healthy collaboration?

I try to get along with everyone I work with. I worked with David Mitchell, and I've seen how he works with Theoni Aldredge and Tharon Musser. I know how important it is to have a group of people you know you can work with, but at this point in my career I'm always working with new people. I'm not at that point where I can sit back and wait for someone to call me. But that's good because I'm allowing myself to work with people. I might talk with the producer if I anticipate trouble, but I don't think I've ever turned down a project for that reason.

What do you want from the director? What kind of information do you find useful?

I don't want details up-front. What I want is just a general feeling for the project — usually a word or a picture. I love it when directors show me pictures because it in-

wants. And it may not be that he doesn't know what he wants, it's just that he hasn't seen it yet. Eventually, when I feel the director connecting with what I'm doing, that's when the ice breaks and I can get more specific. That's when collaboration gets exciting.

Good collaborations are what keep me in theatre. I'm not a masochist. I don't enjoy bad collaborations. This is a tough business, especially now that budgets are being slashed and people who used to work exclusively on Broadway are designing Off and Off-Off Broadway. You have to have a reason, a purpose to continue to dicates that they've made a connection with the play within themselves. I like being told to read something. I was doing a video for Spike Lee and he told me to go see *Talk Radio*. He didn't say anything else, just "I want you to see *Talk Radio*." So I knew there was something in *Talk Radio* that he wanted me to look at in order to do the project.

But that wasn't the first time you worked with Spike Lee, so you had some idea of how he might see Talk Radio.

True, but directors will say, for instance, go and look at so-and-so's backyard. And you know that the director was in that backyard and thought, wow, this would be great for *Picnic*.

It's that tangible quality again, isn't it?

Absolutely.

What do you dislike about working in the theatre?

What I don't like is when a theatre comes to me with a project at the last minute. Sometimes it happens because they've just gotten the money. I can understand that, but I hate being expected to cough up a design on the spur of the moment. I can read the play once and come up with something, but what I miss is not having the time to do it properly.

Having time to work out the kinks in a design is very important. I've had to turn out shows in New York in a couple of weeks. I can do it, but it's not the way I prefer to work. I researched *Ma Rainey's Black Bottom* for four months, which was a luxury. I looked at newspaper clippings from the *Chicago Defender*, circa 1925, and went through the Historical Sound Recordings archives at Yale. I went to New York to talk with guys who had worked in the early jazz business. I went into picture collections, libraries, even into people's homes. I wish I could do that again. I wish I could afford to do that again. For me, that's where the passion is, in the discovery of a life, in bringing a person back to life—what they did, their period, the whole atmosphere of their world.

And the reality of the business doesn't really allow for that.

Not now, not where I am as a designer. I have to juggle three or four projects at a time in order to stay afloat, "pay the bills" as they say. Maybe at some point in the future I won't have to do it this way, but for now I do.

What do you think characterizes your work? Is there a particular look by which people can identify a McClennahan set?

I wouldn't know. A lot of people tell me that they can identify one of my sets, but I have no idea what it is they see. It's like looking in a mirror and trying to figure out what it is about your face that is you. I can look at work by other designers and tell who designed the set, but I don't know what distinguishes my work. I can design a minimalistic set and I can design a set that is heavily detailed. I can also design sets for film and television, which don't necessarily have to show any sign of the designer's influence. It's like designing a hotel room—they all look alike. But I think it's only on the stage that a designer can control what is seen. You could look at my work and see my mark, but I can't.

What has been your favorite design work?

My favorite projects are the ones I do for the small black theatres in New York. They're very special to me. The sets may not have a great dynamic to them—sometimes, in fact, they'll just be simple sets—but the theatres love them because they're simple and inexpensive. And it's for these sets that I win most of my awards. Although I haven't won any awards that put me in the same category with David Mitchell or Robin Wagner, it's the little sets that cost two hundred dollars that are important to me. I can go to the theatres, hang out, paint a little bit . . . just have fun. And I feel free to do this because the producers aren't concerned about paying overtime, about when we're going to leave the theatre.

Ma Rainey *was something of an unusual situation. I mean, you were young, still at Yale, and then on Broadway.*

Yes, it was my third year in the Drama School. I was twenty-three when *Ma*

Rainey opened on Broadway. There's a lot that goes along with being a minority designer on Broadway, and a lot with being a young minority designer. It was a very frightening experience, but an enlightening one as well. A lot of the union guys, for instance, didn't want to believe I was the set designer. But I had to get beyond that. I had to focus on the work and my responsibilities to the producer. I couldn't use condescending remarks or attitudes as an excuse for why work on the set wasn't get-

ting done. After I put that behind me, I enjoyed doing the show on Broadway.

I've had two more Broadway credits since then, one was a Philip Morris event and one was with Maurice Hines. I'm not very attracted to what happens backstage on Broadway shows. Having to prove myself to the stagehands was always aggravating to me. And it only happens when I'm in the theatre. Everything is fine when I talk on the phone. Even at Carnegie Hall, when I did *A Tribute to Harry Chapin*,

THE WPA THEATRE PRODUCTION OF FRED GAMEL'S *WASTED*, DIRECTED BY CLINTON TURNER DAVIS.

the guy I talked with over the telephone, when I got to the hall, asked me what I was doing there. He talked to me, but he never looked directly at me. And when I said I wanted certain things done, he would never address it right then. He'd walk around, take a telephone call, and then ask a crew member to take care of it. It was those kinds of situations that inspired me to develop Minority Designers and Technicians Network, or MINDTEK.

There has to be some sort of education, especially within the black community, about the importance of blacks in the technical areas of theatre. And unless we push more of us into the technical areas, there'll always be a certain reluctance about the amount of theatre knowledge minorities have. There are a lot of us out there, but we work up to a certain level and then we start to trickle down. I'm not sure why. It may have something to do with the unions, I don't know, but it has nothing to do with design. Some of the people I worked with right out of Yale are no longer in the business, they just gave up—and it hasn't been that long. Others are leaving all the time, and it's getting worse. The economics doesn't help.

I had to learn how to stay in theatre and do other things, like work a computer. Now that I've learned how to do that, I'm trying to help other minority designers do the same. We have to stay because if we don't, there won't be any of us in the the-

atre. I just got a letter the other day from a young lady at the University of Georgia, a black lighting designer, who is concerned about what she is going to do. I can empathize with her because there isn't any program, other than what I'm trying to develop now, that can bring in people, work with them, and get them to the point where they can effectively compete as professionals. That was the problem I had in North Carolina.

Are other people working with you in developing MINDTEK?

No, I founded it myself. I wasn't getting very much work around 1985 and 1986, so I started doing research to figure out what was going on. I discovered a lack of communication, a lack of networking, among minority artists and theatres. So I set up my own network, contacting and referring people.

This business is ninety-nine percent press. If you don't keep your name out there, let people know you're available, people forget about you. It may sound terribly commercial, but it's the only way to survive. You can have great technique and do great sets, but if people don't know that you are available, you don't work. I could be working in Timbuktu, but when I get back to New York I have to let people know that I'm back—or that I'm coming back. So I set up this line of communica-

tion to let people know what I'm doing, where and when. I also know where other people are, so I can recommend someone if I get a call for a job I can't do. I know a lot of black set designers and lighting designers in California, for instance, and they'll call me when they're coming to New York to find out what's available. It's networking, but it also provides a certain camaraderie.

How do you get work?

A lot of it comes from theatres I've worked with before. Or people see my work—or they hear about me—and call. I also meet people at parties. I'll meet a director and tell him that I'd like to work with him. Or I'll tell someone what I do and find out that they're working on a project. I tell people who contact MINDTEK that they have to go to shows, they have to go to the theatre, because that's where the people are, that's their job source, where they need to network.

How did working with Spike Lee come about?

A friend of mine introduced us in the lobby after a panel discussion sponsored by the Black Filmmaker Foundation. His brother had gone to Yale, and I told him I knew his brother. Spike had seen *Ma Rainey* so he knew my work. He was doing

TOP LEFT, ALONZO D. LAMONT, JR.'S *THAT SERIOUS HE-MAN BALL*, DIRECTED BY CLINTON TURNER DAVIS FOR AMERICAN PLACE THEATRE. TOP RIGHT, P.J. GIBSON'S *LONG TIME SINCE YESTERDAY*, DIRECTED BY BETTE HOWARD FOR NEW FEDERAL THEATRE. RIGHT, MARTIN JONES'S *WEST MEMPHIS MOJO*, DIRECTED BY RICK KAHN FOR THE NEGRO ENSEMBLE COMPANY.

a video the next week and asked if I wanted to work on it. He took my telephone number and said he would call. Spike is one of the few black directors who will work with someone new on a project.

There are a lot of minority production companies in New York, and I've worked with some of them, but they tend to work with the same people. What's so nice about Spike is that he breaks down that barrier. Although it can be good working over and over again with people you trust, Spike brings people in because he's interested in having people, especially minorities, work in film. Bill Cosby is concerned about this too. Sometimes the situation is beyond his control, especially in terms of the unions, but I've found many people who are very concerned about helping minorities in the business.

But first you have to have the skills, then you have to have the endurance. Some people will do one show and then decide they don't want to do this kind of work anymore, which can leave a bad taste in the mouths of the people who hired them. It can also reinforce particular stereotypes. So anyone who is attempting to change this business must realize that something has to be done to help sustain people when they're not doing a show for Bill Cosby or a film for Spike Lee, which come along only once in a while. There has to be something to sustain them both financially and emotionally.

What do you tell young designers, or would-be designers, who come to you for advice?

I've said this so many times to friends who have been beaten down by this business, I tell them, "Don't give up. It's going to get hard and you're going to feel like giving up, but it's the job that comes along tomorrow or next week that will open a door and give you an experience with people and the money you could only dream about. It's that moment when you say 'no more' that the door is shut on you." That's the frightening thing about this business, you never know what's going to happen, what will be the spin-off point for your career.

What would be an ideal project for you?

I like the South and the literature about it, like Tennessee Williams, probably because I spent most of my life in North Carolina. I loved working on Leslie Lee's *The Rabbit Foot* because it indulged that part of myself. I also love the look and smell of weathered wood because it reminds me of some of the farms I worked on in North Carolina. The visual images of all of those places—the tobacco farms, the cucumber farms, the narrow dirt roads—have stuck with me. Very few writers are writing about that time period and using those images, especially here in New York

where the writing tends to be about what is happening in an urban environment.

What influences your work?

I'm influenced by everything around me. I'm always investigating what's around me—making discoveries, recording, trying to understand why things happen. Like why, when the sun is setting, the light through a window on this side of the room gets blue and the light on the other side stays warm. I also buy books. I'll stop at a yard sale, buy an unusual book, and three or four weeks later, or a year later, I'll be doing a project and that book will be the very thing I need. As an artist I have to be constantly recording and reaffirming my ideals. I have to be sensitive to what is going on around me both visually and socially. That's what's special about designers in the theatre. We bring to our work a certain sensitivity that helps others understand what a play or musical is all about. That's why we do this work, I think.

Much of your work has been done with new scripts. Is this by choice?

No, it's not. Although I did Ben Jonson's *Bartholomew Fair* at Juilliard, in 1985, I haven't done any Shakespeare since Yale. I do them in my mind all the time because, for a lot of the projects I work on, I deal

TOP, COMPUTER SKETCH FOR AUGUST
WILSON'S *FENCES*. BOTTOM, SET FOR THE
STAGEWEST PRODUCTION OF *FENCES*,
DIRECTED BY CLINTON TURNER DAVIS.

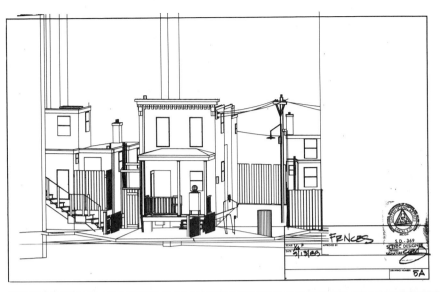

with the set as if I were doing a set for a play by Shakespeare. The set for Charles Fuller's *We* is a good example. In a certain sense what Charles wrote was a Shakespearean tragedy, and you could do any Shakespearean play on the set I designed for *We*.

I would love to do more classical plays, but they're not happening in New York. Unless you can put everything else aside and take your portfolio to regional and academic theatres, you aren't going to do them. Doing the classics takes time and commitment. Producers don't want you flying all over the United States while you're working on a Shakespearean piece, especially when they're paying you good money for it.

Do you want to do more film?

Yes, although I'm not in a hurry to throw myself into it. It's a big step, a big responsibility, especially when you are coming out of the theatre. I did the production design on one film, and the work wasn't as enjoyable as theatre. Film is more abrasive than theatre. It could never replace theatre for me, but I think I would enjoy it.

In what way is film abrasive?

All of the work is done for the camera. You do a lovely wall over here and the director decides to shoot the scene in another corner, where there's nothing. So you've done all of this work, spent thousands of dollars, and it's never used.

To do film you also have to be able to stop everything and say, for the next three to four months I'm just going to work on this film. Preproduction, production and postproduction take a lot of time. You turn down work because you're doing a film, and then people stop calling you. That's why I like to do videos. I know that they will take a week and that I can usually continue to work in theatre. The only person I know who can do both film and theatre—and do them well—is Santo Loquasto.

Do you use assistants?

I call up people on a freelance basis, but I don't have anyone continually working with me. I can't afford that. And unfortunately, a large part of this business is based on what you as a designer can afford to design. The contracts I sign now—the pay schedules I work out with the theatres—are crazy. Sometimes I spread my payments out over a period of four months, and at the end of the four months the theatres are in worse shape than when I signed the contract. But I guess I stay in this business because it's what I've always known, it's what I love as an artist.

MICHAEL MERRITT

ALTHOUGH MICHAEL MERRITT has on occasion considered moving to either the East or the West Coast, his emotional connection to the Midwest—and specifically, to the prairies—has kept him in Chicago, "a city on the edge of the prairie." As a result Merritt may have less national recognition than designers who skip from regional theatre to regional theatre, but he has developed an extraordinary body of work which also includes, since 1985, production design for both film (*The House of Games* and *Things Change*) and video (*Brewster Place*).

Merritt's best work, like his set for *Glengarry Glen Ross*, tends to be sculptural. It can also be deceptively simple, emphasizing a particular element which supports the action of a play rather than defining a character or the play's narrative (the green sofa in the Lincoln Center production of Arthur Miller's *Clara*, or the eight-sided table for *The Shawl*, for example). "If I have any style," Merritt explains in this interview, "if there is any sense of form in the work I do, it comes partially out of the fact that I don't have intensive training in the traditional theatre. A lot of my ideas come from the experience of working with specific people." Among these

FACING PAGE, THE GOODMAN THEATRE PRODUCTION OF NIKOLAI GOGOL'S *THE GOVERNMENT INSPECTOR*, DIRECTED BY FRANK GALATI.

"specific people" Merritt includes David Mamet (whose scripts he likens to the "hyperrealism" of Thomas Pynchon's novels) and Gregory Mosher.

MARCH 18, 1990—
MICHAEL MERRITT'S OFFICE AT
HARPO STUDIOS, CHICAGO, ILLINOIS

I was born in South Dakota and raised in Sioux Falls. Then, when I was about ten or eleven, I moved to La Crosse, Wisconsin. Most of my family had grown up on farms in that area and were working class, so I wasn't exposed to much theatre as a child. Much of my experience was through films and, in the 1950s, through television. I became interested in painting and being an artist when I was very young. Always in the back of my mind I wanted to be a painter, or do something in the arts. I did do some theatre in high school, and I enjoyed it, but it never occurred to me that theatre could provide a possibility for a career. In fact, I went to the University of Chicago as a math and physics major—I was the first in my family to go to college—and found after a year or so that I wasn't going to be interested in doing that for the rest of my life. So I switched to an arts program. Unfortunately they didn't have any theatre—and they still don't have a theatre department—but I got involved with a local theatre group and started to do a lot of work with them.

Designing?

No, first as an actor. But I soon discovered that I enjoyed myself more backstage, so my third and fourth years there I started to design. After I graduated I spent a year at the Court Theatre, which at that time was a summer theatre connected to the university. I met a designer, James Ascaragi, who convinced me that theatre was something I could make a living at. I loved working in the theatre. It felt very comfortable to be able to apply my need to paint to working with other people and creating these large sculptures, which was what I imagined design to be. So after I got out of the military, I went back to the Chicago Circle Campus of the University of Illinois and started doing lots of small theatre projects locally for little or no money. It was very exciting because it coincided with the blossoming of Chicago theatre.

Which was when?

The early to mid-1970s. I met Robert Falls when he first came to Chicago. I met David Mamet before his plays were being produced. In fact, I designed a very early production of *A Midsummer Night's Dream* for the summer festival in Oak Park in which David played Oberon with a cigar and toga. It was a great production. We had a lot of fun. Bill Macy was also in it, and Steven Schachter directed it, so it was the entire group.

A lot of it was just fortunate timing. I got involved with the Steppenwolf people when they first moved into the city. I met Gregory Mosher when he first came to Chicago as an assistant to Bill Woodman at the Goodman. Gregory and I started working together early on in his career here. There was so much happening; it was very exciting. I probably learned more then than I did in my graduate studies.

Was there ever a point at which you were going to study painting professionally?

Like many people from that period, I lacked direction when I came out of college. So no, there was never a time when I thought I would make a profession out of painting. In a way, the theatre presented itself to me. It was there, it was available, and it was, at that time, the most exciting thing to be involved in. In some ways I had very little concern about what was going to happen. Unlike a lot of people in the theatre now, I didn't have a sense of creating a career out of it. That came later

as opportunities opened up and I saw that I could plan what I wanted to do. Even to me, at this point, it sounds like drifting, but in a way it has served me well. If I have any style, if there is any sense of form in the work I do, it comes partially out of the fact that I don't have intensive training in the traditional theatre. A lot of my ideas come from the experience of working with specific people. Perhaps design is a little more personal thing for me.

THE GOVERNMENT INSPECTOR, DIRECTED BY FRANK GALATI.

ABOVE, THE WISDOM BRIDGE THEATRE
PRODUCTION OF WILLIAM SHAKESPEARE'S
HAMLET, DIRECTED BY ROBERT FALLS.
FACING PAGE, DAVID MAMET'S *LAKEBOAT*,
DIRECTED BY GREGORY MOSHER FOR THE
GOODMAN THEATRE.

At what point did you realize that you were committed to working in theatre?

I think it happened when Gregory Mosher took over the Goodman Theatre as artistic director. It also happened when David Mamet's career started to blossom, when it became apparent that what we were doing in Chicago was on a level with work being done across the nation. Certainly when we did *Glengarry Glen Ross* and took it to Broadway. That experience convinced me that the theatre was something I could do. And indeed I was doing it.

Chicago is a strange town. People in the theatre were, and to a certain extent still are, treated as children. They're not seen as serious. Everything in Chicago is about business. If you're not doing business, you're not really serious about your life. When I went to New York and talked to bank tellers, they wanted to know what I did in the theatre, what I was doing. It was a very moving experience because I was being accepted as a serious adult. It touched me deeply, and I felt that the theatre was real and legitimate and not just a plaything.

It has changed a bit in Chicago. There's more of an audience for Chicago theatre now. When I started working in theatre, everyone—except for the young North Side audiences—went down to the Loop and saw shows at the road houses. Only a few people saw these experimental groups up on the North Side. But that has changed. The road houses have just about died out, except for the big blockbusters, and we're building larger theatres on the North Side.

I'd like to talk about how Gregory Mosher and David Mamet influenced your work.

David has been a big influence on me. I don't find his writing at all realistic, and in our discussions he obviously doesn't see it as realistic. There has evolved a need to visually create a sense of supporting the action of the play rather than becoming

descriptive or narrative. So rather than describing the character through the design, I try to support the action of the character. To me this means simplifying, and emphasizing a given element.

A good example would be *The Shawl*. It's a play about a psychic. During my discussions with David and Gregory it became increasingly clear that we had to have something I thought of as a ceremonial place. The trick was to suggest a Chicago railroad flat but still keep an element of spirituality that would support David's ambivalent feelings about what was happening in the play. I remember

several discussions about whether or not this character really had psychic powers, and of course David would never say. I came up with two windows and a door, each covered with drapes—three simple drapes in what could be considered a very realistic room. All of the furniture was suggestive of real furniture, and we had to build an eight-sided table, which was used almost like an altar.

Going back to your question, my work in the fine arts, even when I was in college, tended to be stylistically simple. It tended to be simple shapes that had a certain theatricality about them. And then, as I started working with artists like Gregory and David and Robert Falls—although Bob's views are a little different—they encouraged me to develop a very simple style.

I've been doing a lot more film and television in the last two years, partially because it is very lucrative, but also because I enjoy creating a product. I have to admit that the ethereal quality of theatre sometimes bothers me. It's very frustrating at times to see it just fade away. My first experience in film was working with David on his first films, which again were not realistic. They're like Thomas Pynchon novels—so hyperrealistic that they're almost abstract. I think the heightened reality of David's language calls for a simple visual style that also emphasizes certain real elements.

When *Glengarry Glen Ross* was first done in London, it was done in a realistic restaurant with people moving from booth to booth. When Gregory and I were dis-

BERTOLT BRECHT'S *MOTHER COURAGE*, DIRECTED BY ROBERT FALLS FOR WISDOM BRIDGE THEATRE.

cussing how to do it in Chicago, it was apparent that what we wanted to do was really present it, thrust these people forward into the audience. The set was originally going to be very abstract. It was going to be done in an empty theatre with booths. Then David came back from the London production and suggested that the play needed more visual support than we were giving it. Because we had started with a simple, abstract structure, it was just a matter of bringing in certain elements to reinforce the realistic quality. I was very pleased with it because it didn't become overwhelmingly real, but there was no question about where you were.

Where did you learn the mechanics of design?

I was in the theatre program at the University of Illinois for a while, which was helpful. At the same time I was working as a carpenter at the Goodman, so much of my experience has come from on-the-job training and working with other designers. I would assist designers who came to town. I read and studied as much as I could. I still feel a certain lack because I don't have the formal training. It's a mixed blessing. My experience of people coming out of very intensive design programs is that they often develop habits or ideas about design that take some time to shake

off. I didn't have to overcome that. What I did have to overcome was my own lack of experience.

Your career has been founded on the work you've done with people in Chicago, but was there ever a time you thought about living and working someplace else?

Yes, there have been times. There was a program at Yale for servicemen, and after I got out of the service I actually applied, thinking I might move East to pursue theatre. I also spent six months in Los Angeles in the early 1970s. But I don't know,

DAVID HALLIWELL'S *HAIL SCRAWDYKE! OR LITTLE MALCOLM AND HIS STRUGGLE AGAINST THE EUNUCHS,* DIRECTED BY MICHAEL MAGGIO FOR GOODMAN THEATRE II.

maybe it's because of my nature, my need to be comfortable. I see Chicago as a city on the edge of the prairie, and I have a deep affection for the prairies. When I moved east, even when I first moved into Wisconsin, I suffered from claustrophobia because of all the trees around me. But there was a real sense that if I could make a living for myself in Chicago, Chicago was really where I wanted to be.

I'd like to know how you approach a new project.

Obviously, the director is the major influence, but the process usually involves working heavily with the text. I spend a lot of time with the script and collecting material. Not so much visual material, but literary material that relates to the period or the author—anything I can find that can give me more clues about the text. I think directors feel most comfortable with designers because, in many ways, our experience of the process is similar. Both the director and the designer have to grasp the action of the play in an Aristotelian sense. So this becomes my major objective: to understand and get an almost intuitive sense—as opposed to an intellectual sense—of the emotional content in the play.

I am sometimes slow to begin to put things down on paper, which some direc-tors complain about. But I have to have a clear understanding of what the play is about before I can really start to visualize it. Then I'll bring sketches and visual material to my discussions with the director. My first ideas about the play tend toward creating spatial relationships that support the action of the play. Are we going to have to expose the character? Is he going to have to be trapped? Are we going to have the sense that he has no way to rest, that he's constantly moving? Only then do I start thinking about the detail, about period and architectural elements. I don't usually start with texture. I start with the space.

I read some of Adolphe Appia's work when I was in college. I was very impressed with his designs and was intrigued with the rhythmic use of space. I like to work very closely with directors to try to get a clear sense of their vision, which is often difficult. If it's a very complex piece with lots of scenes, if we're doing Shakespeare, for instance, I'll try to create certain visual moments and then build out from them. I hesitate to describe my process, but I would say that I start within the play and build out. This sounds very awkward—and I'm sure the reality changes from play to play—but if there is a common thread to my method of working it is that I like to start with a very deep understanding of the text.

Do you do much sketching?

Yes. I'm reluctant to start working on paper, but once I do it contributes greatly to solving problems. I may rely too heavily on the text sometimes and resist putting ideas down, but once I start I usually find that it helps to clarify things, which then helps the director. But it depends. Some directors are much more visual that others. You can discuss an idea and they'll have a sense of what you are talking about. Other directors will feel very uncomfortable until they see something. I also like to work with models. I like to put things down three-dimensionally. It helps me, of course, but it also helps the director. Color is always problematic for me. Color comes in last, probably because I have so much trouble with it.

Is there a reason for that?

I don't know. I've often wondered. I think it's just a certain fear of putting color together. I've always been a sketch artist, working in black and white. My focus is on understanding the rhythms of the text. Michael Maggio and I did *Romeo and Juliet* at the Goodman in 1989. Because the Goodman has no fly system, everything tends to be horizontal, which we wanted to avoid. We ended up with a huge turntable, with periaktoids that moved within it. The design came out of the rhythmic needs. My process is to understand the rhythm of the action, and then try to match that visually.

What do you think have been your most successful productions?

There have been a number of productions with Mamet and Mosher—*Glengarry* and *The Shawl* come to mind, of course. And I love working with Chicago directors like Michael Maggio and Frank Galati. A number of projects I've done with Robert Falls: *Mother Courage* and *Curse of the Starving Class*, which John Malkovich was in.

Curse of the Starving Class was a very simple design. I had read an article about farmers in Montana who were suing the electric company because of the power lines that ran over their land. They claimed that the lines produced electromagnetic radiation that was affecting their milk cows. So I designed this sweeping, abstract landscape with a huge Georgia O'Keeffe drop in the back. I had an electrical power line running right through it. I had a huge electrical leg on one side of the stage, then a medium-size tower, and then another smaller one, so it was in forced perspective. Then I put little electrical appliances on the landscape. It was very simple, but very effective, I thought.

Mother Courage is another favorite. Brechtian technique had become so accepted that we were looking for new ways to startle a contemporary audience. We did it so that each section of the play had a different style. For each scene we chose what we thought supported the action of that scene. If it required realism, we did it realistically. If it required fourteenth-century costumes, we used them. It was intellectually very successful. Sometimes I wonder if I shouldn't have been a director. I sometimes like dealing with the ideas more than anything else.

THE GOODMAN II PRODUCTION OF SAM SHEPARD'S *CURSE OF THE STARVING CLASS*, DIRECTED BY ROBERT FALLS.

THE GOODMAN PRODUCTION OF *ROMEO AND JULIET*, DIRECTED BY MICHAEL MAGGIO.

Would you like to direct?

Yeah, I think so. But I still don't understand the actor's process. My one regret is not being involved with one company on an extended basis. Maybe it's my need for nesting, which is why I stayed in Chicago, but I've always regretted not having a company with which I could work closely. At one time Mosher and Mamet and a number of designers started The New Theater Company, which looked promising, but then Gregory took the position at Lincoln Center and it faded away.

What would a permanent company provide for you?

A consistent opportunity to develop along a certain line. Freelancing in American theatre—for me, at least—has often been an experience of going into regional theatres and dealing with seasons. But I want all of the forces of the theatre to be focused on the production I'm working on. I have a hard time being told that this is just one of six plays and that the real product being provided is the season, that the individual play within the season is not the final product. It's not a very creative situation. As much as people berate Broadway producers, my experience on Broadway has been that this is the product and every effort is made to make it work. I find that very exciting.

Unfortunately, a lot of theatre in America has gotten tied into providing a generic product. A lot of regional theatres try to break out of that, they try to provide special projects, but it doesn't happen a lot. Particularly not when you are coming in for one show with a director you may not know. I think a play has an internal life, and if it needs to run for a year then it should be allowed to run for a year. Every time you do a play, on a certain level it is the last play you are ever going to do.

Have you done a lot of work outside of Chicago?

I've done some regional work, but it has been fairly limited. Maybe this is why.

Were you pleased with Speed-the-Plow?

Not altogether. It was originally designed for the small theatre at Lincoln Center, but at the last moment, after some of the set had been built, it was decided to move the show to Broadway. There were enormous pressures to make changes, but in some way we got caught up in just getting it up on the stage. I'm not displeased with it, but it didn't work the way I had imagined.

How did it change in moving from the Mitzi Newhouse to the Royale?

In many ways it didn't, which was the problem. The legs were already prepared, so I had to adapt them to a much larger space. Gregory was so focused on making the change—and dealing with the personalities he was working with—that we didn't have time to communicate about the design. We had a very tight schedule. I thought the production in London was a little more successful. The National wanted a much more naturalistic set, so I designed a rather elaborate patio for the second act and a more complete office for the first and third acts.

Let's talk a bit about your film and television work.

I did David Mamet's two films, *House of Games* and *Things Change*, and then two films for television that were shot here in Chicago: *The Howard Beach Story* and one for the Disney Channel that was aired in the fall. Now I'm doing this series, *Brewster Place*.

Do you feel as if you have less control of your work than you do in theatre?

No. It has to be shared more than in the theatre, but there can be a real exchange. I've heard horror stories about cinematographers who don't talk to designers, who treat them like slaves, but that hasn't been my experience. All of the people I've worked with have been very open to discussions and suggestions about the look of the pieces. The money is much better than it is in theatre, but it doesn't replace the excitement of theatre. There really isn't any comparison for me.

Then why do film or television?

Well, they pay better. And more people will see my work, so it's giving me a place in history that I might not otherwise have. I suppose, psychologically, it all ties into how I started working in theatre and my sense of myself in the theatre. Attempting to take myself seriously as an artist has been a real issue for me. I came from a lower-middle-class background—this is a little like being on my analyst's couch—and my family doesn't really understand the type of work I do in the theatre. They do, however, have a clearer understanding of what I do in film and television. Maybe this is part of the reason I'm attracted to these other mediums. Certainly the theatre is personally more exciting, but these other forms supply solace for other needs.

How many projects a year do you do?

Between eight and nine, but that has dropped since I've gotten involved in television. Last year I did four theatrical productions. I don't know how *Brewster Place* is going to pan out. Obviously, I'm drifting away from the theatre to some degree. And right now I'm considering going back to teaching, which would allow me more time to design.

Why teach?

Teaching is a wonderful learning experience. I enjoy exchanging ideas with students. The way they challenge me gives me insight into the choices I make. Every piece of theatre, every piece of art, creates a universe out of the chaos around it. It makes something real and coherent out of a lot of confusion. Coming to understand that universe is a wonderful experience.

I developed some ideas when I was teaching at Columbia College that I would like to expand on. One class was about cultural history. I would draw parallels between the art I love of a particular period and the intellectual ideas of that period, and then how they got expressed not only in the plays, but also in the way plays were put on. It was a fascinating course that I would like to explore some more.

I suspect that on some level I'm looking to take elements from the theatre that will serve my other interests. There's a love of the theatre, but I'm trying to couple it with my other needs, which tend to be more prosaic. I never sought from theatre the more traditional returns. I've used my experience of theatre to support my other needs, like staying in Chicago, for instance, or trying to create a family. One of

TWO STILLS FROM THE MOVIE *HOUSE OF GAMES*, WRITTEN AND DIRECTED BY DAVID MAMET.

my great experiences in theatre has been to work with David. David has a very strong sense of family. He is very concerned about the relationship behind the curtain or screen, about how that relationship affects the product that goes on stage or up on the screen.

I sometimes believe that this can be a very cruel way to create art. It can be very brutal on the people who make it. But I don't believe you create great art through a process that is painful. Maybe part of my search has been to find a good life and still be able to create art. I have great hopes about the future, and I am very excited about it. I feel as if I am in the midst of a lot of changes that are going on in American theatre. The line between film and theatre is blurring, for instance. My experience in the past has been that film people were leery of getting involved with theatre people, but it is now becoming more and more common. Because of communication changes, like computers and faxes, you can live wherever you want and still participate in the community.

What would you recommend to people who want to go into theatre or design?

I would certainly caution them against going into a theatre program too early. Everything seems to me to be focused on getting on the fast track. It's a funny thing, but a lot of American film today is manneristic. The popular filmmakers are basically making movies about movies. They don't compare to the wonderful films of the 1940s and 1930s, where people came out of real life and brought their experiences to the film. If you don't have any real experience to fall back on, you can get theatre about theatre, too. In terms of a career, it's important to get the right training, make the right contacts. But as an artist in the theatre, I think it is very important that you get some experience of life apart from the theatre. Those are the things that give the work some special quality, that create a certain vision that will give the audience a new view—which in some sense is what it means to be an artist.

Where do you see theatre going?

I hope that more attention will be paid to regional differences. It has always struck me as very strange that the whole of American theatre—what is good, what is bad—has been defined by one city in this country. I think this is changing. New York is still the center, it's where the bulk of the talent goes, but you also see something like Steppenwolf, with its commitment to Chicago. Even though many members have become famous in their own right, they still try to maintain a connection here. The style that came out of the Chicago experience, back to Second City and Paul Sills' Story Theatre, this tearing down the walls of naturalism, can be related to other things that are happening here. I would hope that this kind of recognition of regional differences would not only continue but be nurtured.

I'd like to stay in this area, work with other artists, and develop some ideas about the theatre that are more peculiar to the Midwest. When I go to the top of very tall buildings in Chicago I can see the prairies, and I have a real clear sense of being on the edge of where I was born, of having a real connection to the land. Maybe my work reflects a little bit of that prairie emptiness. I love the open prairies. I love seeing the clouds form eighty miles away and then feeling them blow over me. This excites me, and maybe my work reflects a little bit of that. I'd like to be able to explore these feelings, and I'm not sure I could do it someplace else. Maybe this is too emotional, but on some level I don't want to lose contact with the earth.

What would be an ideal theatre project for you?

I love doing Shakespeare. I'd love to do a series of the histories, or the classic Greek plays. I'm not a writer, but I would also love to develop a piece based on a writer of the Midwest, say Willa Cather. It's very

DAVID MAMET'S *GLENGARRY GLEN ROSS*,
DIRECTED BY GREGORY MOSHER.

strange. People from the coast who haven't had the experience of the prairies don't really understand it. If I could find a writer I could work with, I would like to develop something that dealt with the experience of the prairie states.

Designers don't generally develop projects, do they?

No, they don't. I suppose most designers want someone else to take the responsibility, and then they enjoy working within the framework presented. It must be something in our natures that we become designers. That's exciting in its own right, but it also has limitations—at least for me it does. And I think that as I grow more confident in theatre, I want to develop more of my own voice.

I feel as if I've been in a learning period for the past ten or fifteen years. I've finally gotten to a point where I understand a little bit about the nature of the art form and I feel optimistic that there'll be future opportunities to explore these feelings I have. Maybe in design, maybe I'll direct, who knows, maybe in film. I would really love to develop a company; there are enough artists in Chicago committed to staying here and working in this area.

What are your interests outside of theatre?

I love to read. I read a lot, in fact. My background is in art and art history, and that has been very influential. I love painting and I still paint, although less than I used to. Like many people in the theatre, my life is pretty much consumed by the work. I don't know if it is healthy, but it certainly feels good. I'm happiest when I'm working—or involved with something that is related to my work.

It seems to me that part of bringing something fresh and original and exciting to the theatre depends upon your own experience of life. As I said, I came into the theatre very late. I have had a fair amount of life experience that I would like to bring into my work. I was in Vietnam and it is an issue that is a major part of my consciousness. I would eventually like to explore that. A lot of theatre available to me doesn't interest me very much. Ultimately, I'd like to pull back and really focus on the things that mean the most to me.

TONY STRAIGES

UNLIKE MANY other designers who, for various reasons, tend to juggle several design projects concurrently, Tony Straiges prefers working on only one project at a time. "When I'm working on a project," he explains in this interview, "that's where I'm focused, that's really all I can think about." As a consequence (particularly in recent years), Straiges's chronology may contain fewer titles that those of his contemporaries, but the work, much of it for Broadway, has had an undeniable impact on American theatre.

Straiges, who was raised in a small coal-mining town in eastern Pennsylvania, worked for the Library of Congress, helped found the American Puppet Theatre, and assisted John Priest at the San Francisco Opera before he finally decided to actively pursue set design as a profession. Once the decision was made, however, Straiges wasted no time in seeking out programs and/or designers he thought he could learn from, like the design program run by Eldon Elder at Brooklyn College and then Ming Cho Lee, at Yale.

Although Straiges is probably best known for his designs for *Sunday in the Park*

FACING PAGE, MODEL FOR THE AMERICAN BALLET THEATRE PRODUCTION OF LEO DELIBES' *COPPELIA*, CHOREOGRAPHED BY ENRIQUE MARTINEZ.

with George and *Into the Woods*, he appears to be equally comfortable with serious dramas (like *Long Day's Journey into Night*, directed by Jonathan Miller) and comedies (Neil Simon's *Rumors*). Besides his numerous Broadway credits, Straiges has also designed Off Broadway (Manhattan Theatre Club, Circle Repertory, Circle in the Square and The Second Stage), for regional theatres (including Yale Repertory Theatre, Arena Stage, Williamstown Theatre Festival, the Guthrie Theater) and for dance (Joffrey Ballet, American Ballet Theatre).

FEBRUARY 24, 1989—
TONY STRAIGES'S APARTMENT,
BROOKLYN, NEW YORK

I grew up in Pennsylvania, in a small coal-mining town called Minersville. The Catholic Church played a large part in the life of the community. The services, especially those of the old Catholic Church, were very theatrical, and even though I didn't associate the services with theatre, when I think about it now, that sense of spectacle and ritual probably influenced me in choosing theatre as a profession.

Did your parents take you to see theatre?

Nothing that was professionally staged, except for ice shows and circuses. The Catholic school presented operettas, however, and I was involved with them. It was a very primitive theatricality. I acted and painted drops, although at the time I didn't know that was what they were called. I didn't know that you could actually study design until after I graduated from high school and moved to Washington, D.C., where I met John Priest, who ran a scene shop.

Why did you move to Washington?

I couldn't afford to go to college, so I accepted a job with the Library of Congress. At that time government agencies would travel to depressed areas and hire graduating high school students for government work. Minersville had been a mining community, but the mines were closed and the possibility of finding work in the area was poor. A young person did not have much of a future in Minersville. The Library of Congress offered a real job, which I needed to support myself.

I wasn't particularly interested in going into government service, but when you are seventeen you want to be out on your own, make some dough. I didn't especially like the job, but the people were very nice. I was a microphotographer in the photoduplication department. I photographed newspapers, lithographs and rare books. It was interesting up to a point, but I didn't like having a nine-to-five job, a twenty-minute lunch break. I didn't enjoy the restrictions. So on the side I started exploring theatre projects, which I supported with my salary from the government.

What kind of projects?

A group of us started The American Puppet Theatre. Most of the people involved were my age—some younger, some older. They also worked at the Library of Congress and were bored with their jobs. We didn't know anything about puppets, but because we worked in this great library we had all of the research in the world. The project became successful and very rewarding. I met John Priest through the puppet theatre—his shop built our traveling rigging and theatre—and it was John who told me about Carnegie and Yale, and suggested I should become a designer. I liked drawing and painting, but I didn't think about designing as a job until I turned twenty-one or twenty-two.

Was The American Puppet Theatre a touring company? What kind of work did it do?

We toured throughout D.C., Virginia and Maryland, but our home base was Georgetown University. The university had a small theatre which we used during the summer, then we toured during

THE CENTER STAGE PRODUCTION OF
CHRISTOPHER HAMPTON'S *SAVAGES*,
DIRECTED BY JACKSON PHIPPIN.

the rest of the year. We were all fairly young, and it was the 1960s. There were, you know, a lot of hippies around at the time, and they were attracted to our work. Audiences seemed to enjoy our show, we made some good friends, and it was a lot of fun.

Some of the work was scripted, but most of it was done to music. Some pieces were based on popular entertainers like Pearl Bailey, but we had different nationalities in our company—Brazilian, German, oth-ers—and they had a large influence on what we did, like what music we used. For example, we were intrigued with a collection of South American suites by the composer/conductor Waldo de los Rios. We took his evocation of the ruins at Cuzco, the ancient site of Inca culture, and created a story using puppets and marionettes. Because I was in charge of the company—and interested in sets and costumes—the visual element became an important part of the production.

ATHOL FUGARD'S *A LESSON FROM ALOES*,
DIRECTED BY JACKSON PHIPPIN FOR
CENTER STAGE.

Did you also work the puppets?

Oh yes, we all did. The show was large. It took us over a year to make it, and thirteen people to put it on. We built everything ourselves. We worked every day after library hours and every weekend. It still was incomplete when we were asked to try it out. What happened was actually very funny. A committee from the House of Representatives had heard about our group and invited us to perform at the annual variety show they hold for Congressmen and staff. We performed three

completed production numbers. We thought of the show as being for the entire family, but this particular gala was "adults only." Besides The American Puppet Theatre, the program included Italian singers, belly dancers, and an entertainer named Rusty Warren, who played the piano and told lewd jokes. There had been a lot to drink, and the audience was feeling very good. We closed the first act. We were a big hit with the audience. As we were taking down the set, one Congresswoman—I don't remember her name, but she was really drunk—came over and

asked, "Can I go with you? I know I'm old, but I really want to join your show. Can I join your show?"

The production played for two years, and as it got larger and more complicated I realized I didn't like being in charge. I didn't like having to deal with the daily problems, like clearing copyrights, appeasing the fire marshals. So I decided to go to Carnegie Tech to study design. I started the undergraduate program, but didn't stay very long. I was there for a month, in fact. At that time, as an undergraduate, you took all of these art courses:

figure drawing, calligraphy, sculpture. They were terrific courses, but I was interested in theatre design and was receiving only one one-hour theatre course a week. So I quit.

I went to Europe for three months, using my returned college fee for a bankroll. When I got back to the States I decided to put together a portfolio to see if I could get work with the Ice Capades. I had friends skating with the show. I took my portfolio to their studio in Hollywood, showed them my designs, and told them I was willing to take any position. They were already into their new season, but said they might hire me for the next season. That was encouraging, but I needed a job. John Priest, who had left Washington and was now the technical director of the San Francisco Opera, hired me as his assistant. This was my first opportunity to work with real designers, all of whom were European.

What year was that?

It must have been 1970 or 1971. I learned a lot assisting John. He taught me how to draft, and I picked up how to build models. The Opera also asked me to design three summer productions, which were on a small scale. After two years with the Opera it seemed time for a change. I had heard that Eldon Elder was sponsoring a design program at Brooklyn College—funded by the Ford Foundation and the Rockefeller Foundation—and was looking for people to fill the program. They asked me to join. We worked hard, but they provided us with generous stipends that allowed us to go to Europe for the summer. It was a good program.

Then, after two years with Eldon, I felt that I should see how another designer approached theatre. At that point Ming Cho Lee was one of the leading designers in the country, so I applied to Yale. I loved Yale. I don't remember how old I was when I went there, but because I had traveled and worked in a real theatre I was more aware of what I wanted to do with my life, which was design.

Robert Brustein was still at Yale, and it was a very stimulating environment. No one did box sets; everything was more abstract, which appealed to me. And I liked Ming. I learned a lot from him. I was at Yale for a long time—about five years, I think—because I didn't have an undergraduate degree. You could receive a master's degree if you took courses for five years. Except I didn't do my light plots or theatre-history program, so I never received the degree. I may have been in New Haven for seven years, in fact, because I was hired as an associate designer at Yale Rep. I liked Yale and New Haven. Friends from class moved to New York, and I would visit them, but I didn't like New York. The city scared me. I finally moved to New York when Heidi and Rocco Landesman asked me to move into this place.

You did the Broadway production of Timbuktu while you were still living in New Haven. How did that production come about for you?

I had designed a production of *A Midsummer Night's Dream*, directed by Alvin Epstein. It was a wonderful production, and it received a good deal of coverage in the national press. Geoffrey Holder's wife, Carmen de Lavallade, played Titania. Geoffrey saw the show and asked me if I wanted to design *Timbuktu*. I didn't know anything about Broadway, and was apprehensive knowing that Geoffrey was such an excellent artist. I wasn't sure how it would be working for another artist. Geoffrey told me at the beginning that he might make recommendations and suggest changes, but in the end he would respect my decisions concerning what the scenery would look like. And that was the way it worked. He designed the costumes first, and then I designed the set, working around his colors.

A first-time Broadway show is quite an experience. I remember attending the bid session. Both Steve Graham, my associate, and I were nervous. There you are in a room with all of the representatives from the shops—and you don't know any of them. That's where I met Pete Feller, whom I knew only by reputation. He was very reassuring as we went through the drawings. I felt he really wanted to help. His shop got the show, and he sort of watched out for me. He knew I didn't know what I was doing, in the sense of how the game was played.

You can get into trouble on your first Broadway show. Arnold Abronson had painted these large umbrellas for *Timbuktu*, and they arrived in Philadelphia, where we were doing tryouts. Geoffrey and I hadn't seen them completed in the shop, so I opened them up and spread them all over the stage. They were really very beautiful. The production manager pulled me aside to ask if I knew what I had just done. I didn't know that the designer isn't allowed to touch the props when the prop crew is on a lunch break. The prop people had to be paid an hour and a half overtime.

How do you approach a project?

I read the play and try not to think about the design as I'm reading. It's difficult, but I try. Then I meet with the director. I usually let the director tell me what he or she feels about the play, while I listen and take notes. Then the research period begins. I'll browse through picture collections, libraries, bookstores and art galleries, searching for visual images that might relate to the play or something the director said. Then I'll meet with the director again and we'll look at the research together. For *Dangerous Games*, for example, I went to the Argentinean embassy to find photos of Argentina—of the architecture, the landscape, the earth. I also went to many Latin American bookstores in New York and found a book about an American/Spanish artist who did large, textured paintings and sculptures, which suggested a mixture of religion and violence. The work was beautiful and grotesque at the same time.

I also found a book about an artist who glued fabric to the canvas and then textured and painted the fabric. His colors were incredible: orange reds with Prussian blue and acid green. One of his paintings inspired the brothel set, in fact. I showed these books to Graciela Daniele, who directed *Dangerous Games*, and got her response. She really liked the colors and textures. Then, inspired by these two artists, I designed the production based on Graciela's emotional, visual choice for the show.

Is your response generally to the texture of something?

Yes, texture and color and environment. I seldom do much reading when I'm researching a project because there isn't enough time. I did read Gypsy Rose Lee's memoirs when I thought I was doing *Gypsy*, but that was an exception.

What happens after you talk to the director?

We build a stage house and I work out a rough ground plan. We'll put together a rough blueprint model, which is when we discover the space. The blueprint model is really the director's first opportunity to see what I am doing, and we'll move things around, or change the proportions, as needed. It's part of the discovering period. I seldom show the director finished sketches. Sketches are wonderful, but they can be deceptive. I'm deceived by sketches, and the director can be deceived too. After the blueprint model is approved, I'll talk to the costume designer about color and the lighting designer about space for the lights. I try to work very closely with the other designers. The good drafting is begun after the color model is approved. Sometimes things change when rehearsals start, but if you and the director have had enough time to plan how the piece moves—or how the actors will move through the space—the design usually stays close to what was planned.

Do you do the drafting yourself?

I do some of it, but I always work with another person. I don't know why, but I

MODEL FOR THE GUTHRIE THEATER PRODUCTION OF JOHN GAY'S *THE BEGGAR'S OPERA*, DIRECTED BY ALVIN EPSTEIN.

THE BROADWAY PRODUCTION OF NEIL SIMON'S
RUMORS, DIRECTED BY GENE SAKS.

can't seem to do a show by myself any-more. I'm fortunate to have Richard Taris, an excellent colleague, working with me. It's easier and more fun working with an-other person. You can bounce ideas off of each other.

Does this allow you to do more shows?

I get a lot of requests, but I don't do many shows because I don't like working on

more than one project at a time. And when that project is over, I like to take two weeks off to relax, put the studio back in order, have my teeth cleaned. When I'm working on a project, that's where I'm fo-cused, that's really all I can think about. I can't do three projects at one time. I also don't have the setup for it. Although I have had up to five people working in here, you can't move. Three people is about the limit. This is also where I live; I don't have a separate apartment. As you can see, there isn't even a sofa. I would love to have a sofa, or a room for myself, but I can't afford a larger space.

Another reason for not doing more than one show at a time is that no matter how small the show is, there are always complications. Propping *Rumors* is a good example. It's a straight set, but we went all over the city to get the furniture. Then we had to get the fabrics. Then we had to have the fabrics dyed. We had to deal with what's behind the bathroom door. How much of a bathroom do we need to put there? We had bedroom doors, so how much of the bedrooms should we see? It takes a lot of time. Every show is so demanding. And once you say yes to designing a show, you're really into it. They call you all the time. It's like joining the army.

How many shows a year do you do?

Four or five. But *Into the Woods*, including the San Diego production, took a year and a half, and I didn't do anything else during that time. *Sunday in the Park* and *Copperfield* each took a year to design.

Can you do a ballet and a theatre production at the same time, or is that too much, too?

I'm doing a ballet for the Joffrey now. The Joffrey has a certain look, I'm told, so I

have to work within their restictions. But that's fine because it's easier to make decisions when you're given restrictions. Although it seems like a ballet uses less scenery, they're calling me every week. The choreographer called again to say he wants to talk. We've already talked a lot, and I haven't done anything yet, but he wants to talk some more.

Why did you agree to do it?

Although I didn't vote for him, the ballet was commissioned for President Bush. I thought it might be interesting to try

TOM STOPPARD'S *ON THE RAZZLE*, DIRECTED BY DOUGLAS C. WAGER FOR ARENA STAGE.

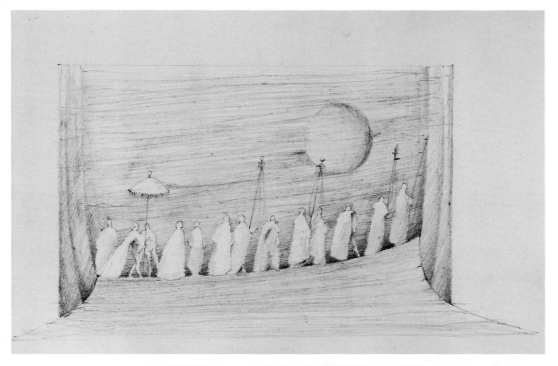

something different, do a ballet. We haven't discussed salaries yet, nor the time needed to do the project. People call you about these projects and they want to talk about the artistic look of the piece, but no one wants to talk about money. Paying the designer always seems to be the last thing on the producer's mind. So I call my agent, Helen Merrill, and let her discuss the financial arrangement.

So she deals with the contracts?

Yes, always. It's horrible stuff. Helen handles all of the contract work. I don't know what kind of money to ask for, so I rely on her to be up on that kind of stuff. A designer can earn good money doing television or film, but theatre is another story. The salaries from regional theatres provide enough to pay the rent and eat, but no more. Off Broadway doesn't provide even that. The only time a set designer can actually earn money is on a Broadway show. If the show is successful, then the designer receives royalties. So you depend on your agent to place you in a decent royalty pool.

Do you find producers difficult to deal with?

Sometimes. I finally got a contract for the bus-and-truck tour of *Into the Woods* the week before the bid session. Problems usually occur because everybody is negotiating. Your agent is asking for something the producers aren't willing to give, but the project needs to start. I finally had to call the union. The union told us not to have the bid session until we got a contract. We told that to the producers and got a contract. Some offices, like Manny Azenberg's, are wonderful; others are not so wonderful. There are good joints and bad.

Do bus-and-truck productions present more problems than Broadway productions?

I think it depends on the show. A bus-and-truck's main concern is getting in and out of a theatre in a short period of time. One tour producer actually said to me, "We don't want art up there. We just want something behind the actors." I must say, however, that the bus-and-truck company of *Into the Woods* really is a fine show. Some of the scenery is good and some of it isn't, but it's a good show. But I wonder what an audience actually sees of a set. They probably don't see what we see—designers wrestle with height, proportions and harmony—but maybe it doesn't really matter. I don't know.

Do you pick projects because you think they're going to be commercially successful?

That was what I was being told to do on one show recently. The producers said, "This is going to play out of town for fifteen weeks, and you'll get five or six hundred dollars a week in royalties." I really wanted to design the show, but as it went along it turned into another bus-and-truck production. I was originally told that it would play four cities before it came to New York. Then it turned into fourteen cities. We didn't even have the design completed before it became about how it would get in and out of theatres, how much time was needed for load-ins. I could have stayed with the show and received royalties for fifteen weeks, but that wasn't why I wanted to design it. It's great getting a check every week, and you certainly hope a show will be successful, but I can't do a show for that reason alone.

You've designed two shows for James Lapine and Stephen Sondheim—Sunday in the Park with George *and* Into the Woods. *I'd like to hear you talk about your experience working with them.*

Sunday in the Park was my favorite. I liked that show a lot.

Why?

Because the design was so integrated into the piece. Also, it was about an artist,

FACING PAGE, TOP, SKETCH FOR THE BROADWAY PRODUCTION OF *TIMBUKTU!*, DIRECTED BY GEOFFREY HOLDER. BOTTOM, MODEL FOR EDWARD BOND'S *SUMMER*, DIRECTED BY DOUGLAS HUGHES FOR MANHATTAN THEATRE CLUB.

THE CENTER STAGE PRODUCTION OF
THORNTON WILDER'S *OUR TOWN*,
DIRECTED BY JACKSON PHIPPIN.

model, which we then took over to Steve's house.

Although I admired Steve's work, I hadn't met him before that. I was nervous about showing him the set. Steve went for refreshments while I was setting up the model on his desk. I remember wondering if he would notice my knees trembling. He came back into the room and asked if he could take a look. Then he sat down on the floor, looked at the model, and said he really liked it.

Was the process for Into the Woods similar?

Jim and I did a lot of the work together on *Into the Woods*. For *Sunday in the Park with George* the designers would meet at Steve's house, Jim would read us new parts of the script, and Steve would play and sing the new songs. That didn't happen with *Into the Woods*. I did, however, spend weekends at Jim's farm house in upstate New York. Jim and I would take walks through the woods at sunset, soaking up the atmosphere.

I read the script for *Into the Woods* before it was finished. I did a drawing and showed it to Jim, but he thought it was too literal. He wanted a more simple approach for the production. He wanted the audience to fill it in with their imaginations—a "story theatre" kind of production. The Old Globe production of *Into*

what being an artist is like: balance, harmony, confronting a white canvas, take that tree out and try this one instead. It shared the same anxiety one experiences as a set designer.

What about working on that design?

Jim is a fine photographer and graphic artist, so he has a good visual sense. You can talk to him about your design problems and he can help you. Jim always told the designers what Steve was doing, and he told Steve what we were doing. Jim and I worked together until I got to the white *the Woods* was very presentational. The New York production was more elaborate. We used many of the same ideas, but we expanded them into a physically larger production.

Who decided to make the giant a woman?

I thought it was an odd choice; it was made by Jim and Stephen. All of the giants I researched were men. I don't think we were very successful with the giant in New York. The back of her head looked good, which wasn't easy considering we only had a foot of space to work in, but it's hard to have scenery crash on stage realistically. You can't do that kind of crash every night without breaking something. It's the same with the chandelier in *Phantom of the Opera*. To me, the way that chandelier should fall is impossible to do on stage. We wanted our giant to really fall and then bounce off the stage. We tried it once and were told by Pete Feller not to do it again. He warned us that it would crack the floor and injure the grid structure. The head was eliminated entirely for the road tour. The audience assumes that the giant has fallen offstage.

What other changes were made for the tour?

Well, the trees are just painted flats, similar to the Albrecht Durer-style drawing on the main drop in the Broadway production. The moving ramps are gone. And the tower doesn't come up through the floor anymore, it just moves on stage. Actually, no scenery or actors come up through the floor. The touring show is a much simpler production than what was seen in New York.

Before we get to your work in regional theatres, I'd like to talk about the production of Long Day's Journey into Night *that Jonathan Miller directed on Broadway.*

Working with Jonathan Miller was wonderful. I first met him in New York, but

MODEL FOR THE YALE REPERTORY THEATRE PRODUCTION OF *JULIUS CAESAR*, DIRECTED BY ALVIN EPSTEIN.

then I went to England to show him the model. Being in London with Jonathan Miller was quite a treat. Everyone knows him, so it's always "Oh, Mr. Miller." He's treated like a member of the royal family. His knowledge of painting, architecture and history is amazing. He can tell you why the moss is growing on this tree and not on that one.

At our first meeting he said he wanted the set to look like a house by Edward Hopper. We started building a large, realistic house based on our research of Eugene O'Neill's home in Connecticut. Then I received a call from Manny Azenberg, the producer, who said, "Stop building the model. Jonathan doesn't want that artist anymore. He wants George Segal." When I asked what Jonathan meant, Manny said he didn't know, that I should call Jonathan in London. Which I did. Jonathan said he had been thinking about the play and realized that it moved quickly, and that it would take the actors too long to move around a large house. He wanted a smaller playing area, one less encumbered by walls. I couldn't figure out how George Segal's white plaster sculptures related to the design of the set, but Jonathan pointed out that usually behind each figure was a piece of architecture—a door, a framed window, a section of a porch—floating in black. Jonathan was right. Segal's work provided the same sense of loneliness as Hopper's.

Jonathan wanted pieces of architecture, but they had to be solid, so that the actors could lean on them, slam them, or hit them. So I designed a piece of the staircase, two pieces of wall, and a window nook. The wood was stained dark, as it was in O'Neill's home, and the surround was black. Willa Kim designed white costumes, which were left unironed. Because they were rumpled, they looked like Segal figures. Some critics thought the place looked drafty, but no one really mentioned the look of the show in the reviews. I thought the design conveyed O'Neill's family: how isolated they were from the world and from each other—lost.

Let's talk about working in regional theatres.

Yes, I enjoy working in regional theatres. I like the Broadway proscenium, but I also like the people in regional theatres. There's a tremendous pool of talent in these organizations. I find the snobbish attitude some New Yorkers hold toward the regional theatres odd. A lot of the regional work is more adventurous than the work you'll find in New York.

I also like the "family" feeling in the regional theatres, like at Arena Stage and Old Globe. I feel protected. I also know the show will have a run. In New York you don't know what will happen with a show. We worked on *Copperfield* for a full year,

and, after all that work, it closed very quickly. I remember the stagehands with tears in their eyes. It's terrible when a show closes so quickly.

What have been your favorite productions?

The *Midsummer Night's Dream* I did with Alvin Epstein and *Sunday in the Park with George*. But I also liked John Guare's *Women and Water*, which we did at Arena Stage. It's a beautifully written play, and Doug Wager did a tremendous job directing it. I liked the way Doug used the arena space. Tom Stoppard's *On the Razzle*, another Arena Stage production, was very successful. The arena space forces you to be more imaginative.

I would imagine that doing On the Razzle in an arena would be difficult. How did you approach the design?

Someone told me that Roger Stevens, from the Kennedy Center, purposely came to the show to see how the play, which contains a lot of hide-and-seek, could be done without doors. There are two main locales in the script: the first and last acts take place in a country store, the second act takes place in many different locations in Vienna. When we went from the store to Vienna, actors dressed like Viennese soldiers came out and rolled up

TOP, SKETCH FOR THE WILLIAMSTOWN THEATRE FESTIVAL PRODUCTION OF ANTON CHEKHOV'S *THREE SISTERS*, DIRECTED BY NIKOS PSACHAROPOULOS. BOTTOM, ERIC OVERMYER'S *ON THE VERGE OR THE GEOGRAPHY OF YEARNING*, DIRECTED BY JACKSON PHIPPIN FOR CENTER STAGE.

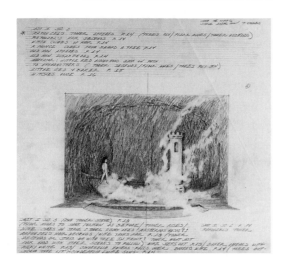

SKETCH FOR *INTO THE WOODS* (BOOK BY
JAMES LAPINE, MUSIC AND LYRICS BY
STEPHEN SONDHEIM), DIRECTED BY
JAMES LAPINE.

the store ground cloth, under which was a Viennese ceiling—the floor was painted to look like a beautiful plaster ceiling. For the first scene we flew in large Plexiglas panels on which were etched and tinted images of Vienna street life. They played at different angles so that they formed small streets. The actors moved through and about the transparent panels, so you could always see them.

There is a restaurant scene in the second act in which the characters need to hide and eavesdrop. Doug is very clever. On one side of the stage he had a folding screen which an actor used to hide behind. Then a waiter walked over to the screen, folded it up, and no one was there. The waiter walked to the other side of the stage, opened up the screen, and the actor appeared from behind it. It's a simple trick—the actor went down through a trap on one side of the stage and up through another on the other side—but in a bare, open space it was a fantastic bit.

For the big chase scene, which takes place in a garden, we had castered hedges with people inside them. The hedges were about five feet tall and eight feet long, and we had maybe ten of them. They came rolling out on stage at quite a clip. They took their positions, forming a garden and capturing the actors within the configuration. Then they would move again and the actors were free until they

formed another configuration, which trapped the actors again. The production was dazzling, a lot of fun to watch.

It doesn't sound like something that would work as well behind a proscenium.

No, it wouldn't work. The space dictates the design.

But you indicated earlier that you prefer working in proscenium theatres?

I do, but after working at Arena Stage I came to appreciate the beauty of the arena space.

Do you teach?

Only periodically, and only if it's kept very informal. I have been going to Carnegie-Mellon once a year to conduct some classes. I can talk about design up to a point, but I don't have the gift of articulation. Students ask me questions and I sometimes don't know how to answer them.

What show, or shows, have you seen recently that you thought were particularly well designed?

Black and Blue. Visually, it's a knockout. It's beautiful, very elegant. It's like Robert

Wilson goes to Rio de Janeiro. It has a very European look, not American at all. And I thought the costumes were gorgeous. I always like watching how Robin Wagner moves a show. His designs for *On the Twentieth Century* and *Dreamgirls* were great. And I like David Mitchell's work. And Ming Cho Lee's. Tony Walton's set for *Anything Goes* was wonderful.

What would be an ideal project for you?

I would love to do a classical American musical. I would love to do a *Pacific Over-* *tures* or *My Fair Lady* or *Follies*. I enjoy listening to classical music, but I don't like watching opera. I can't relate to it. I relate more to plays and musicals, which seem to deal with real life.

One more question: How would you characterize your work?

People sometimes say there's a similarity between my sets and David Mitchell's. Maybe. I think my work is very detailed. It might have a simple form on stage, but within that form there is a lot going on. Designers like Oliver Smith and Peter Larkin had a distinct style of painting, so did Jo Mielziner. Their painting and drawing hand appeared even when they did realistic interiors. Many designers today, including myself, do not have easily identifiable styles. We rely on color xeroxes and collage forms; renderings seem to be photographs or xerox copies of something. I wish I was more familiar with watercolors and could paint better, maybe then I might produce my own style.

PRODUCTION PHOTOGRAPH FROM *SUNDAY IN THE PARK WITH GEORGE* (BOOK BY JAMES LAPINE, MUSIC AND LYRICS BY STEPHEN SONDHEIM), DIRECTED BY JAMES LAPINE.

GEORGE TSYPIN

Gᴇᴏʀɢᴇ ᴛsʏᴘɪɴ's theatre sets tend to be angular, aggressive, sometimes even dangerous. They are probably best understood in terms of a relatively recent movement known as deconstructivist architecture. (Tsypin is a graduate of the Architectural Institute in Moscow, and supported himself after he moved to New York City by working in an architectural firm.) Such architecture, sometimes referred to as an architecture of fantasy or of the mind, undermines the traditional notions of composition and unity, and is considered by many to be "unbuildable," which has also been said of Tsypin's sets. But as Tsypin explains in this interview, it was John Conklin, his set design teacher at New York University, who taught him that the initial creative impulse takes precedence over technical considerations.

Another distinguishable element of Tsypin's work is the way in which he layers various historical references and/or scenic elements within a single set. This layering can provide a visual density so complex that, as Tsypin admits, "you can't watch everything." In Peter Sellars' controversial 1987 production of *Don Giovanni*, for example, Mozart's opera was presented in present-day Spanish

Harlem, but Tsypin also included various references to medieval paintings and altarpieces. The resulting mix provided a somewhat unsettling experience, supporting Sellars' interpretation of the opera. And in JoAnne Akalaitis's recent Guthrie production of Jean Genet's *The Screens*, Tsypin stretched a net over much of the acting area, providing a second level on which cast members, moving in slow motion to counterbalance the bounce of the net, appeared to be floating over the action occurring on stage.

FEBRUARY 13, 1989 AND
AUGUST 30, 1990—
GEORGE TSYPIN'S APARTMENT,
ASTORIA, NEW YORK

I was born in Russia. My father is a painter, and my mother was an actress for a short time. I was educated as an architect in Moscow. It was a very traditional, old-fashioned art education. In order to get into the school you had to pass an examination in painting, sculpture and drawing. I was part of a circle of people in Moscow that included musicians, poets and theatre people. I had several friends who were set designers and directors. I also entered different kinds of competitions, conceptual competitions. One was called "New Spontaneous Ideas for the Theatre," which was where I found out about theatre.

Were you planning on being an architect when you moved to New York, or were you thinking about going into theatre?

I didn't have a precise plan, and I certainly wasn't planning to work in the theatre. We had this notion in Moscow that you couldn't really work in theatre in America, that you couldn't really make any money, which is partially true. So I worked as an architect. But I also felt that I wanted to do something in theatre, so I studied set design at New York University. It wasn't until I got out of NYU in 1984 that I started working in theatre.

What fascinates me about your sets is the way the stage space is handled architecturally. What is it about the stage space that interests you?

The architecture is one element, certainly, but I think theatre is a much more synthetic art form. It includes all the arts—poetry and music and sculpture and painting. It is an architecture of the mind, rather than of the space. I was very inspired by the set designers I met in Russia. At that time there was a real boom in set design. For some reason, it was the only thing that was really alive. I do theatre—as opposed to some other form—because I can use all of the skills I acquired.

Who did you study with at NYU?

John Conklin, Oliver Smith, Lloyd Burlingame. I also studied film design with Steve Hendrickson and costume design with Carrie Robbins.

What kind of influence did they have on you?

John Conklin was a big influence, but it wasn't an influence on my work per se. People didn't think I was going to be able to build anything because I didn't have a technical background. Everybody would say no, no, you can't do that—and I must admit that I didn't know some very basic things—but John never said that. He understood that you do eventually realize something, but that's not where you start, with the technical aspects. Some schools or teachers start with the technical elements, but I feel that that immediately limits the imagination.

What kinds of projects did you do for Conklin?

Mostly opera.

Did you do any professional work in theatre while you were at NYU?

No, not in theatre. I was still working in an architectural firm once in a while, but I had no theatre experience at all when I got my first professional job.

Which was what?

Assisting David Mitchell on *Biloxi Blues*. It was a terrific experience. It was one of the more complicated nonmusicals on Broadway, and I got to do everything. Technically, it was very useful for me. It was like a crash course on designing a Broadway show.

What was the first show you designed?

It was for the Philadelphia Drama Guild— *The Power and the Glory*, directed by William Woodman. Then, shortly after *The Power and the Glory*, Peter Sellars called. Someone had seen my work at the portfolio review at Juilliard, which was also how I got the show in Philadelphia, and had told Sellars about me. We met and I showed him my stuff. He had just started the American National Theater, in Washington, D.C., and he asked me to design *The Count of Monte Cristo*. I don't know why he asked me to do it, but we did it, then we did another and another and another. I did four productions for Peter at the Kennedy Center.

What do you think it was about your work that Peter responded to?

I don't know. He didn't really like it, in fact. He said, "But I love this because

SKETCH FOR THE CHICAGO LYRIC OPERA'S PRODUCTION OF RICHARD WAGNER'S *TANNHAUSER*, DIRECTED BY PETER SELLARS.

nobody could ever build it." My projects were totally unbuildable. Also, at that time, he had just come back from Russia and was very much into Taganka Theatre. Even though my work didn't look like Taganka's at all, we understood each other, I guess.

What do you think characterizes your work?

The scope. The scale is very large. Obviously, I don't do realistic sets, and Peter doesn't do small, kitchen-sink dramas. He does large, philosophical works, where you need to have this large scale. I also believe that I think like a director, so I can see the subtle moments in a show with actors, with music. It's always a collaboration with the director, but designing a set very much involves directing. I do think about the actors and how to get them physically involved.

I am thinking about the Don Giovanni I saw at PepsiCo Summerfare. The set was both real and abstract at the same time.

Two things were studied very carefully for that set. It was almost like doing research for a film. I did go to Harlem, where I took a lot of photographs. But at the same time I was looking at medieval paintings, altarpieces and lithographs. So it was Hell as a combination of both Harlem and something medieval.

The set also forced the actors to be more physical than we normally expect them to be in an opera.

Yes. We wanted you to feel that you were about to fall down. There is this long hole, the orchestra pit, that you could fall in. Or in another sense, it suggests the earth opening up. Then there is a ditch on the side, too. The acting space is very narrow,

so you feel constantly that these people are literally on the edge. It was maybe a little too dangerous, but the singers were young and physical and they were able to handle it. But a lot of my sets are dangerous.

Can you give me another example?

The Guthrie production of *Leon and Lena*, which was directed by JoAnne Akalaitis. I made this highway in the air above the audience. It was nothing, just a broken-off slab. But when the actors danced on it, your heart started pounding just looking at them. You felt they were going to fly off this highway at any moment.

How would you describe your working relationship with Peter Sellars? How do the two of you approach a project together?

Well, for example, the script for *Ajax* did not exist when we started. The play existed, but the final script was a modern adaptation. *Ajax* was a long and painful process. Sometimes Peter and I will work very closely, as we did on *Ajax*, but it was painful for everybody. The play itself is so great and so difficult, but Peter also made many, many changes. On other projects, like *Tannhäuser*, for instance, we barely spoke at all. Peter had a general idea about what the opera was about and where it could take place, and I took it from there.

Did you do a lot of research for Tannhäuser?

Yes, I always do lots of research. I read a lot, everything that is written about the play. It sometimes seems unnecessary because I still don't know how to design it, but the research makes me think about the piece. I read one thing and an image comes up. Then I'll read something else and another image, completely different, comes up. Criticism can help a lot, too. I also believe that both the director and the set designer must see the play as a whole. But where the director can choose to work on a play moment by moment, the set designer can't. The set designer has to build something that works for the entire play.

Do you complete your research before you start designing?

I do all the reading before I start designing. Then I do the visual research. I like to take photographs if I can find something in real life that is appropriate.

Do you do a lot of sketching?

Not really. I used to do more, but now I basically work with models. Sometimes I will give the director a real quick sketch to let him know what I'm doing, but sketches don't mean anything to me. They don't show the space or the scale. If I do a sketch, I do it to suggest the atmosphere. I like to construct with models—and I like to make large models—because the model is something else, another thing. I'll get an idea for a set, for example, but by the time I complete the set model it has nothing to do with what I originally intended. It's out of my control a little bit, which is fine. It's like my hands take care of it. You have to trust your hands.

More so than your eyes?

It's the same thing. You have to watch. It can be very painful. I'll make a piece and then it'll have to be painted some color. So I'll put down newspaper and I'll spray-paint the piece, but all of a sudden it's the paper I'm spraying on that is much more interesting than the piece itself. So I end up using the paper and throwing away the piece. Designing is like that; it's watching for accidents.

Is working with JoAnne much different than working with Peter?

No, the two are very similar. Peter is usually more prepared, but with JoAnne I have a little more freedom. Some directors give you total freedom, others want very much to be involved. I like both approaches, but I prefer the director who gives me a chance. Except that Peter is such a visual person himself, he can take an idea even further. Also, my sets need directing. It doesn't make any sense for me to come up with something that the director doesn't understand, something he doesn't know what to do with. The set is a machine that has to be dealt with imaginatively, like with actors.

THE AMERICAN NATIONAL THEATER PRODUCTION OF ANTON CHEKHOV'S *THE SEAGULL* (RENAMED *A SEAGULL*), DIRECTED BY PETER SELLARS.

Is your approach to designing opera different than your approach to designing theatre?

Yes. If I am designing a large opera, like *Tannhäuser*, I have more limitations. The budget and the scale may be bigger, but because of the limited rehearsal time I have to be very careful of what I ask the singers to do. Also, because opera is usually done in larger houses, I'm dealing less with detail. The image is much larger.

Tannhäuser *got a lot of attention.*

Peter had a modern context for the opera, which is something he always does. But it didn't quite come together until the Jimmy Swaggart thing hit the press. It was so perfect. I was reading all of these stories in *Time* magazine and the *Village Voice* about what had happened in this little motel. There were these pictures of the motel, and all of a sudden the opera sort of designed itself. Peter had originally planned to do the first act on a beach, but when the Swaggart story surfaced we moved it to the Southwest and this strange little motel in this sleazy town. The second act took place in the Crystal Palace, which is so beautiful. But the opera also contains this mythological background—plus references to Wagner's own story—so we decided to put all of these things in the same space.

Both Don Giovanni *and* Tannhäuser *incorporated research of medieval art. Would it be fair to say that medieval art has been a major influence on your work?*

Yes, it has had more influence on me than, say, classical art or the Renaissance. I feel that the medieval period has much more in common with our own times.

Why is that?

It's very personal and subjective, but New York feels like a medieval city to me. It's dirty, it's vertical, and it's kind of barbaric. You could argue with that, I guess, but for me it is true. I use a lot of classical elements, too, but in terms of stylized lines, medieval drawings are the best.

What else influences your work?

I look at a lot of architecture. I still follow what architects are doing. This whole deconstructivist movement that is happening now—the more imaginative, freer architects who do these wonderful conceptual projects—has been a big influence.

Do you have any interest in doing film or television?

I am working on a film right now, in fact. And depending on if he can get the fund-

FACING PAGE, THE NEW YORK SHAKESPEARE FESTIVAL PRODUCTION OF *CYMBELINE*, DIRECTED BY JOANNE AKALAITIS.

FACING PAGE, SKETCH FOR W.A. MOZART'S
DON GIOVANNI, DIRECTED BY PETER
SELLARS. LEFT TOP AND BOTTOM, PHOTO-
GRAPHS FROM THE PEPSICO SUMMERFARE
PRODUCTION. ABOVE, TSYPIN'S SCULPTURE
BASED ON HIS SET DESIGN FOR THE
PRODUCTION.

THE GUTHRIE THEATER PRODUCTION OF *THE
SCREENS*, DIRECTED BY JOANNE AKALAITIS.

ing, I might be doing another film with Peter, a remake of *The Cabinet of Dr. Caligari.* He wants to do it as a silent film, but set it in contemporary New York. What interests me about films is that they are usually about real people, but they're deceptive. They have to feel real, but first you have to create a believability.

But your primary interest is to continue to design theatre and opera, correct?

Film is financially more satisfying than theatre, but artistically I think film is less satisfying. You have less control. You can design something beautiful and no one

will ever see it. The actor's face takes up the whole screen, so who cares what's in the background. On the other hand, film is in some respects much freer than theatre. You think of an image and there's no reason why you can't have it. You don't have to think about how to get from this point to that point. In the theatre, however, everything is connected. The way I design theatre, it is all one machine, one mechanism, that changes and transforms all the time. But it is one thing. In film, the interconnections are handled through the editing, so getting from point A to point B isn't really an issue in the design.

Where do you see your career going from here?

I was approached about doing a gallery show, so I've been thinking about that. I spend a lot of time and energy doing theatre—I try not to do any shows that are just routine, I try to invent something new for each production—but then the show is over very quickly and the sets are destroyed. Theatre is so ephemeral. What's left after the show closes is often just a memory. Except I'm the one working with hard materials, so the nature of my craft is very different from that of, say, the director or lighting designer or actor. What's

left after a production are my sketches, the slides and the model, which take on an existence of their own, almost independent of the original production. I was thinking that I should pursue that a bit more, that I wanted to give it a more permanent shape, even if it was just for myself.

Another reason for doing the gallery show is that I don't like traditional models or sketches. The ones I've seen have an old-fashioned, provincial feel to them. Often, however, I'll go back after a production has closed and work on one of my models. I want to use the gallery show to explore what it is that keeps me excited about these old models I still have. Then, when I started thinking about the gallery space, I realized that I could create something in another form, but which would have certain connections with the theatre. I wanted to develop the models in such a way that they become objects, or sculptures, that captured the essences of the sets.

Could you give me an example?

Yes. Take *The Screens*, which JoAnne and I did at the Guthrie. We stretched a net over much of the acting area, but I wanted it over the entire audience. That's what I dreamed of doing in the theatre, but it couldn't be done for a number of reasons. But in the model I could. There is nothing I can't do in the model.

So the model, or sculpture, becomes the ideal theatre space?

Exactly. Something I can do without the constraints of budget or practicalities, where I can really dream.

But you want people to view these sculptures as objects in and of themselves, not as models for something you once did in a theatre?

Right. I want them to be approached as ideas.

Which is also how you approach theatre design.

Yes. What I am trying to do is explode the box. Usually the theatre model is in a box, but the box is irrelevant. In fact, you try to overcome the box whenever you design for the theatre. You design a world that is not in the box, that is much larger than the box. So I just got rid of the box.

How many sculptures have you designed for the gallery show?
Fifteen.

One per show?

No. I actually have four pieces from *Tannhäuser*—one for each act, and then one more. And for the other shows, usually one per show.

The other thing about the gallery show is that it will also incorporate lights and sounds. After a production has closed, I remember images. I remember the way the lighting hit something, or some piece of music—not the narrative shape of the production. So I wanted to create that kind of situation in the gallery. The sculptures will include little lights, but I'll also design the lighting for the gallery. And I'm planning on using sound in some way.

Before we end this interview I would like to talk about The Screens. *I'd like to know how you and JoAnne approached that play.*

The Screens was written in the 1960s, some thirty years ago, so the first thing we did was to discuss how we would look at it now. Although Jean Genet asks that his plays not be set in very specific locations, JoAnne decided to use Algeria in the late 1950s and early '60s for this production. JoAnne also included some contemporary references in the production, but they were not important elements in terms of the design. I tried to deal with the play as a philosophical statement rather than as a political document.

What kind of research did you do?

JoAnne and I went to Morocco. It was an incredible experience. I had never been

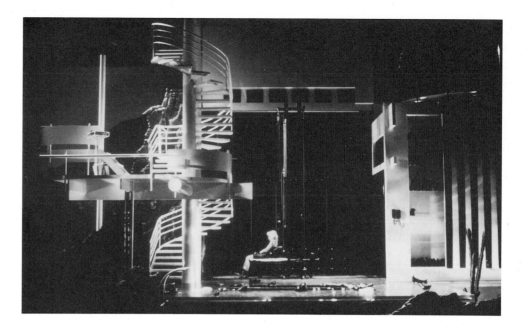

to that part of the world before. I took thousands of slides.

And what did you see in Morocco?

It's another civilization. In a way, the place in Russia where I was born had a very strong Islamic influence, but I didn't realize that until I went to Morocco. It brought back these incredible childhood memories. Some parts of Morocco are modern, of course, but we went specifically to look at the architecture in the medieval towns. And then we went into the desert.

JoAnne really wanted to create an environmental event at the Guthrie. In fact, we were going to use another space run by

THE GUTHRIE THEATER PRODUCTION OF GEORG BUCHNER'S *LEON AND LENA* (TRANS-LATED BY HENRY J. SCHMIDT), DIRECTED BY JOANNE AKALAITIS.

the theatre, but then decided to do it at the Guthrie because it's right beside the Walker Arts Center. The museum, basically, is an incredible center for Western art, and our major impulse was to have it clash with this unbelievable Third-World culture. All of the lobby windows were painted with wild, violent drawings, so as you passed the Guthrie you were already pulled into the world of the play.

How did you approach the theatre space?

I wanted to get rid of all of the notions of Western theatre, and I had two ideas about how to do it. One was to take out all of the seats and make people sit on this desert-like yellow fabric. I thought it would work like an Arabic theatre, or like watching a spectacle in a marketplace.

My second idea was to continue the fabric up and over the audience to create another acting level. Within the structure of the play, these two worlds—the world of the living and the world of the dead—are very important. People die in the world of the living and then appear in the world of the dead.

But I couldn't do both. I couldn't take out the seats, which is labor intensive, and create this upper level for the world of the dead. So I decided to go with the world of the dead. I suspended a huge net over the stage. It wasn't supported in any way, but was stretched from many different points in the theatre. We had to hire an architect and go through walls to reach the main beams of the building. Even then we weren't sure that the tension would be great enough to sustain the weight of the actors.

But it worked. The image was like that of the desert. It was shaped like the desert. And when the characters walked across the net, which they had to do slowly, in slow motion, they sank into it—like into sand. It was like they were weightless. It was very beautiful.

How did you treat the rest of the space?

I covered the stage with yellow fabric, and then had lots of transparent screens which moved during the performance. The screens had different images on them, but the actors also drew on them during the show, so you had these many different layers of images.

Were the images based on the research you did in Morocco?

No, nothing of what I saw in Morocco ended up in the show. Out of all of the photographs I took in Morocco, I didn't use a single one of them. I eventually realized that the details I thought I would use for ethnic flavor were not important.

Why not?

Because they would take away focus. *The Screens* is a terribly profound play. It's not about little, decorative, Arabic detail. The play is so much more suggestive than that.

Who designed the lighting for the production?

Jennifer Tipton. Genet writes that the first scene takes place on the road, in the desert. So naturally you assume hot, bright, yellow sunlight, which was the first image JoAnne and I had. But Jennifer decided she wasn't going to do that. She said, "Genet says cold blue light, so I'm going to do cold blue light." No, no. It's a desert. It's noon in the desert. But no, Jennifer

wanted cold blue light. She drove JoAnne and me crazy with her cold blue light. But we eventually realized she was right. You either go with Genet's directions, or you don't. But if you go with them, you can't question them.

But you didn't follow his directions for the set.

No, for two reasons. First, I had no choice. Genet's directions are written specifically for a proscenium stage, which we didn't have at the Guthrie. And second, I didn't really throw them out. I don't remember why, but I reread his directions after the show opened and discovered his description of lots of lines running from the top of the set out over the audience. I had completely forgotten about them, but on some subconscious level they must have registered because there they were—the net.

It sounds as if you are pleased with this production. Are you?

By the time a show is over, I never know what I feel about it. I'm too close to it. I'm too immersed in the details, and all I see are the imperfections. Then, a few months later, I'll look at the slides and decide what I think of the show. But I have pretty good memories of this show. Whatever it was, it was an event.

THE AMERICAN NATIONAL THEATER PRODUCTION OF SOPHOCLES' *AJAX*, ADAPTED BY ROBERT AULETTA AND DIRECTED BY PETER SELLARS.

MICHAEL
YEARGAN

MICHAEL YEARGAN, who was born in Dallas, is a teacher and a designer, balancing the demands of both professions in such a way that neither appears to suffer. As he explains in this interview, "Teaching provides a wonderful forum for keeping up on what's happening in the theatre. The nature of this work is that you go from project to project to project. If I wasn't teaching, I'd be a pretty insular person."

Although Yeargan is hesitant to use "metaphor" to describe his work, many of his sets exhibit a remarkable, subtle and sophisticated understanding of the use of theatrical metaphor. Reluctant to describe what it is he does, Yeargan says "it's just a visual expression of the play that has nothing to do with the play's reality." But in Mark Lamos's recent production of *A Midsummer Night's Dream* at Hartford Stage, the various scenic elements scattered over the stage provided metaphoric clues to understanding Lamos's own interpretation of the play.

Yeargan studied set design at Yale with both Donald Oenslager and Ming Cho Lee. He has been teaching at Yale since 1974, and in recent years has been designing for theatre and opera in both Europe and the United States.

FACING PAGE, THE HARTFORD STAGE
COMPANY PRODUCTION OF *A MIDSUMMER
NIGHT'S DREAM*, DIRECTED BY MARK LAMOS.

I was born in Dallas, and was fortunate to have a wonderful music teacher in the fourth grade who introduced me to opera. Miss Paar would bring huge photographs of opera singers to class. Then she would tell us the stories of the operas—in cleaned-up versions, of course—and we would make little shadow boxes of the scenes. But the first real production I designed was in high school. We did *Plain and Fancy*. And then, the following year, I designed *Bye, Bye Birdie*. That's how I got started.

It was an incredible time to be in Dallas. The Metropolitan Opera was coming through on its national tour every year, and the Dallas Civic Opera was just forming. Franco Zeffirelli, who was relatively unknown in this country at that time, was making history in Dallas with his productions with Maria Callas. The *La Traviata* he did with Callas was incredible. I also saw her *Medea* the night she was fired from the Met. You couldn't experience that without wanting to throw yourself into it.

What was it about those productions that appealed to you?

It was pure, unadulterated magic. The first opera I saw was *La Bohème*. I must have been in the fourth or fifth grade. It was an afternoon performance, and my grandmother took me. We had tickets in the fifth or sixth row. I remember the curtain going up on this huge garret with a huge window and all this light coming through it. I looked at it and thought, how did they do that? How did they make that sky? How did they make that window look so dirty? I couldn't wait to get home and make a little model of it.

I never wanted to be an actor or a singer. I was obsessed with design. I would take *Opera News* magazine and copy sets out of it, thinking maybe it would look better if I did this or this. And I would spend hours in the library on Saturday reading every book about theatre I could find, looking at pictures, checking out play scripts. I hate reading scripts now, but I loved it then.

I didn't see a straight play until I was in high school. Eva Le Gallienne had a touring company called the National Repertory Theatre. They did *Ring Round the Moon*, *The Crucible* and *The Seagull*, which was the first play I saw. Because I was ushering for the Dallas Summer Musicals, I also ushered for them. I saw those three plays over and over. I must have seen each of them six times. I was completely blown away by the idea that the actors could be so different in each play.

Was there someone in Dallas who offered advice, or guided your interest in design?

Yes, Peter Wolf, who designed all of the productions, six or seven each season, for the Dallas Summer Musicals. His sets were spectacular. The shows would play for two weeks each, and I would usher for them. This was when you had *Wildcat* and *Destry Rides Again*—all those musicals nobody thinks about anymore. My parents arranged for me to meet Mr. Wolf to discuss how one got into this business. I couldn't work for him, he said, because his shop was completely unionized, but if I was really interested in becoming a designer the place to go was Yale. He also suggested that I should get an undergraduate degree in liberal arts first, but I immediately wrote to Yale for a catalog.

My parents also thought that I should get a good liberal arts education, but I didn't want to go to a large university. My father was a traveling salesman and then a regional manager for the John B. Stetson Hat Company, in Texas. He discovered that John B. Stetson, who had a summer home in Florida, supported Stetson University, also in Florida, which had a small theatre program. So that's where I went. You had to do everything in the theatre department: act in shows, light them, design and make costumes. It was small and wonderful.

After two years, however, I was frustrated with the program. I considered transferring, but decided instead to do my junior year abroad. You could go to Spain, Germany or France. I went to Spain because Spanish was the only foreign language I knew. I loved that year in Europe. I did a lot of traveling and took a lot of pictures. What interested me at the time was seeing all the places where the operas and plays were set, like the Rome that *Tosca* is all about.

I returned to Stetson University, finished my senior year, and then taught Spanish and drama for a year in a public high school in Eustis, Florida. I was also to direct the school play. Eustis was a tiny place, and the school was being integrated for the first time. I couldn't find anything that used a mixed cast, so I finally decided we should do *Spoon River Anthology*. It's the one point in my life where I feel I did something for humanity. For a time I thought it was what I wanted to do—that I should just stay in Eustis and teach—but I eventually applied to Yale.

I was terrified of Yale, but I got accepted, only to arrive the following year to discover that Donald Oenslager was leaving and that this Chinese designer, Ming Cho Lee, whose work I sort of knew from photographs, was taking over. I was in Mr. Oenslager's last class. He retired in the middle of the year, so I had them both for one semester and then Ming for the next semester, which nearly gave me a nervous breakdown.

How were the two men different? Was one more influential than the other in your development as a designer?

It might be more interesting to look at the school Donald ran then and the school Ming runs now. Donald was a great gentleman of the theatre, and he ran his classes like an old school. The classes were two hours long, on Thursday, and were all

critique-based. He would assign a project one week, and you were expected to bring it in the next week. The project consisted of a matted, color sketch and, on the back, in ⅛″ scale on graph paper, the ground plan. You put it on the table in the front of the room when you entered and then took your seat. If you came in late, you couldn't put it on the table.

Donald was tall, big. We called him "the Big O." He usually wore a gray suit with a tie, a gabardine overcoat and a hat. He would usually trip over the trash can on his way in, take off his coat, and say, "Good day, all." The first hour was a lecture on a very specific subject, but almost always on the history of stage design. Sometimes he would come to class with a

brown paper bag under his arm. He would talk about so-and-so's design for a production and then unwrap his package, which usually contained an original sketch or engraving by that designer. He had an incredible collection, like Robert Edmond Jones' sketches for *The Green Pastures*. All these things that as a child I had seen in books. I was totally awed by it.

His lectures lasted exactly one hour. Then he would assign a project that was related in some way to the subject. The first project was always *Candida*. Somewhere along the line you did *Medea*. Always one a week. And it never went beyond that, it never got into models. It was purely about first impressions.

The class would take a short break after

the assignment had been given and then come back for the critique. Donald would walk around the room with the rendering so that everyone could see it while he looked at the ground plan taped on the back. Then he would put it on the chalk rail of the board. His critiques could sometimes be matter-of-fact. I remember this distinctly: "Yeargan," he once said to me, "why did you make it so mauve?" I answered with some reason I've now forgotten, and he simply said, "I think it's too strong a color for this particular play." Or he would ask another student, "Why is that entrance there?" Then he would say, "When I did this play with Kit Cornell, the entrance had to be in the center of the stage because . . ." and then he would

THE YALE REPERTORY THEATRE PRODUCTION OF ARISTOPHANES' *THE FROGS*, ADAPTED AND DIRECTED BY BURT SHEVELOVE, WITH MUSIC AND LYRICS BY STEPHEN SONDHEIM.

leave the room and make a grand entrance like Cornell's. He would say only one or two things about the design, but you never forgot it. His remarks were very concise.

He also had an incredibly dry wit and the curiosity of a child. I remember our final project, which was *Macbeth*. One of the students came in with about six sketches, all in pink-mauve and blue-gray—these funny colors. It looked like one of those illusions where you can't tell whether it's a cutout or a profile. Donald looked at the student and asked how she proposed shifting the set. She was very shy and said, "Well, some of the pieces would fly in, others would come from stage left, perhaps some from stage right, and at times the backdrop would lift up and units could also come from upstage. There is also the possibility that some of the pieces would come up through a trapdoor in the stage. Then, during intermission, pieces on stage would go into the shop and other pieces would be moved from the shop to the stage." Basically, she was covering all of her options. He turned to her and said, "Yes, but then where would the rest of it come from?"

Although the department has loosened up a bit, this is still the basis of what we do today. We follow the same format for the first year: we assign one project a week. It gives you just enough time to get a sense of what the play is about and your first impressions down on paper. It also means that you have to be able to draw. And you learn to talk about a play—what it means, why you put what you did on the stage. But now we also give a second week to each project so that students can do a rough model—like a sketch model—in ⅛″ scale. That and the choice of plays are the major changes in the first-year program.

Does Ming include more conceptual discussion in his class critiques?

The classes now meet on Saturdays, so they can go all day. So yes, discussions are much more directed toward conceptual concerns. They can go on for hours. But the classes also cover everything from the ground plan to inadequacies of drawings. Ming will discuss whatever comes to his mind.

What did you do after you graduated from Yale?

I graduated in 1973, and rather than jump right into the design world, I accepted a teaching position at Boston University. Then, a year later, Howard Stein called to say that Robert Brustein wanted to hire me as a resident designer at Yale Rep. So I accepted the invitation—and have been there ever since.

What were the major influences on your work during that period?

There were two or three momentous things that changed the way I thought about design. The first occurred during my second year as a student when I was asked to do a production of *Woyzeck*, which Tom Haas was to direct for Yale Rep. He wanted to do the play in a space with no visible entrances, no doors. I didn't know what to do, but I remember saying to Tom that maybe it had to be like a section of a tunnel. I eventually came up with a design that was like a tunnel piercing through a big wooden wall. It actually refers to those horrible barracks and bunks I saw at Dachau while I was in Europe. I didn't talk to anybody about what I was doing. I just brought it into class, and Ming liked it. He thought it was a major breakthrough for me. Tom loved it, too, so that's what we used.

The next thing happened at the Rep after I came back from Boston. Andrzej Wajda directed a production of *The Possessed*, for which I was the associate designer. It was a stage full of mud, with a stormy sky at the back. Christopher Lloyd was in it, so was Meryl Streep. It was an amazing, totally metaphorical production—and very theatrical. The actors wore these incredibly real costumes with mud on the bottom of them. It was all this beautiful furniture and crystal chandeliers on this mud floor. It changed my life. I mean, I had always been fascinated with the magic of design, but this was the first time I understood what power design could have.

The third major influence was Andrei Serban. He had just done *The Cherry Orchard* in New York, at Lincoln Center, and Bob brought him to the Rep to do *The Ghost Sonata*. That was our first production together.

You've done a number of productions with Serban, haven't you?

A lot, yes. It was always difficult, but he has a brilliant mind and an incredible

sense of the theatrical. He's also very daring. He feels that art can't come out of anything except chaos. If something is planned and ordered, then it is boring. So a show wasn't finished until opening night, which meant that the set was constantly changing. This would drive everyone crazy, but I found it exciting. The way to work with him was to come up with a general world for the play and then let it evolve as opening night got closer and closer. It meant walking a tightrope between what the shop had to have and how to get it on stage.

How did you and Serban approach **The Ghost Sonata?**

We started very realistically, as if it were a film. We also talked about the feel of the play. In the first scene, for instance, Strindberg describes the house, and in each window there is something different. I had seen something in a museum where the object was put in a box, which made it very special, so I made little brass boxes and put the things Strindberg talks about in them. In one box was a chair and a mirror, with a woman looking into the mirror because she couldn't directly confront life by looking out the window. I put the front door in another box. I took the boxes to Andrei, who was working at the Public at the time. It was during one of the blackouts, so we went across the street to

Lady Astor's and, by candlelight, looked at all these boxes. That was how the set for *The Ghost Sonata* came about.

Andrei also has an incredible sense of humor, so we had a good time working together. I think we discovered new territory together. He is responsible for me working in European opera as much as I do. While we were doing *The Umbrellas of Cherbourg* at the Public, Andrei got a telegram from Brian McMasters at the Welsh National Opera asking if he would be interested in directing *La traviata*. Andrei thought it was a joke and threw it away. Then, toward the end of *Cherbourg's* run, this little man appeared at the theatre, introduced himself, and asked if Andrei had ever gotten his telegram. It was Brian McMasters, of course. *La traviata* had come and gone, but they wanted Andrei to do a production of *Eugene Onegin*. It was Andrei's first opera, and it was the first opera we did together. We did Handel's *Rodelinda* the following year. Then we did Bellini's *I Puritani*, a *Merry Widow*, *Norma*, and a scaled-down version of *Aida*.

What was it about Serban's work that attracted the Welsh National Opera?

He blasted things wide open. His type of theatre was extremely visual. A lot of times I didn't know why he would do something, but when I tried to argue with him he would say, "How do you know until you've tried it? Just try it." That was his standard line. Jane Greenwood designed the costumes for *The Umbrellas of Cherbourg*. There was a scene in which the young girl was to enter in her nightgown, and Jane had done a beautiful white flannel nightgown with a Peter Pan collar. Andrei thought it was all wrong. Well, why was it wrong? "I don't know," he said, "it should be more Strindberg." And what did that mean? "Make it red." So Jane made a little red nightgown, and it was absolutely right. When the girl came on stage it was so striking.

Andrei would work the same way with actors. For *Eugene Onegin* we had two neoclassical doors, one downstage and one upstage. There's a line in the music with this beautiful melody where Tatiana says, "Happiness was once so close for us yet now so far away." Onegin was in black in the downstage door, and Tatiana was in red—very Strindberg—in the upstage door. Andrei had Tom Allan, who was singing Onegin, fall to his knees on Tatiana's line. Tatiana was in the upstage door directly behind him and suddenly you felt like all the planets had lined up. You knew exactly what that moment was about. There was no reason for Onegin to fall to his knees, but it worked beautifully.

The last thing Andrei and I did together was *The Juniper Tree*, at American Repertory Theatre. Maybe we knew each other too well by then. We're still great friends,

but that was the end of our working relationship. You reach the end of a road and it's time to move on.

You used the word metaphor earlier. Would you describe your work as metaphorical?

"Metaphor" is Peter Brook's word. I think he uses it in *The Empty Space*. It's a dangerous word now because it can get out of hand. For example, I did the set for Robert Brustein's production of *The Wild Duck*. Susan Sontag's book *On Photography* had just come out and Bob was fascinated by some of her ideas. His Hjalmar Ekdal was not just a retoucher of photographs, but an actual photographer. So we put the play inside this abstract camera. I felt it was like hitting you over the head with a hammer. It was effective, but it was too strong. I'm not sure that "metaphor" is the right word to describe what I do. A lot of times I come up with something that's just a visual expression of the play, but it has nothing to do with the play's reality.

Would Mark Lamos's recent production of A Midsummer Night's Dream be a good example?

I have no idea why, finally, I designed that show the way I did. We had another whole idea for the show, but were having second thoughts about it. Late one night I thought, no, it shouldn't be this, but if we do this and put this there . . . and it all came together. Mark originally wrote a wonderful letter to me in which he said he thought the images were all black, that it had to do with water, that he saw orbs floating on water. He saw the production as this black, damp, wet world of reflections and duality. So I starting working with black, shiny, sliding panels and about three inches of water. But then I had to ask, what about the rustics? And what about the palace of Theseus? It wouldn't accommodate these worlds.

The more I work on Shakespeare, the more I realize how easy it is to get locked into a metaphor. The set has to be expansive enough to accommodate all the worlds. And Shakespeare's plays are about worlds. They are like states of mind in a way. The forest of Arden in *As You Like It*, for example. If you go through the script and analyze the different kinds of trees, you can't have a literal forest.

It occurred to me that if you had a painted flat of a tree and then put a real tree next to it, something interesting happened. Or when you looked into a mirror, instead of seeing yourself you saw your mate or your alter ego. A man and a donkey. Double images: water, reflections. Instead of a glitzy floor, what if it's just gray and we find a way of presenting all these things on the floor? So I made these things and stuck them in the model and took it from there. Why was that? You can't really say that it was a metaphor for anything. For what? For duality? I don't think so. Maybe it was just a dream.

What was your first show with Mark Lamos?

The first show Mark and I did together was *As You Like It*.

How did that come about? Had Mark seen your work?

No, nor had I seen Mark's. Another designer was supposed to do *As You Like It*,

THE LONG WHARF THEATRE PRODUCTION OF *TOBACCO ROAD*, ADAPTED FROM THE ERSKINE CALDWELL NOVEL BY JACK KIRKLAND AND DIRECTED BY ARVIN BROWN.

ALLAN HAVIS'S *MOROCCO*, DIRECTED
BY MARK LAMOS FOR HARTFORD
STAGE COMPANY.

but they weren't getting along. The costume designer, Dunya Ramicova, suggested that Mark and I meet. So I talked with him, talked to the other designer because I felt terrible about the situation, and then agreed to do the show. I found Mark's work exhilarating. He opened up Shakespeare for me, made me realize how free it could be.

Then we did *The Tempest, Twelfth Night, Morocco*, which was the first thing we did that wasn't Shakespeare, *Midsummer Night's Dream* . . . and then he decided he wanted to do *The Importance of Being Earnest*. He said he wanted to do it like it was the most beautiful classical production—as if Cecil Beaton had de-

signed it. That's the way I wanted to do it, too, but it didn't seem right for that theatre. I designed several interiors, but the space wouldn't let me do them. There's all that vertical space at Hartford Stage, so a room is down here with a big void over it. And I couldn't put ceilings on any of the sets because they would block the sightlines. We ultimately began to think, not metaphorically, but of ways of treating that world in a more theatrical manner. I designed this big sweep of Morris wallpaper and a sort of pavilion that could work for both exterior and interior scenes. It became an envelope of that Victorian world in which we could emphasize the actors and their costumes, which is what the play is really all about.

I was a little surprised that Mark took such a straight approach to the play.

I know, everyone was. But it's so easy to typecast people—actors, directors, designers. In Europe, designers have a signature and you know who designed a set. But I've always felt that you should be as eclectic as possible. You should be able to do the big bare floor with dead leaves and then turn around and do *Hay Fever* on Broadway. I enjoy that.

Was there ever a point in your career when you were typecast?

I may have been typecast at one point because of my work with Serban, but I don't really know what people think of my work now. No one would have come to me to do *The Importance of Being Earnest*, but that changed when I started doing more realistic things. But it wasn't like I made a conscious choice to do more realistic sets—it had a lot to do with the space. The Long Wharf, for example, is a smaller space where I could present reality.

How do you approach a script?

I read it, which is torture. I can't just buzz right through it. I always hear a cast acting it. I also get visual flashes, so I make a set of cheat sheets as I'm reading it. I'll do rough ground plans and make note of things that are important to the action, like where the telephone has to be.

You do this as you are reading?

Yes. A lot of people like to read through the script and then go back, but I really like to work things out during the first reading. Then I'll go back and read it again when I don't have to think about it anymore. If it's Shakespeare, on the other hand, I like to listen to it. I like to find a recording of it—I don't care who did it— and listen to it. Otherwise I get so bogged down in all those little footnotes that I don't get the flow of it.

Then you'll meet with the director?

It depends. If it's a script I know, I immediately sit down and talk with the director. I'm currently working with Doug Wager on a production of *Pygmalion* at Yale Rep. I can't tell you how many meetings we've had. It's a much more difficult play than one would think. First, you have to get over all of your associations with *My Fair Lady*. Then you have to find a way to do it that is fresh and for today. You have to decide whether you are going to set it in 1912, which was when it was written, or in the 1930s, which was when it was presented in the film. Then there are all those little scenes inserted for the film, scenes that you can't really do on stage without incredible stage equipment. But are you going to do them because you can blow them wide open, or, as we discovered, not do them because they just weaken the stage experience? We found the original play to be much stronger, so we're doing the play as it was originally written.

What do you usually present to the director?

Thumbnail sketches. These horrible roughs that I never think are really good enough, but I show them because it's the last minute and I have nothing else to show. Then I usually do a rough white model as quickly as I can. It's usually very messy. For *Pyg-*

malion I drew and drew and drew. I got stuck until I got into the model, then some things started to happen.

You have a number of Broadway credits, don't you?

Yes, including *The Ritz* and *Bad Habits* — another whole aspect of my career we haven't talked about.

How did they come about?

Terrence McNally did *The Tubs*, which was the original title for *The Ritz*, at Yale Rep, which was then moved to New York. It was a wonderful production, hysterically funny, and because of that, we did *Bad Habits* Off Broadway. We met and worked with Adela Holzer, the producer who is now in prison. I did a whole string of terrible plays for her, all on Broadway.

What were they?

Oh, you'll remember them instantly. One was called *Me Jack, You Jill*. It was one of the worst things I have ever read in my life. It was directed by Harold J. Kennedy, who wrote a book called *No Pickle, No Performance*. He did a lot of summer stock. Adela found the play and cast Lisa Kirk, Barbara Baxley and Sylvia Sydney. It was about three women who are plotting to kill a husband. It was a disaster. Then we did *Something Old, Something*

New, with Hans Conrad and Molly Picon. Another disaster.

Why did you do them?

It was exciting. It was Broadway. It's easy to say, oh I don't do this or I can't do that, but you do. You sometimes regret it, but you end up with great stories—like the first rehearsal of *Me Jack, You Jill*. These three actresses had the most impossible reputations. There wasn't one costume designer in New York who would touch them. And because I happened to be in the costume-design part of the union, Adela asked me to design the costumes as well as the set. I agreed, not knowing what I was getting into. I just went in and said, "Listen, you tell me what you want to wear and I'll go get it." Lisa Kirk wanted to wear Halston, so we went to Halston. We went to Jerry Silverman for Sylvia Sydney. It was great fun. I still have a scarf Lisa Kirk threw on the floor. I couldn't take it back to the store so I framed it and hung it over my mantel.

You and Bob Israel are the only designers in this book who both design and teach on a regular basis. Why do you teach?

Because I love it. Sometimes, when I'm very busy, I think I should stop teaching, but Yale is a wonderful base from which to work. It's like a family there. Ming and I have gone from a student/teacher relationship to being best friends. And no matter how hard I'm working on something, the fact that I have to get away from it to go in and teach a class is very healthy. It gives me an opportunity to think about somebody else's problem for a few hours. Then I come back to my work refreshed and it isn't the crisis that I thought it was. And I learn from the students. I'm amazed at what they'll dare to do sometimes . . . and amazed at what they don't think of when it seems so obvious to me.

Teaching also provides a wonderful forum for keeping up on what's happening in the theatre. The nature of this work is that you go from project to project to project. If I wasn't teaching, I'd be a pretty insular person. Plus it's fun just to share things. We always give *La Bohème* as a project in the first year. So we bring in a tape player and we play a recording of it. A number of the students have never heard opera before. To watch them be moved and get excited is wonderful. Then I think, this is what teaching is all about.

How many productions do you do in a year?

Too many. It works into a cycle. At the beginning of the year, in the fall, I'm usually doing the first show at Hartford, the first show at Long Wharf, and the second show at Yale. Then I'm also working on an opera. It's been about one opera a year for the last several years, but suddenly I'm doing three. And then additional things come along. So it's five or six productions a year.

Which is a heavy schedule for someone who is also teaching.

It is, but fortunately the schedule is flexible. I wouldn't be able to lead the life I do if it weren't for Ming. He covers for me and, when he is away, which is rarely, I cover for him. It's a little like an English department, I guess, where it's important to publish. We feel that we can't teach design unless we're out there doing it. And the minute we stop doing it, we lose something. It provides a nice balance.

How have students changed over the years?

I don't know whether it was a function of being very young when I started teaching, or whether the students have actually changed, but they seem less arrogant now. They are also incredibly demanding, hungry for whatever you can give them. If you missed a class in the early days, they didn't care. But if you miss a class now, they want it rescheduled.

Has design changed over the years?

That's a tough question. American theatre was kitchen plays, family plays—"plays about relationships," as Ming says. Then a Robert Wilson comes along, or performance art, and the theatre becomes more open to ideas. MTV comes along and makes audiences much more receptive to theatrical ways of saying things. So I would have to say that design has moved further away from the realistic box set and closer to a much more free way of expression.

Do you think that's going to continue?

Yes, I think so. Except that in Europe now, especially in opera, I feel that design has gone so far that you haven't a clue what it is. Why does *Un ballo in maschera* have a huge moon sitting on the stage with a hand reaching down to touch it? Maybe the metaphors have become so obtuse that we don't know what they mean anymore. Rather than think about the actor and the play, the audience sits there wondering what is that, why is that there, and then they miss important dialogue. But for me, the actor is the most important thing on the stage. If I tend to put less on stage than other designers, it may be because i want to put more focus on the actor.

Your career has included a wide variety of work: opera, classics, new plays. Has this been a conscious decision on your part?

It's just what they call and ask me to do. But I love the variety of it. I'd be very bored if all I did was opera. I do two or three operas and I can't wait to get back to a play. It's almost like drawing. To me there are two kinds of drawing: drawing sets and drawing costumes. I don't really do costumes, except in opera where it is expected of you, but it takes me a good week to get back into figure drawing. It's the same with designing an opera and then doing a play or a musical. They're such different languages, and it can be a real struggle, but it keeps the work interesting.

THE YALE REPERTORY THEATRE PRODUCTION OF THOMAS MIDDLETON'S *THE CHANGELING,* DIRECTED BY ROBERT BRUSTEIN.

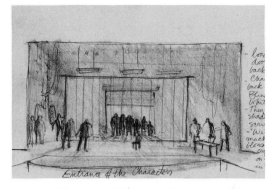

Entrance of the Characters

Fluorescents flicker on· at moment of shot· making scrim opaque· real trees, moon translucency in loading door — Pipe-trees in front; aquamarine vinyl over trap

Do you ever design the lighting for a production?

I did lights once for an opera based on *Of Mice and Men*. It was great fun, but it took a long time. I can't design a set without thinking about the lights, but I'm so unmathematical. I don't know what all those numbers on the colors mean. I think a lot of set designers and a lot of lighting designers don't know how to talk to each other. The designer might have a very specific idea about how the set should be lit, and he should talk to the lighting designer about that. Jennifer Tipton will ask at the beginning of a project—and I think this is brilliant—about the quality of the light in the room. You're not talking about white light or yellow light coming through a window, but about the atmosphere.

From where do you draw your inspiration?

I'm a terrible hoarder of things: books, magazines, videotapes, newspaper clippings. I never have enough time to organize or file it away, but I know it's there somewhere. I read a play and think, that's like such-and-such. It is all influential. You need to have a knowledge of painting and of what is going on in the world today. You're walking down a street and you take a picture. Everything feeds your visual vocabulary. Movies. The lighting in 1930s movies. I'm working on a production of *Rigoletto* right now, and the director said, "If you could do a Renaissance film noir, that's what it would be like." Why film noir? Well, it's the lighting and the angles of the lighting, the long shadows, which comes out of German Expressionism. Then you put it into a Renaissance world. Is it Titian? I don't know. But somehow it all gets mixed up together and comes out through the designer.

What would you recommend to people who want to go into design?

Don't get too bogged down in the beginning with doing theatre. Learn how to draw. It's what we seem to tell every other applicant who comes to Yale. Until you can express yourself with a pencil or a pen or watercolor, it is very difficult to express yourself to a director. When you sign your name, you can either look at the paper or you can close your eyes, but it'll look the same because it's second nature. You have to be able to do that when you are drawing, too. When you can draw the lamp without looking at the paper, it's because you are coordinating what your eye is seeing with what your hand is drawing. It's the basic building block of design. Do the plays, work on crews, but don't neglect the drawing. And the word "rendering" should be banished from every vocabulary. Some people still do finished, framed renderings, but they become the end product. They don't give you room to go on to the next step.

Have you done any film or television?

Just *The Resurrection of Lady Lester*, which was done at Yale Rep and then taped by CBS Cable. It was great fun, although I feel it misses an entire step. In the process of making theatre you eventually have an opening-night catharsis and it's over. In film, however, you do all of this work and then you go away for six months. You never see it.

Does this mean that you aren't interested in working in film or television?

Oh no, I'd love to do film or television if it were the right project.

Is there a particular project that you would like to do?

No. My favorite part of the process is working with the director, so I just go blank when I'm asked what I would like to do. It depends on the director. The initial conversations with the director, in which we're trying to discover what the play is about, are the most fulfilling part of the process for me. I'll come back here and work by myself until I get totally stuck. Then I'll meet with the director again and be rejuvenated because I'll feel like we're in it together. I see over there on the shelf

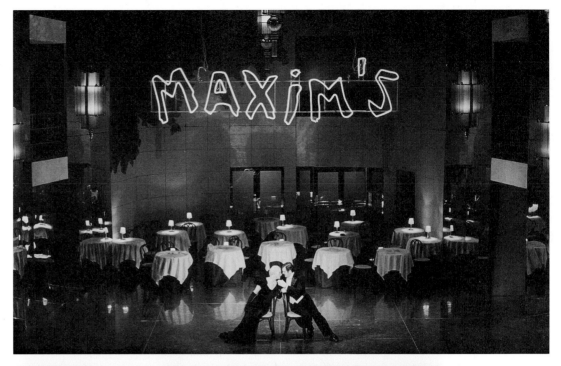

THE WELSH NATIONAL OPERA PRODUCTION OF PETER ILYICH TCHAIKOVSKY'S *EUGENE ONEGIN*, DIRECTED BY ANDREI SERBAN. FACING PAGE: LEFT TOP, ACT 1, SCENE 1; BOTTOM RIGHT, ACT 1, SCENE 2; BOTTOM LEFT, ACT 2. THIS PAGE: TOP, ACT 3, SCENE 2; BOTTOM, ACT 3, SCENE 1.

that incredible recording of *Show Boat* that came out last year, and I think, that's what I would love to do. But I would love to do it with this or that director.

Before we conclude this interview, I'd like to talk about a musical you designed for the Yale swimming pool that has become something of a legend.

The Frogs, yes, with Burt Shevelove. Burt was one of the funniest, most wonderful people I have ever met in my life. He was a delight. Burt was a student at Yale a long time ago, in the 1930s. He and some of his friends decided they wanted to do a production of *The Frogs*. So they got the Yale swimming team, dressed them up like frogs, and did the play in the Yale swimming pool. It was a huge success. So years later, I guess, he decided he wanted to do it again, and he wanted Stephen Sondheim to write the score. Sondheim liked the idea—they had just finished working together on *A Funny Thing Happened on the Way to the Forum*—and they approached Brustein with the project. It was supposed to be a lark, an extension to the regular season, but it ended up practically killing all of us.

Burt again wanted to use the swimming team and the swimming pool, which is huge. My first idea was to float platforms in the pool, but Burt didn't like that idea. He wanted to treat the pool as a classic amphitheatre. All he cared about was having three large doors at one end of the pool; the pool was to be free and the cast could act on the sides. He also wanted the audience to come in and see Charon, with his long white beard, asleep in a boat.

What we ended up with were three terra-cotta doors. We painted the doors to go with the aquamarine green tiles around the pool and then added beige lines for detail. We also silkscreened a Greek key on contact paper—we did thousands of them—that we stuck on the tile all around the pool and up around the doors, to try to tie it all together. Then, because I felt it needed a little color, we took yards and yards of the cheapest fabric in the world at that time, white cheesecloth, and dyed it saffron yellow. As it dried on battens on the main stage, it looked like laundry day in a Buddhist monastery.

Then we moved everything into the pool room—the doors, the saffron material, and all the lighting equipment, which we had to hang ourselves. Everything was in place and we were going to do our first preview performance that night. The fire marshal came in to test the set and it was like it had been soaked in kerosene. The only explanation was that there was a chemical reaction between the fumes from the chlorine and the fireproofing solvent. So we had to cancel the show that night.

I remember the whole thing as one huge nightmare. Sondheim was sending the music up in a chauffeur-driven limousine. The music was being handed to these students right before they were going on in front of the audience. The music was very witty, but it was also very difficult to hear. Plus the fumes. You got dizzy from the chlorine fumes. At one point we tried to repaint the doors, and the paint came up like chewing gum because it dried so fast from the chlorine. So instead of paint, we tried using masking tape. I was sitting in a performance one night and the panels disappeared before my very eyes—the masking tape was peeling right off because the adhesive wouldn't stick.

What a nightmare.

Oh, it was. But the climax was the night that Sondheim's and Burt's friends chartered a bus to come up from New York. It was Leonard Bernstein, Larry Kert, Phyllis Newman, Adolph Green, Betty Comden . . . a who's who of that world. And there were no reserved seats. Some seats had been blocked off, but because people, especially the students, wouldn't acknowledge that they were reserved, a fight broke out. All these people had arrived from New York and they had no place to sit. It was a huge free-for-all, and was written up in all the papers. But despite everything—and in retrospect—it was great fun, a "once-in-a-lifetime" experience.

CHRONOLOGIES

The following year-by-year listings were supplied by the designers, some of whom do not keep complete records of their work. While every effort has been made to verify the information, it was impossible to do so for all of the productions. These listings, which include productions through December 1990, are as complete and accurate as possible.

In general, each entry includes the name of the production, producing organization (or theatre), and director. Unless noted, the designer was responsible for the set only. ("S & L" indicates that the individual designed both the set and the lighting; "S & C" indicates set and costumes.) Nontheatre work—i.e., work done for film, video or dance—is identified as such when not immediately apparent in the credit.

LOY ARCENAS

1978

Amphitryon 38, Soho Repertory Theatre, Jude Schanzer.

1979

The Barber of Seville, Soho Repertory Theatre, Alison MacKenzie.

Everest Hotel, New York Theater Studio, Richard Romagnoli.

Vampire, New York Theater Studio, Richard Romagnoli.

When the War Was Over, Impossible Ragtime Theatre, Jude Schanzer.

The Shem Plays, Impossible Ragtime Theatre, Ted Storey.

Take Death to Lunch (S & C), Impossible Ragtime Theatre, Amielle Zemach.

October 12, 410 B.C., Soho Repertory Theatre, Alison MacKenzie.

Wed-Lock (*The Color of Heat* and *Trifles*), Impossible Ragtime Theatre, Michael Bloom and Darlene Kaplan.

1980

An American Story (costumes only), Pan Asian Repertory Theatre, Tisa Chang.

Vera, With Kate, Cherubs Guild, Matt Williams.

Perch/Powder, Cherubs Guild, Victor Bumbalo and Hillary Wyler.

Resident set and costume designer, Williamstown Theatre Festival (Second Stage).

1981

Redback, New York Theater Studio, Richard Romagnoli.

Frugal Repast/Cubistique, New York Theater Studio, Ted Walch and Dorothy Lyman.

Murder in the Cathedral (S & C), St. Malachy's Theaterspace, NYC, Gregory Abels.

La buona figliuola, Juilliard Opera Theatre, Norman Ayrton.

1982

Finding Donis Anne, The Ark Theater Company, Rebecca Guy.

1983

The Quilling of Prue, New York Theater Studio, Cheryl Faraone.

Four Lanes to Jersey, Shelter West Repertory, Jude Schanzer.

Gunplay (S & C), White Barn Theater, Westport, CT, Carey Perloff.

Sea Marks, Berkeley Stage Company, Angela Paton.

Stars, Stripes . . . Forever (S & C), Berkeley Stage Company, Robert MacDougall.

Second Lady, The Production Company, Carey Perloff.
Dementos, The Production Company, Ted Pappas.

1984

Souvenirs, New York Theatre Workshop, Stephen Katz.
The Man Who Could See Through Time, The Ark Theater Company, Carey Perloff.
Blue Window, The Production Company, Norman Rene.

1985

Leverage/Baby Steps, The Production Company, Carey Perloff.
Maneuvers, South Street Theater, Fielder Cook.
Blue Window, Long Wharf Theatre, Norman Rene.
Resident designer, New York Theatre Workshop (New Directors Project).

1986

Dry Land, New Arts Theatre Company, Kay Matschullat.
Spring Awakening, Double Image Theater (Vassar College), Gerald Chapman.
Bosoms and Neglect, New York Theatre Workshop, Larry Arrick.
The Merchant of Venice, CSC Repertory Ltd., James Simpson.
The Skin of Our Teeth, CSC Repertory Ltd., Carey Perloff.
Bedroom Farce, The Hartman Theatre, David Trainer.
The Day Room, American Repertory Theatre, Michael Bloom.
Resident designer, New York Theatre Workshop (New Directors Project).

1987

Butterfly, The Goodspeed Opera House, Jack Hofsiss.
Roosters, INTAR Hispanic American Arts Center, Jackson Phippin.
The Real Thing, Studio Arena Theatre, Kathryn Long.
Mrs. Sorken Presents, American Repertory Theatre, R.J. Cutler and Wesley Savick.
The Ribman Plays, American Repertory Theatre, David Wheeler.

Gillette, American Repertory Theatre, David Wheeler.
Three Postcards, Playwrights Horizons, Norman Rene.
Three Postcards, South Coast Repertory, Norman Rene. (Los Angeles Critics Circle Award, *Drama-Logue* Award)

1988

Welcome Back to Salamanca, INTAR Hispanic American Arts Center, George Ferencz.
The Debutante Ball, Manhattan Theatre Club, Norman Rene.
Benefactors, Studio Arena Theatre, Kathryn Long.
Precious Memories, Milwaukee Repertory Theater, John Dillon.
Right Behind the Flag, Playwrights Horizons, R.J. Cutler.
Prelude to a Kiss, Berkeley Repertory Theatre, Norman Rene.
Prelude to a Kiss, South Coast Repertory, Norman Rene. (*Drama-Logue* Award)
Reckless, Circle Repertory Company, Norman Rene.
For Dear Life, New York Shakespeare Festival, Norman Rene.

1989

Spunk, Crossroads Theatre Company, George C. Wolfe.
The Heiress, Long Wharf Theatre, Kenneth Frankel.
Italian-American Reconciliation, The Cleveland Play House, Michael Breault.
The Glass Menagerie, Arena Stage, Tazewell Thompson.
The Birthday Party, CSC Repertory Ltd., Carey Perloff.
Mountain Language, CSC Repertory Ltd., Carey Perloff.
Life Is a Dream, American Repertory Theatre, Anne Bogart.
Nebraska, La Jolla Playhouse, Les Waters.
IBM—The Solution (commercial, 9 segments), Richard Avedon.

1990

Prelude to a Kiss, Circle Repertory Company, Norman Rene.

Prelude to a Kiss, Helen Hayes Theatre, NYC, Norman Rene.
Spunk, New York Shakespeare Festival, George C. Wolfe.
Once on This Island, Playwrights Horizons, Graciela Daniele.
Imagining Brad, Circle Repertory Company, Joe Mantello.
Life During Wartime, La Jolla Playhouse, Les Waters.
Fences, Arena Stage, Tazewell Thompson.
Daytrips, Hartford Stage Company, Michael Engler.
Once on This Island, Booth Theatre, NYC, Graciela Daniele.
Once in a Lifetime, American Repertory Theatre, Anne Bogart.
Caucasian Chalk Circle, Arena Stage, Tazewell Thompson.

JOHN ARNONE

1974

Gammer Gurton's Needle, Lion Theatre Company, Gene Nye.
Kitty Hawk, Lion Theatre Company, Garland Wright.

1975

Casserole, Lion Theatre Company, Garland Wright.
Twelfth Night (costumes only), Lion Theatre Company, Garland Wright.
End as a Man, Lion Theatre Company, Garland Wright.

1976

Kerouac, Lion Theatre Company, Kenneth Frankel.
Vanities, Lion Theatre Company, Garland Wright. [Subsequent productions of *Vanities* designed for Mark Taper Forum, American Conservatory Theatre, Ford's Theatre, Fisher Theatre, Charles Playhouse, The Egg (Albany, NY), Coconut Grove Playhouse, Studio Arena Theatre, Drury Lane Theatre, PAF Playhouse, Westwood Theatre and John Drew Theatre, 1976-78.]

Love's Labours Lost (costumes only), Lion Theatre Company, Garland Wright.

Marathon '33, Lion Theatre Company, Garland Wright.

1977

K: Impressions of Kafka's The Trial, Lion Theatre Company, Garland Wright. (OBIE Award)

1978

Killing of Yablonski, PAF Playhouse, Peter Mark Schifter.

Patio/Porch, Century Theatre, NYC, Garland Wright.

The Sound of Music (national tour), Stockton Briggle.

Music Hall Sidelights, Lion Theatre Company, Garland Wright. (Joseph Maharam Foundation Citation)

The World of Sholom Aleichem, Syracuse Stage, Steven Kaplan.

New Jerusalem, New York Shakespeare Festival, Garland Wright.

1979

Private Lives, Playwrights Horizons, Garland Wright.

Loved, Syracuse Stage, Arthur Storch.

Lone Star/Pvt. Wars, Century Theatre, NYC, Garland Wright.

Split/Domino Courts, The Acting Company, Jonathan Furst and Richard Hamburger.

Cold Storage, Indiana Repertory Theatre, Edward Stern.

Naked, Syracuse Stage, Arthur Storch.

1980

Star Treatment, Lion Theatre Company, Garland Wright.

Twelfth Night, Indiana Repertory Theatre, Hal Scott.

Old World, Syracuse Stage, Arthur Storch.

Matter of Opinion (costumes only), Stratford Shakespeare Festival, CT, Garland Wright.

Limbo Tales, Westbeth Theatre Center, Len Jenkin. (Villager Award)

1981

A Man's a Man, Towson State College, Paul Berman.

Talley's Folly, Studio Arena Theatre, Lawrence Kornfeld.

Candide, The Guthrie Theater, Garland Wright.

The Ghost Sonata, University of Dallas, Patrick Kelly.

Creativity with Bill Moyers, PBS Television, Bill Moyers.

Dark Ride, Soho Repertory Theatre, Len Jenkin. (Villager Award)

1982

Red and Blue (S & L), New York Shakespeare Festival, JoAnne Akalaitis.

Buffalo Notes, Studio Arena Theatre, David Marlin-Jones.

Looking-Glass, Entermedia Theatre, NYC, David Bell.

Dead End Kids (film), JoAnne Akalaitis.

The Infernal Machine, University of Dallas, Patrick Kelly.

1983

The Imaginary Invalid, Arena Stage, Garland Wright.

Buck, The American Place Theatre, Elinor Renfield.

My Uncle Sam, New York Shakespeare Festival, Len Jenkin.

The Good Person of Setzuan, University of Dallas, Patrick Kelly.

The Beniker Gang (film), Ken Kwapis.

Resident set designer, Circle Repertory Company (Young Playwrights Festival).

1984

Happy End, Arena Stage, Garland Wright.

Chain Letters (film), Mark Rappaport.

As You Like It, La Jolla Playhouse, Des McAnuff.

Infidelities, University of Dallas, Patrick Kelly.

The Tempest, Arena Stage, Garland Wright.

1985

Life Is a Dream, The Ark Theatre Company, James Simpson.

A Wimp's Revenge, Scholastic Productions (television), James Scott.

Lautrec, The American Place Theatre, John Ferraro.

Life and Limb, Playwrights Horizons, Thomas Babe.

The Seagull, La Jolla Playhouse, Des McAnuff.

The Good Person of Setzuan, Arena Stage, Garland Wright.

Tales From the Darkside, Laurel Entertainment (television).

1986

Rum and Coke, New York Shakespeare Festival, Les Waters.

Shout Up a Morning, La Jolla Playhouse, Des McAnuff.

Gillette, La Jolla Playhouse, Des McAnuff.

Worstward Ho, Mabou Mines, Frederick Neumann.

The Piggy Bank, Arena Stage, Garland Wright.

Highest Standard of Living, Playwrights Horizons, Don Scardino.

1987

On the Verge or The Geography of Yearning, The Acting Company, Garland Wright.

Stand Up Shakespeare, 890 Broadway, NYC, Mike Nichols.

The Piggy Bank, The Guthrie Theater, Garland Wright.

The Crucible, Williamstown Theatre Festival, Nikos Psacharopoulos.

Spalding Gray's Terrors of Pleasure, Home Box Office (television), Tommy Schlamme.

The Invisible Thread: Penn and Teller, Showtime (television), Bob Balaban.

The School for Wives, La Jolla Playhouse, Mark Lamos.

Prison-made Tuxedos, Music-Theatre Group, David Warren.

Haddock's Eyes, Music-Theatre Group, David Warren.

Frankenstein: Playing with Fire, The Guthrie Theater (tour), Michael Maggio.

The Voyage of the Beagle, Music Theatre Works, JoAnne Akalaitis.

Mondo Beyondo with Bette Midler, Home Box Office (television), Tommy Schlamme.

Silent Edward, La Jolla Playhouse, David Warren.

Rap Master Ronnie, Home Box Office (television), Jay Dubin.

1988

Made in Bangkok, Mark Taper Forum, Robert Egan.

American Notes, New York Shakespeare Festival, JoAnne Akalaitis.

My Heart Belongs to Daddy, Pittsburgh Public Theater, David Warren.

The School for Wives, Hartford Stage Company, Mark Lamos.

Frankenstein: Playing with Fire, The Guthrie Theater, Michael Maggio.

Lulu, La Jolla Playhouse, Sharon Ott.

Penn and Teller Get Killed (film), Arthur Penn.

1989

Pravda, The Guthrie Theater, Robert Falls.

The Winter's Tale, New York Shakespeare Festival, James Lapine.

Nothing Sacred, Arena Stage, Garland Wright.

A Walk in the Woods, Arena Stage, Paul Weidner.

Lulu, Berkeley Repertory Theatre, Sharon Ott.

Macbeth, La Jolla Playhouse, Des McAnuff.

Women and Wallace, American Playhouse (television), Don Scardino.

Hyde in Hollywood, American Playhouse (television), Gerald Gutierrez.

1990

The Miser, Hartford Stage Company, Mark Lamos.

Candide, The Guthrie Theater, Garland Wright.

Sex, Drugs, Rock & Roll, Orpheum Theatre, NYC, Eric Bogosian.

A Cool Million, Dance Theater Workshop, NYC, Dan Hurlin.

A Funny Thing Happened on the Way to the Forum, La Jolla Playhouse, Des McAnuff.

A Long Day's Journey into Night, Stella Adler Theatre, NYC, Milton Justice.

The Days and Nights of Molly Dodd (television), Don Scardino.

Hamlet, Great Performances (television), Kevin Kline.

DAVID GROPMAN

1976

Bingo, Yale Repertory Theatre, Ron Daniels.

1977

Mister Puntila and His Chauffeur Matti, Yale Repertory Theatre, Ron Daniels.

The Last Analysis, Berkshire Theatre Festival, Arthur Sherman.

I Married an Angel, Berkshire Theatre Festival, Allan Albert.

Two Gentlemen of Verona, Folger Theatre Group, Louis W. Scheeder.

1978

Hamlet, Folger Theatre Group, Jonathan Alper.

Conjuring an Event, American Place Theatre, Douglas C. Wager.

The Pretenders, The Guthrie Theater, Alvin Epstein.

Buried Child, Theater for the New City, Robert Woodruff.

The 1940s Radio Hour, Arena Stage, Walton Jones.

1979

Two-Part Inventions, Goodman Theatre, Michael Feingold.

The Dybbuk, Habimah National Theatre of Israel, Tel Aviv, Joseph Chaikin.

Goodnight Grandpa, PAF Playhouse, Jay Broad.

Bonjour, là, Bonjour, Hartford Stage Company, Paul Weidner.

Buried Child, Circle Repertory Company, Robert Woodruff.

The 1940s Radio Hour, St. James Theatre, NYC, Walton Jones.

Death and the King's Horseman, Goodman Theatre, Wole Soyinka.

1980

The Winter's Tale, BAM Theater Company, David Jones.

Billy Bishop Goes to War, Arena Stage, John Gray.

Billy Bishop Goes to War, Mark Taper Forum, John Gray.

Billy Bishop Goes to War, Morosco Theatre, NYC, John Gray.

Billy Bishop Goes to War, Edinburgh International Festival, John Gray.

Mass Appeal, Manhattan Theatre Club, Geraldine Fitzgerald.

Passione, Playwrights Horizons, Peter Mark Schifter.

Passione, Morosco Theatre, NYC, Frank Langella.

True West, New York Shakespeare Festival, Robert Woodruff.

1981

Romeo and Juliet, Long Wharf Theatre, Barry Davis.

Lena Horne: The Lady and Her Music, Nederlander Theatre, NYC, Arthur Faria.

I, James McNeill Whistler (S & C), Hartford Stage Company, Jerome Kilty.

I, James McNeill Whistler (S & C), Provincetown Playhouse, Jerome Kilty.

Billy Bishop Goes to War, Comedy Theatre, London, John Gray.

Billy Bishop Goes to War, Royal Alexandra Theatre, Toronto, John Gray.

Children of a Lesser God, Schauspielhaus, Dusseldorf, Daniel Freudenberger.

Family Devotions, New York Shakespeare Festival, Robert Allan Ackerman.

Mass Appeal, Booth Theatre, NYC, Geraldine Fitzgerald.

1982

Pantomime (S & C), Goodman Theatre, Gregory Mosher.

Come Back to the 5 and Dime, Jimmy Dean, Jimmy Dean, Martin Beck Theatre, NYC, Robert Altman.

Come Back to the 5 and Dime, Jimmy Dean, Jimmy Dean (film), Robert Altman.

Lena Horne: The Lady and Her Music, Showtime (television), Arthur Faria.

Mass Appeal, Lyric Theatre, London, Geraldine Fitzgerald.

A Little Family Business, Ahmanson Theatre, Los Angeles, Martin Charnin.
A Little Family Business, Martin Beck Theatre, NYC, Martin Charnin.

1983
The Comedy of Errors, Goodman Theatre, Robert Woodruff.
Snow White, Paul Taylor Dance Company, choreographed by Paul Taylor.
Trouble in Tahiti/A Quiet Place, Houston Grand Opera, Peter Mark Schifter.
O.C. and Stiggs (film), Robert Altman.

1984
Open Admissions, Music Box Theatre, NYC, Elinor Renfield.
Byzantium, Paul Taylor Dance Company, choreographed by Paul Taylor.
Mr. & Mrs., WPA Theatre, David Trainer.
Danny and the Deep Blue Sea, Circle in the Square Downtown, NYC, Barnet Kellman.
A Quiet Place, Teatro alla Scala, Milan, Stephen Wadsworth.
A Quiet Place, The Kennedy Center, Washington, D.C., Stephen Wadsworth.
Key Exchange (film), Barnet Kellman.
The Laundromat, Home Box Office (television), Robert Altman.

1985
Eden Court, Promenade Theatre, NYC, Barnet Kellman.
Home of the Brave: A Film by Laurie Anderson, Laurie Anderson.
The Last Days of Frank and Jessie James, NBC/TV, William Graham.

1986
Sweet Lorraine (film), Steven Gomer.
Campus Man (film), Ron Casden.

1987
Death and the King's Horseman, Lincoln Center Theater, Wole Soyinka.

The Comedy of Errors, Lincoln Center Theater, Robert Woodruff.
A Time Exposure, Eliot Feld Ballet, choreographed by Carolyn Carlson.
Miles From Home (film), Gary Sinise.

1988
Danbury Mix, New York City Ballet, choreographed by Paul Taylor.
Slaves of New York (film), James Ivory.
Life Under Water, American Playhouse, Jay Holman.
Babycakes, CBS/TV (television), Paul Schneider.

1989
Quick Change (film), Howard Franklin and Bill Murray.
Mr. & Mrs. Bridge (film), James Ivory.

1990
Once Around (film), Lasse Hallstrom.

ROBERT ISRAEL

Note: Except for the work with Martha Clarke, the following are opera productions for which both sets and costumes were designed (unless listed otherwise).

1966
The Good Soldier Schweik, Minnesota Opera Company, H. Wesley Balk.

1967
The Minute Operas, Minnesota Opera Company, H. Wesley Balk.
The Harpies, Minnesota Opera Company, H. Wesley Balk.
Socrates, Minnesota Opera Company, H. Wesley Balk.
The Sorrows of Orpheus, Minnesota Opera Company, H. Wesley Balk.

1968
A Midsummer Night's Dream, Minnesota Opera Company, H. Wesley Balk.

1969
Horspfal, Minnesota Opera Company, H. Wesley Balk.

1970
The Abduction from the Seraglio, National Educational Television, Rhoda Levine.
Punch and Judy, Minnesota Opera Company, H. Wesley Balk.

1971
Men at Play, St. Paul de Vence, France.

1972
Transformations, Minnesota Opera Company, H. Wesley Balk.

1974
The Good Soldier Schweik, National Opera of the Netherlands, Rhoda Levine.

1975
The Magic Flute, Minnesota Opera Company, H. Wesley Balk.
Eight Songs for a Mad King, Minnesota Opera Company, H. Wesley Balk.
Seven Deadly Sins (costumes only), The National Opera of Belgium, Helmut Krek.
Gulliver, Minnesota Opera Company, H. Wesley Balk.
Macbeth, National Opera of the Netherlands, Rhoda Levine.
The Kaiser of Atlantis, National Opera of the Netherlands, Rhoda Levine.

1976
The Love for Three Oranges, National Opera of the Netherlands, Rhoda Levine.
The Kaiser of Atlantis, Festival of Two Worlds, Spoleto, Italy, Rhoda Levine.
The Kaiser of Atlantis, The National Opera of Belgium, Rhoda Levine.

The Magic Flute, Michigan Opera Theatre, Rhoda
  Levine.

1977
The Combat of Tancredi and Clorinda, San Francisco
  Opera Company, Rhoda Levine.
The Kaiser of Atlantis, San Francisco Opera Company,
  Rhoda Levine.
Savitri, San Francisco Opera Company, Rhoda Levine.
Transformations, National Opera of the Netherlands,
  H. Wesley Balk.
Transformations, The National Opera of Finland, H.
  Wesley Balk.

1978
Lulu (incomplete version), National Opera of the
  Netherlands, Rhoda Levine.

1980
Lulu (complete version), National Opera of the
  Netherlands, Rhoda Levine.
Satyagraha; Rotterdam, Amsterdam, Utrecht, the
  Hague; David Pountney.

1981
Satyagraha, Brooklyn Academy of Music, David
  Pountney.

1982
The Yellow Sound, Guggenheim Museum, NYC, Ian
  Strassvogel.
The Yellow Sound, Frankfurt, Germany, Ian
  Strassvogel.

1983
The Turn of the Screw, Santa Fe Opera, David Alden.
Intelligent Systems, Frankfurt, Germany, Karsen
  Kievman.

1984
Akhnaten, Houston Grand Opera and New York City
  Opera, David Freeman.

1985
Die Walküre, Seattle Opera, Francois Rochax.

1986
Vienna: Lusthaus, Music-Theatre Group/New York
  Shakespeare Festival, Martha Clarke. (Joseph
  Maharam Foundation Award)
Vienna: Lusthaus, The Kennedy Center, Washington,
  D.C., Martha Clarke.
Die Walküre, Seattle Opera, Francois Rochax.
Das Rheingold, Seattle Opera, Francois Rochax.
Siegfried, Seattle Opera, Francois Rochax.
Götterdämmerung, Seattle Opera, Francois Rochax.

1987
The Hunger Artist, Music-Theatre Group, Martha
  Clarke. (OBIE Award, American Theater Wing
  Award)
The Ring Cycle (revised), Seattle Opera, Francois
  Rochax.
The Fiery Angel, Los Angeles Music Center Opera,
  Andrei Serban.
The Fiery Angel, Geneva Opera, Andrei Serban.
The Fiery Angel, English National Opera, Andrei
  Serban.

1988
Satyagraha, Chicago Lyric Opera, David Pountney.
Miracolo d'Amore, Spoleto Festival of Two Worlds,
  Charleston, SC, Martha Clarke.
Miracolo d'Amore, New York Shakespeare Festival,
  Martha Clarke.
Vienna: Lusthaus; Venice, Vienna, Madrid, Paris;
  Martha Clarke.

1989
The Rise and Fall of the City of Mahagonny, Dorothy
  Chandler Pavilion, Los Angeles, Jonathan Miller.

1990
Don Giovanni, Maggio Musicale Fiorentino, Italy,
  Jonathan Miller.
Endangered Species, Music-Theatre Group/Brooklyn
  Academy of Music, Martha Clarke.

HEIDI LANDESMAN

1979
Holeville, Dodger Theatre Company, Des McAnuff.
Leave It to Beaver Is Dead, New York Shakespeare
  Festival, Des McAnuff.
The Vienna Notes, Playwrights Horizons, Andre
  Ernotte.
The Vienna Notes, Mark Taper Forum, Gwen Arne.

1980
The Marriage Dance, BAM Theater Company, Andre
  Ernotte.
Table Settings, Chelsea Theatre Center, NYC, James
  Lapine.
Split, The Second Stage, Carole Rothman.

1981
Twelve Dreams, New York Shakespeare Festival, James
  Lapine.
How It All Began, New York Shakespeare Festival, Des
  McAnuff.
Penguin Touquet, New York Shakespeare Festival,
  Richard Foreman.
Treats, Indiana Repertory Theatre, William Peters.
A Midsummer Night's Dream, Arena Stage, David
  Chambers.

1982
A Midsummer Night's Dream, New York Shakespeare
  Festival (Delacorte), James Lapine.
Pastorale, The Second Stage, Carole Rothman.
Maybe I'm Doing It Wrong, Astor Place Theatre, NYC,
  Joan Micklin Silver.
'night, Mother, American Repertory Theatre, Tom
  Moore.
A Midsummer Night's Dream, The Acting Company,
  David Chambers.

1983
'night, Mother, John Golden Theatre, NYC, Tom
  Moore.
Painting Churches, The Second Stage, Carole
  Rothman.

Painting Churches, Lamb's Theatre, NYC, Carole
   Rothman.
The Lady and the Clarinet, Lucille Lortel Theatre,
   NYC, Gordon Davidson.
Romeo and Juliet, La Jolla Playhouse, Des McAnuff.

1984

Big River: The Adventures of Huckleberry Finn,
   American Repertory Theatre, Des McAnuff.
Big River: The Adventures of Huckleberry Finn, La
   Jolla Playhouse, Des McAnuff.
Traveler in the Dark, American Repertory Theatre,
   Tom Moore.

1985

Big River: The Adventures of Huckleberry Finn,
   Eugene O'Neill Theatre, NYC, Des McAnuff. (Tony
   Award)

1986

Miami, Playwrights Horizons, Gerald Gutierrez.
Big River: The Adventures of Huckleberry Finn
   (national tour), Des McAnuff.

1987

Urban Blight, Manhattan Theatre Club, John Tillinger
   and Richard Maltby, Jr.
The Kathy and Mo Show, Los Angeles Theatre Center,
   Carole Rothman.
Emily, Manhattan Theatre Club, Gerald Gutierrez.
Hunting Cockroaches, Manhattan Theatre Club,
   Arthur Penn.

1988

Romeo and Juliet, New York Shakespeare Festival, Les
   Waters.
Dutch Landscape, Mark Taper Forum, Gordon
   Davidson.
Approaching Zanzibar, The Second Stage, Carole
   Rothman.

1989

The Secret Garden, Virginia Stage Company, R.J.
   Cutler.

1990

The Cherry Orchard, La Jolla Playhouse, Tom Moore.

HUGH LANDWEHR

1974

Short Eyes, Hartford Stage Company, Marvin Camillo.

1975

Oh, Coward!, Hartford Stage Company, Roderick
   Cook.
A Raisin in the Sun, Hartford Stage Company, Irene
   Lewis.

1976

The Blood Knot, Hartford Stage Company, Paul
   Weidner.
A Touch of the Poet, Williamstown Theatre Festival,
   Olympia Dukakis.
Born Yesterday, Williamstown Theatre Festival, Paul
   Sparer.
Born Yesterday, Hartford Stage Company, Irene
   Lewis.
Dream on Monkey Mountain, Hartford Stage
   Company, Charles Turner.
The Threepenny Opera, Trinity College, Roger
   Shoemaker.

1977

Past Tense, Hartford Stage Company, Paul Weidner.
After the Fall, Williamstown Theatre Festival, Austin
   Pendleton.
The Learned Ladies, Williamstown Theatre Festival,
   Norman Ayrton.
Sleuth, Trinity College, Roger Shoemaker.
The Oldest Living Graduate, Trinity College, Roger
   Shoemaker.
Candida, Hartford Stage Company, John Going.
A History of the American Film, Hartford Stage
   Company, Paul Weidner.

1978

A Christmas Carol, Center Stage, Robert Allan
   Ackerman.
Catchpenny Twist, Hartford Stage Company, Irene
   Lewis.
Dracula, American Stage Festival, Harold DeFelice.
A Moon for the Misbegotten, American Stage Festival,
   Stanley Wojewodski, Jr.
The School for Wives, Williamstown Theatre Festival,
   Jean-Bernard Bucky.
They'd Come to See Charlie, Hartford Stage Company,
   Irene Lewis.
Holiday, Hartford Stage Company, Edward Berkeley.
The Animal Kingdom, Hartman Theatre Company,
   John Going.
The Runner Stumbles, Center Stage, Stanley
   Wojewodski, Jr.

1979

Ladyhouse Blues, St. Peter's Church, NYC, Tony
   Giordano.
The Recruiting Officer, Milwaukee Repertory Theater,
   William Ludel.
Children of the Sun, Williamstown Theatre Festival,
   Nikos Psacharopoulos.
Tartuffe, American Stage Festival, Stanley
   Wojewodski, Jr.
Ladyhouse Blues, Playwrights Horizons, Tony
   Giordano.
Bonjour, là, Boujour, Center Stage, Stanley
   Wojewodski, Jr.
Measure for Measure, Center Stage, Stanley
   Wojewodski, Jr.
The Little Foxes, Hartman Theatre Company, Tony
   Giordano.
White Sirens, New York Shakespeare Festival, Eleo
   Pomare.
Hillbilly Women, The Actors Studio, NYC, Peter
   Bennett.

1980

Sly Fox, Actors Theatre of Louisville, Jon Jory.
Joe Egg, Philadelphia Drama Guild, Irene Lewis.
Agnes of God, Center Stage, Stanley Wojewodski, Jr.

The Chekhov Sketchbook, The Harold Clurman Theatre, NYC, Tony Giordano.
Watch on the Rhine, Philadelphia Drama Guild, Irene Lewis.
The First Lady, Berkshire Theatre Festival, Michael Montel.
Cyrano de Bergerac, Center Stage, Stanley Wojewodski, Jr.
Crimes of the Heart, Center Stage, J. Ranelli.
Shout Across the River, Phoenix Theatre, Robert Woodruff.
Resident designer, Eugene O'Neill Theater Center (National Playwrights Conference).

1981

A View from the Bridge, Long Wharf Theatre, Arvin Brown.
This Story of Yours, Long Wharf Theatre, John Tillinger.
Nude with Violin, Williamstown Theatre Festival, Nikos Psacharopoulos.
Feathertop, American Stage Festival, Larry Carpenter.
A Life, Long Wharf Theatre, William Ludel.
Inherit the Wind, Center Stage, Jackson Phippin.
The Nerd, Milwaukee Repertory Theater, John Dillon.
Sally's Gone, She Left Her Name, Center Stage, Stanley Wojewodski, Jr.
The Front Page, Philadelphia Drama Guild, Irene Lewis.
Close Ties, Long Wharf Theatre, Arvin Brown.
Resident designer, Eugene O'Neill Theater Center (National Playwrights Conference).

1982

Manon, Juilliard Opera Theatre, Norman Ayrton.
The Miser, Center Stage, Stanley Wojewodski, Jr.
Last Looks, Center Stage, Jackson Phippin.
Two by A.M., Long Wharf Theatre, Arthur Miller.
Miss Lulu Bett, Milwaukee Repertory Theater, John Dillon.
Wings, Santa Fe Festival Theatre, Stanley Wojewodski, Jr.
Hay Fever, Williams College, Jean-Bernard Bucky.
Terra Nova, Center Stage, Stanley Wojewodski, Jr.

Snow Orchid, Circle Repertory Company, Tony Giordano.
The Workroom, Center Stage, Stanley Wojewodski, Jr.
An Enemy of the People, Alaska Repertory Theatre, Irene Lewis.
The Carmone Brothers' Italian Food Products Corp's Annual Pasta Pageant, Long Wharf Theatre, William Ludel.

1983

The Hostage, Long Wharf Theatre, Joseph Maher.
Billy Bishop Goes to War, Sante Fe Festival Theatre, Thomas Kahn Gardner.
True West, Sante Fe Festival Theatre, Daniel Sullivan.
Holiday, Williamstown Theatre Festival, Nikos Psacharopoulos.
Time and the Conways, The Huntington Theatre, Elinor Renfield.
The Vinegar Tree, Seattle Repertory Theatre, Daniel Sullivan.
The Woman, Center Stage, Jackson Phippin.
Wings, Center Stage, Stanley Wojewodski, Jr.
A View from the Bridge, Ambassador Theatre, NYC, Arvin Brown.

1984

Execution of Justice, Center Stage, Stanley Wojewodski, Jr.
The Devil's Disciple, Milwaukee Repertory Theater, Gregory Boyd.
Danton's Death, Center Stage, Stanley Wojewodski, Jr.
Ducks in a Row, Santa Fe Festival Theatre, Thomas Kahn Gardner.
The Tale of the Wolf, Williamstown Theatre Festival, Nikos Psacharopoulos.
Black Comedy, Santa Fe Festival Theatre, William Peters.
Ohio Tip-Off, Center Stage, John Pasquin.
Stem of a Briar, The Hartman Theatre, Leonard Peters.
You Never Can Tell, Center Stage, Stanley Wojewodski, Jr.
Make and Break, Seattle Repertory Theatre, Daniel Sullivan.

1985

All My Sons, Seattle Repertory Theatre, Edward Hastings.
Glengarry Glen Ross, Syracuse Stage, Tony Giordano.
She Loves Me, Center Stage, Stanley Wojewodski, Jr.
Tonight at 8:30, Williamstown Theatre Festival, Ellis Rabb.
The Royal Family, Williamstown Theatre Festival, Edward Payson Call.
Painting Churches, Santa Fe Festival Theatre, Irene Lewis.
Desire Under the Elms, Hartford Stage Company, Mary B. Robinson.
Who They Are and How It Is with Them, Center Stage, Jackson Phippin.
Cat on a Hot Tin Roof, Long Wharf Theatre, Edward Gilbert.
Hedda Gabler, Center Stage, Irene Lewis.
Crystal Clear, Long Wharf Theatre, Phil Young.

1986

You Can't Take It with You, Seattle Repertory Theatre, Douglas Hughes.
A View from the Bridge, Studio Arena Theatre, Tony Giordano.
A View from the Bridge, Syracuse Stage, Tony Giordano.
A View from the Bridge, Capital Repertory Company, Tony Giordano.
A View from the Bridge, GeVa Theatre, Tony Giordano.
All My Sons, Long Wharf Theatre, Arvin Brown.
On the Verge or The Geography of Yearning, The Guthrie Theater, Stanley Wojewodski, Jr.
Reunion, Center Stage, Irene Lewis.
In a Pig's Valise, Center Stage, Mark Harrison.
Deadfall, Center Stage, Stanley Wojewodski, Jr.
Buried Child, Center Stage, Michael Engler.
"Master Harold" . . . and the boys, Events (Dock St. Theatre), Charleston, SC, Stanley Wojewodski, Jr.
The Foreigner, Events (Dock St. Theatre), Charleston, SC, Charley Lang.
The Normal Heart, Center Stage, Michael Engler.

1987

The Beauty Part, Seattle Repertory Theatre, Douglas Hughes.

The Laughing Stock, Long Wharf Theatre, David Esbjornson.

The Matchmaker, Milwaukee Repertory Theater, John Dillon.

Established Price, Philadelphia Festival Theatre for New Plays, Allen R. Belknap.

Hamlet, Center Stage, Stanley Wojewodski, Jr.

Major Barbara, Center Stage, Stanley Wojewodski, Jr.

Sister Mary Ignatius Explains It All for You, Events (Dock St. Theatre), Charleston, SC, Frank Corsaro.

The Marriage of Bette and Boo, Center Stage, Richard Hamburger.

All My Sons, John Golden Theatre, NYC, Arvin Brown.

All My Sons, The Wilbur Theatre, Boston, Arvin Brown.

All My Sons, Ford's Theatre, Washington, D.C., Arvin Brown.

The Crucible, StageWest, Jean-Bernard Bucky.

Children, Hartford Stage Company, Jackson Phippin.

1988

Les Liaisons Dangereuses, The Cleveland Play House, Robert Berlinger.

Dinner at Eight, Long Wharf Theatre, Arvin Brown.

The Showoff, Williamstown Theatre Festival, James Simpson.

Les Liaisons Dangereuses, Williamstown Theatre Festival, John Rubenstein.

The Price, Berkshire Theatre Festival, Gordon Edelstein.

Sweet Bird of Youth, Royal Alexandra Theatre, Toronto, Nikos Psacharopoulos.

April Snow, Manhattan Theatre Club, David Esbjornson.

Magda and Callas, Philadelphia Festival Theatre for New Plays, Thomas Gruenewald.

1989

Glengarry Glen Ross, Capital Repertory Company, Gordon Edelstein.

Glengarry Glen Ross, The Philadelphia Theatre Company, Gordon Edelstein.

When We Are Married, Long Wharf Theatre, Kenneth Frankel.

Alfred Stieglitz Loves O'Keeffe, Old Globe Theatre, Robert Berlinger.

A Dance Lesson, Long Wharf Theatre, Gordon Edelstein.

Measure for Measure, Seattle Repertory Theatre, Douglas Hughes.

You Can't Take It with You, Studio Arena Theatre, David Frank.

Betrayal, Berkshire Theatre Festival, Gordon Edelstein.

The Rose Tattoo, Williamstown Theatre Festival, Irene Lewis.

John Brown's Body, Williamstown Theatre Festival, Peter Hunt.

Harvey, The Guthrie Theater, Douglas Hughes.

1990

The Front Page, The Guthrie Theater, Douglas Hughes.

Death Takes a Holiday, Williamstown Theatre Festival, Peter Hunt.

The Road to Mecca, Berkshire Theatre Festival, Gordon Edelstein.

Harvey, Williamstown Theatre Festival, Bill Francisco.

Ariadne auf Naxos, University of Wisconsin/Madison, Richard Pearlman.

Anna Christie, Long Wharf Theatre, Gordon Edelstein.

Uncle Vanya, Old Globe Theatre, Jack O'Brien.

ADRIANNE LOBEL

1978

Mad Dog Blues, Yale on the Beach (Yale School of Drama), Andrei Serban.

1979

Buried Child, Yale Repertory Theatre, Adrian Hall.

As You Like It (costumes only), Yale Repertory Theatre, Andrei Belgrader.

The Cocktail Party (S & C), Hartford Stage Company, Paul Weidner.

Artichoke, American Stage Festival, Burke Walker.

1980

Room Service, American Stage Festival, William Peters.

The Inspector General, American Repertory Theatre, Peter Sellars.

1981

Scenes from La Vie de Boheme, Manhattan Theatre Club, Douglas Hughes.

Lulu, American Repertory Theatre, Lee Breuer.

The Man Who Came to Dinner, Arena Stage, Douglas C. Wager.

After the Prize, Phoenix Theatre, Steven Robman.

Play Mas (S & C), Goodman Theatre, Derek Walcott. (Joseph Jefferson Award)

La traviata, Juilliard Opera Theatre, Andrei Serban.

1982

My One and Only, St. James Theatre, NYC, Tommy Tune.

Undiscovered Country, Arena Stage, Garland Wright.

Dwarfman, Master of a Million Shapes, Goodman Theatre, Emily Mann.

1983

The Mikado, Chicago Lyric Opera, Peter Sellars.

Summer Vacation Madness, The Guthrie Theater, Garland Wright.

The Visions of Simone Machard, La Jolla Playhouse, Peter Sellars.

1984

Playboy of the West Indies, The Oxford Playhouse, England, Nick Kent.

All Night Long, The Second Stage, Andre Gregory. (OBIE Award)

Hang On to Me, The Guthrie Theater, Peter Sellars.

The Vampires, Astor Place Theatre, NYC, Harry Kondoleon. (OBIE Award)

1985

The Tempest, Goodman Theatre, Robert Falls.
What's Wrong with This Picture, Manhattan Theatre Club, Claudia Weill.
Anteroom, Playwrights Horizons, Garland Wright.
Man and Superman, Arena Stage, Douglas C. Wager.
Henry IV, Part 1, American National Theater, Tim Mayer.

1986

Così fan tutte, PepsiCo Summerfare, Purchase, NY, Peter Sellars.
Savage in Limbo, Double Image Theatre (Vassar College), Mark Linn-Baker.
Orchards, The Acting Company, Robert Falls.

1987

The Dreamer Examines His Pillow, Double Image Theatre (Vassar College), John Patrick Shanley.
Women of Manhattan, Manhattan Theatre Club, Ron Lagomarsino.
The Taming of the Shrew, Arena Stage, Douglas C. Wager.
The Philadelphia Story, Arena Stage, Douglas C. Wager.
Cheapside, Roundabout Theatre Company, Carey Perloff.
Nixon in China, Houston Grand Opera, Peter Sellars.
Nixon in China, Brooklyn Academy of Music, Peter Sellars.
Nixon in China, The Kennedy Center, Washington, D.C., Peter Sellars.
Playboy of the West Indies, Court Theatre, Tazewell Thompson.
Five Corners (film), Tony Bill.
Bad (music video), Martin Scorsese.
Hard Rock (music video), Peter Sellars.

1988

The Marriage of Figaro, PepsiCo Summerfare, Purchase, NY, Peter Sellars.
L'Allegro, Il Penseroso ed Il Moderato, Monnaie Dance Group, Brussels, choreographed by Mark Morris.

Ask Me Again, American Playhouse (television), Deborah Reinish.
Let's Wait Awhile (music video), Dominic Sena.
Zero Positive, New York Shakespeare Festival, Mark Linn-Baker.
Playboy of the West Indies, Arena Stage, Nick Kent.

1989

Così fan tutte, ORF Media Scope and WNET/TV, Peter Sellars.
The Marriage of Figaro, ORF Media Scope and WNET/TV, Peter Sellars.
Abundance, South Coast Repertory, Ron Lagomarsino.

1990

Abundance, Manhattan Theatre Club, Ron Lagomarsino.
Lohengrin, Theatre Royale de La Monnaie, Brussels, Ansa Silja.
The Magic Flute, Glyndebourne Opera Festival, England, Peter Sellars.
Joe Turner's Come and Gone, The Tricycle Theatre, London, Claude Purdy.
Lake No Bottom, The Second Stage, Carole Rothman.
The Nutcracker, Monnaie Dance Group, Brussels, choreographed by Mark Morris.

CHARLES McCLENNAHAN

1984

Ma Rainey's Black Bottom, Yale Repertory Theatre, Lloyd Richards.
Ma Rainey's Black Bottom, Cort Theatre, NYC, Lloyd Richards.
District Line, Negro Ensemble Company, Douglas Turner Ward.
Bartholomew Fair, Juilliard Opera Theatre, Jeffrey Hitch.
Colored People's Time, Negro Ensemble Company, Horacena J. Taylor.
Late Great Ladies of Blues and Jazz, Cotton Club, NYC, Mike Malone.

1985

Boesman and Lena, Center Stage, Zakes Mokae.
Uptown, It's Hot, Tropicana Hotel, Atlantic City, Maurice Hines.
Pajama Game, Hartford Stage Company, Clay Stevenson.
Long Time Since Yesterday, New Federal Theatre, Bette Howard. (Audelco Award)
Short Change, Samuel Beckett Theatre, NYC, Fred Kolo.
Rommel's Garden, The Harold Clurman Theatre, NYC, Jack Garfein.
Ceremonies in Dark Old Men, Negro Ensemble Company, Douglas Turner Ward.

1986

A Map of the World, Center Stage, Stanley Wojewodski, Jr.
The War Party, Negro Ensemble Company, Douglas Turner Ward.
Time Out of Time, New Federal Theatre, Al Freeman, Jr.
De Obeah Mon, The Actors Studio, NYC, Alba Ohms.
Horn of Plenty, NBC/Saturday Night Live (video), Spike Lee.
No Place to Be Somebody, Hunter College, Dean Irby.
NEC: The First 20 Years, RKB Productions (television), Nick Hutak and Douglas Turner Ward.
Wasted, WPA Theatre, Clinton Turner Davis.
Jonah and the Wonder Dog, Negro Ensemble Company, Douglas Turner Ward and Kevin Hooks.
Black Girl, The Second Stage, Glenda Dickerson.
The Mighty Gents, The Repertory Theatre of St. Louis, Hal Scott.
The Tale of Madame Zora, The Ensemble Studio Theatre, Glenda Dickerson.
Home Street Home, New Federal Theatre, Liz Diamond.
Life Like the Rest, Judith Anderson Theater, NYC, Dean Irby.

1987

Da-Butt (music video), Spike Lee.
A Tribute to Harry Chapin, Carnegie Hall, NYC, Joe Cates.

That Serious He-Man Ball, The American Place Theatre, Clinton Turner Davis.

Moonchildren, The Second Stage, Mary B. Robinson.

Sherlock Holmes and the Hands of Othello, Westbeth Theatre Center, NYC, Gregg Frelon.

Haitian Corner (film), Raoul Peck.

Visit to the Veldt, Amistad Theatre, NYC, Clinton Turner Davis.

Boogie Woogie and Booker T., New Federal Theatre, Dean Irby. (Audelco Award)

A Matter of Conscience, National Black Theatre, Seret Scott.

The Tenant, National Black Theatre, Glenda Dickerson.

The Legacy, National Black Theatre, Terry Morgan.

Resident designer, Eugene O'Neill Theater Center (film department).

1988

Momma's Little Boys, National Black Theatre, Roderick Giles.

Return of the Beentoo, The Door, NYC, Fred Rolf.

Christchild, Rites and Reasons (Brown University), George Bass.

Buck Wild (music video), Spike Lee.

Philip Morris' "Super Band Series," Town Hall Theatre, NYC.

Curves, Circle Repertory Company, Michael Warren Powell.

Splendid Mummer, The American Place Theatre, Woodie King, Jr.

West Memphis Mojo, Negro Ensemble Company, Rick Kahn.

Wet Carpets, Crossroads Theatre Company, Bette Howard.

Lady Day at Emerson's Bar and Grill, Crossroads Theatre Company, Bette Howard.

1989

We, Negro Ensemble Company, Douglas Turner Ward.

The Rabbit Foot, Crossroads Theatre Company, Walter Dallas.

The Talented Tenth, Manhattan Theatre Club, M. Neema Barnette.

Mo' Better Blues (assistant art director; film), Spike Lee.

Black Eagles, Crossroads Theatre Company, Rick Kahn.

Further Mo', Crossroads Theatre Company, Rick Kahn.

Joe Turner's Come and Gone, Studio Arena Theatre, Ed Smith.

Resident designer, Eugene O'Neill Theater Center (film department).

1990

Further Mo', Village Gate, NYC, Vernel Bagerlis.

Ground People, The American Place Theatre, Walter Dallas.

Fences, StageWest, Clinton Turner Davis.

A Doll House, Actors Outlet, NYC, Bryan Delate.

Jazz Thing (music video), Spike Lee.

Harlem Blues (music video), Spike Lee.

Nike/Air Jordan (commercial), Spike Lee.

The Colored Museum, Gilpin Players, Brad Boynton.

Sheila's Day, Crossroads Theatre Company, Mbongeni Ngema.

Hangin' Out with the Home Boys (film), Joe Vasquez.

Resident designer, Eugene O'Neill Theater Center (TV projects).

MICHAEL MERRITT

1973

A Doll's House, Old Town Players, Chicago, Frank Cariotti. (Charles MacArthur Award)

The Lady's Not for Burning (S & L), Old Town Players, Chicago, Frank Cariotti.

1975

All I Want, Victory Gardens, Bruce Hickey. (Joseph Jefferson Award)

A Midsummer Night's Dream (S & L), Oak Park Theater Festival, Chicago, Steven Schachter.

1976

Romeo and Juliet, Oak Park Theater Festival, Chicago, Dennis Zacek.

1977

The Madwoman of Chaillot, Old Town Players, Chicago, Patrick O'Gara. (Joseph Jefferson Citation)

1978

Curse of the Starving Class, Goodman II, Robert Falls.

American Buffalo, Goodman Theatre, Gregory Mosher.

1979

Hail Scrawdyke!, Goodman II, Michael Maggio.

1980

Wings (lighting only), The Wisdom Bridge Theatre, Robert Falls. (Joseph Jefferson Award)

The Crucible, The Wisdom Bridge Theatre, Patrick O'Gara.

The Suicide, Goodman Theatre, Gregory Mosher.

A Life in the Theatre, Goodman Theatre, Gregory Mosher.

1981

Mother Courage (S, C & L), The Wisdom Bridge Theatre, Robert Falls. (Joseph Jefferson Award)

1982

Translations, Body Politic Theatre, James D. O'Reilly.

Rear Column (S, C & L), Northlight Theatre, John Malkovich.

Lakeboat, Goodman Theatre, Gregory Mosher. (Joseph Jefferson Award)

American Gothic, Columbia College, Paul Carter Harrison.

Ladies in Waiting, Civic Theater, Chicago, Michael Maggio.

Othello (S & L), Oak Park Festival Theater, Chicago, Robert Falls.

Filthy Rich, Northlight Theatre, Robert Woodruff.

1983

Glengarry Glen Ross, Goodman Theatre, Gregory Mosher.

Love Life, Columbia Theater Project (Columbia College), Stuart Oken.

City on the Make, Northlight Theatre, Michael
  Maggio.
The Elephant Man, Arizona Theatre Company,
  Michael Maggio.
On the Road to Babylon, Milwaukee Repertory
  Theater, Garland Wright.
Bagtime (S & L), The Wisdom Bridge Theatre, Robert
  Falls.
Travesties, The Wisdom Bridge Theatre, Michael
  Maggio.

1984
The Philanthropist, Court Theatre, Nicholas Rudall.
The Cherry Orchard, Goodman Theatre, Gregory
  Mosher.
The Misanthrope, Court Theatre, Munson Hicks.
Annie, Candlelight Theater, Chicago, Bill Pulinski.
Glengarry Glen Ross, John Golden Theatre, NYC,
  Gregory Mosher.
The Price, Northlight Theatre, Sheldon Patinkin.
Wenceslas Square, Columbia Theater Project
  (Columbia College), Stuart Oken.
The Importance of Being Earnest, The Wisdom Bridge
  Theatre, Robert Falls.
Spokesong, Woodstock Opera House, Michael Maggio.

1985
The Madwoman of Chaillot, Body Politic Theatre,
  James D. O'Reilly and Sheldon Patinkin.
The Art of Dining, Milwaukee Repertory Theater,
  Dilys Hamlett.
The Women, Columbia College, Jane Salhins and Joyce
  Sloan.
Hamlet (S, C & L), The Wisdom Bridge Theatre,
  Robert Falls. (Joseph Jefferson Award)
The Shawl/Spanish Prisoner, Goodman Theatre/New
  Theater Company, Gregory Mosher.
Glengarry Glen Ross (national tour), Gregory Mosher.
  (Los Angeles Critics Circle Award)
Ladies in Waiting, Woodstock Opera House, Michael
  Maggio.

1986
Hay Fever, Milwaukee Repertory Theater, Dilys
  Hamlett.

The Government Inspector, Goodman Theatre, Frank
  Galati. (Joseph Jefferson Award)
The House of Games (film), David Mamet.
Gardenia, Columbia College, Sheldon Patinkin.
Mostly Mamet, Lincoln Center Theater, Gregory
  Mosher.
Hamlet, Civic Theater, Chicago, Robert Falls.

1987
Things Change (film), David Mamet.
Troilus and Cressida, Shakespeare Repertory, Barbara
  Gaines.
War and Peace, Columbia College, Randall Arney and
  Tom Irwin.
Danger Memory, Lincoln Center Theater, Gregory
  Mosher.

1988
After the Fall, National Jewish Theater, Chicago,
  Sheldon Patinkin.
Macbeth, Piven Workshop, Chicago, Byrne Piven.
Romeo and Juliet, Goodman Theatre, Michael Maggio.
Speed-the-Plow, Lincoln Center Theater (Royale
  Theater, NYC), Gregory Mosher.
The Taming of the Shrew, Columbia College, Sheldon
  Patinkin.

1989
Making the Case for Murder (film), Richard Lowry.
Speed-the-Plow, The National Theater of Great Britain,
  London, Gregory Mosher.
Cymbeline (S & C), Shakespeare Repertory, Barbara
  Gaines.
A Mother's Courage: The Mary Thomas Story (film),
  John Anderson.
I'm Not Rappaport, Briar Street Theatre, Chicago,
  Sheldon Patinkin.
84 Charing Cross Road, Northlight Theatre, Russell
  Vandenbroucke.

1990
Shirley Valentine, Wellington Theatre, Chicago, Jeff
  Lee.
Wrong Turn at the Lungfish, Steppenwolf Theatre
  Company, Garry Marshall and Lowell Ganz.
Brewster Place, Hearst Entertainment (television).

Homicide (film), David Mamet.
King John, Shakespeare Repertory, Barbara Gaines.
Much Ado About Nothing, Shakespeare Repertory,
  Barbara Gaines.

TONY STRAIGES

1968
Resident set and costume designer, American Puppet
  Theatre, Washington, D.C.

1969
La Bohème, San Francisco Opera Summer Festival,
  Matthew Farruggio.
Rigoletto, San Francisco Opera Summer Festival,
  Matthew Farruggio.

1970
Man on the Moon (S & C), San Francisco Opera
  Summer Festival, Dennis Rosa.

1971
Exit the King, Brooklyn College.
*Oh Dad, Poor Dad, Mama's Hung You in the Closet
  and I'm Feeling So Sad*, Brooklyn College, Susan
  Einhorn.

1972
Ariadne auf Naxos, Brooklyn College.
The Rose Tattoo, The Juilliard School of Drama, Gene
  Lesser.

1973
Women Beware Women, Yale School of Drama, Tom
  Haas.
The Lower Depths (costumes only), Yale School of
  Drama.
How Music Came to Earth (costumes only), Yale
  School of Drama.

1974
The Rise and Fall of the City Mahagonny, Yale
  Repertory Theatre, Alvin Epstein.

Schlemiel the First (costumes only), Yale Repertory
    Theatre, Isaiah Sheffer.
Victory, Yale Repertory Theatre, Alvin Epstein.

1975

A Midsummer Night's Dream, Yale Repertory Theatre,
    Alvin Epstein.
Enemies, Williamstown Theatre Festival, Nikos
    Psacharopoulos.
Ring Round the Moon, Williamstown Theatre Festival,
    Nikos Psacharopoulos.

1976

Children, Virginia Museum Theatre, Keith Fowler.
The Physicists, McCarter Theatre Company, Gene
    Lesser.
The Three Sisters, Williamstown Theatre Festival,
    Nikos Psacharopoulos.
Troilus and Cressida, Yale Repertory Theatre, Alvin
    Epstein.
Don Juan (costumes only), Yale Repertory Theatre,
    Robert Brustein.

1977

Julius Caesar, Yale Repertory Theatre, Alvin Epstein.
Streamers, Arena Stage, David Chambers.
A History of the American Film, Arena Stage, David
    Chambers.
Timbuktu!, Martin Beck Theatre, NYC, Geoffrey
    Holder.

1978

Comedians, Arena Stage, David Chambers.
The Beggar's Opera, The Guthrie Theater, Alvin
    Epstein.
Gertrude Stein, Gertrude Stein, Gertrude Stein,
    Circle Repertory Company, Milton Moss.
A History of the American Film, Virginia Theatre,
    NYC, David Chambers.
John Curry's Ice Dancing, Minskoff Theatre, NYC,
    choreographed by John Curry.

1979

Tales from the Vienna Woods, Yale Repertory Theatre,
    Keith Hack.

The Winter's Tale, Arena Stage, David Chambers.
Romeo and Juliet, The Guthrie Theater, Ron Daniels.
Don Juan Comes Back from the War, Manhattan
    Theatre Club, Stephen Pascal.
Richard III, Cort Theatre, NYC, David Wheeler.
Idiot's Delight, Arena Stage, Edward Cornell.

1980

Galileo, Arena Stage, Martin Fried.
An American Tragedy, Arena Stage, Michael Lessac.
A Lesson from Aloes, Arena Stage, Douglas C. Wager.
A Lesson from Aloes, Center Stage, Jackson Phippin.
A Midsummer Night's Dream, American Repertory
    Theatre, Alvin Epstein.
Vikings, Manhattan Theatre Club, George Meade.
Harold and Maude, Martin Beck Theatre, NYC, Bobby
    Lewis.

1981

Ghosts, American Repertory Theatre, Robert Brustein.
    (Boston Theatre Critics Circle Award)
Terra Nova, Sante Fe Festival Theatre, Travis Preston.
No End of Blame, Manhattan Theatre Club, Walton
    Jones.
Copperfield, Virginia Theatre, NYC, Rob Iscove.
The Suicide, Arena Stage, Gene Lesser.
Major Barbara, Arena Stage, Martin Fried.

1982

Love's Labor's Lost, Yale Repertory Theatre, Mladen
    Kiselov.
Tennessee Williams: A Celebration, Williamstown
    Theatre Festival, Nikos Psacharopoulos.
On the Razzle, Arena Stage, Douglas C. Wager.
Savages, Center Stage, Jackson Phippin.
Waiting for Godot, American Repertory Theatre,
    Andrei Belgrader.
The Great Magoo, Hartford Stage Company, Mark
    Lamos.
Talking With, Manhattan Theatre Club, Jon Jory.

1983

Buried Child, Arena Stage, Gilbert Moses.
The Importance of Being Earnest, Arena Stage,
    Richard Russell Ramos.

Geniuses, Arena Stage, Gary Pearle.
Our Town, Center Stage, Jackson Phippin.
The Chain, The Hartman Theatre, Elia Kazan.
Summer, Manhattan Theatre Club, Douglas Hughes.
On the Swing Shift, Manhattan Theatre Club, David
    Chambers.
Sunday in the Park with George, Playwrights
    Horizons, James Lapine.

1984

On the Verge or The Geography of Yearning, Center
    Stage, Jackson Phippin.
Diamonds, Circle in the Square Downtown, NYC, Hal
    Prince. (New York Outer Critics Circle Award)
Sunday in the Park with George, Booth Theatre, NYC,
    James Lapine. (Tony Award and Joseph Maharam
    Foundation Award)
Messiah, Manhattan Theatre Club, David Leveaux.

1985

Women and Water, Arena Stage, Douglas C. Wager.
Fighting International Fat, Playwrights Horizons,
    David Trainer.
Follies (concert version), New York Philharmonic, Herb
    Ross.

1986

Into the Woods, Old Globe Theatre, James Lapine.
Coastal Disturbances, The Second Stage, Carole
    Rothman.
Long Day's Journey into Night, Royal Haymarket
    Theatre, London, Jonathan Miller.
Long Day's Journey into Night, Broadhurst Theatre,
    NYC, Jonathan Miller.

1987

Into the Woods, Martin Beck Theatre, NYC, James
    Lapine.

1988

Rumors, Broadhurst Theatre, NYC, Gene Saks.
Into the Woods (national tour), James Lapine.

1989

Two-a-Day, Joffrey Ballet, choreographed by Gerald Arpino.

Dangerous Games, Nederlander Theatre, NYC, Graciela Daniele.

Mandy Patinkin in Concert: Dress Casual, Helen Hayes Theatre, NYC, Mandy Patinkin.

Artist Descending a Staircase, Helen Hayes Theatre, NYC, Tim Luscombe.

1990

Coppelia, American Ballet Theatre, choreographed by Enrique Martinez.

Jake's Women, Old Globe Theatre, Jack O'Brien.

GEORGE TSYPIN

1984

The Power and the Glory, Philadelphia Drama Guild, William Woodman.

1985

The Count of Monte Cristo, American National Theater, Peter Sellars.

A Seagull, American National Theater, Peter Sellars.

1986

Suor Angelica, Opera Company of Philadelphia, Roman Terleckyj.

The Balcony, American Repertory Theatre, JoAnne Akalaitis.

Idiot's Delight, American National Theater, Peter Sellars.

Ajax, American National Theater, Peter Sellars.

Ajax; Theatre Royale de La Monnaie (Brussels), Holland Festival, Vienna Festival, World Theatre Festival (Stuttgart); Peter Sellars.

Measure for Measure, Arena Stage, Douglas C. Wager.

Galileo, Goodman Theatre, Robert Falls.

Death in Venice, Opera Company of Philadelphia, Gray Veredon.

Zangezi: A Supersaga in Twenty Planes

(S & C), Museum of Contemporary Art, Los Angeles, Peter Sellars.

Zangezi: A Supersaga in Twenty Planes (S & C), Brooklyn Academy of Music, Peter Sellars.

1987

Don Giovanni, PepsiCo Summerfare, Purchase, NY, Peter Sellars.

Leon and Lena, The Guthrie Theater, JoAnne Akalaitis.

The Electrification of the Soviet Union, Glyndebourne Opera Festival, England, Peter Sellars.

1988

Landscape of the Body, Goodman Theatre, Robert Falls.

Tannhäuser, Chicago Lyric Opera, Peter Sellars.

1989

Don Giovanni, ORF Media Scope and WNET/TV, Peter Sellars.

The Screens, The Guthrie Theater, JoAnne Akalaitis.

The Misanthrope, La Jolla Playhouse, Robert Falls.

The Misanthrope, Goodman Theatre, Robert Falls.

Cymbeline, New York Shakespeare Festival, JoAnne Akalaitis.

Nothing Sacred, American Conservatory Theatre, Robert Woodruff. (Bay Outer Area Critics Award)

1990

OBIE Award (sustained excellence).

MICHAEL YEARGAN

An asterisk (*) indicates production was designed in collaboration with Lawrence King.

1968

My Fair Lady, Florida Summer Theatre, Bruce Griffiths.

1969

Summer Stock, Florida Summer Theatre, Bruce Griffiths.

1970

La Bohème*, Nevada Opera Company, Ted Puffer.

1971

Woyzeck, Yale Repertory Theatre, Tom Haas.

Tosca*, Nevada Opera Company, Ted Puffer.

1972

Tosca (S & C), produced by Laszlo Halasz and R. Tucker, Michael Posnick.

Happy End (costumes only), Yale Repertory Theatre, Michael Posnick.

Of Mice and Men (S, C & L), Yale at Norfolk, James Crabtree.

A Break in the Skin, Yale Repertory Theatre, Arthur Sherman.

1973

Operation Sidewinder, Boston University, Pirie McDonald.

The Tempest (S & C), Yale Repertory Theatre, Alvin Epstein.

Darkroom, Yale Repertory Theatre, Michael Posnick.

The Tubs, Yale Repertory Theatre, Anthony Holland.

1974

Schlemiel the First, Yale Repertory Theatre, Isaiah Sheffer.

The Frogs, Yale Repertory Theatre, Burt Shevelove.

Dido and Aeneas/L'Heure Espagnole*, Boston Conservatory.

Bad Habits* (S & C), Astor Place Theatre and Booth Theatre, NYC, Robert Drivas.

1975

The Idiots Karamazov, Yale Repertory Theatre, William Peters.

Happy End (S & C), Yale Repertory Theatre, Michael Posnick.

The Father, Yale Repertory Theatre, Jeff Bleckner.

The Ritz*, Longacre Theatre, NYC, Robert Drivas.

The Mikado*, Music Theatre of Wichita, James Lucas.

The Student Prince*, Music Theatre of Wichita, Audrey Needles.

1976

Don Juan, Yale Repertory Theatre, Robert Brustein.

Walk the Dog, Willie (S & C), Yale Repertory Theatre, Walton Jones.

Troilus and Cressida (costumes only), Yale Repertory Theatre, Alvin Epstein.

South Pacific*, Music Theatre of Wichita, Carveth Wilson.

A Streetcar Named Desire*, McCarter Theatre Company, Michael Kahn.

By Bernstein* (S & C), Chelsea Theatre Center, NYC, Michael Bawtree.

Suicide in B-Flat, Yale Repertory Theatre, Walton Jones.

Ivanov, Yale Repertory Theatre, Ron Daniels.

1977

Brigadoon*, Music Theatre of Wichita, Audrey Needles.

The Durango Flash, Yale Repertory Theatre, Kenneth Frankel.

Something Old, Something New* (S & C), Morosco Theatre, NYC, Robert Livingston.

A Month in the Country*, McCarter Theatre Company, Michael Kahn.

A Month in the Country*, Roundabout Theatre, NYC, Michael Kahn.

The Ghost Sonata, Yale Repertory Theatre, Andrei Serban.

1978

Sganarelle: An Evening of Molière Farces, Yale Repertory Theatre, Andrei Serban.

The Wild Duck, Yale Repertory Theatre, Robert Brustein.

The Umbrellas of Cherbourg, New York Shakespeare Festival, Andrei Serban.

Lucia di Lammermoor*, Santa Fe Opera, Lotfi Mansouri.

'dentity Crisis, Yale Repertory Theatre, Frank Torok.

The Rise and Fall of the City Mahagonny, Yale Repertory Theatre, Keith Hack.

1979

The Seagull, Yale Repertory Theatre, Robert Brustein.

Put Them All Together*, McCarter Theatre Company, Michael Kahn.

The Night of the Tribades*, McCarter Theatre Company, Michael Kahn.

The Night of the Tribades*, Helen Hayes Theatre, NYC, Michael Kahn.

Me Jack, You Jill* (S & C), Harold J. Kennedy.

Happy Days*, New York Shakespeare Festival, Andrei Serban.

1980

The Seagull, New York Shakespeare Festival, Andrei Serban.

Eugene Onegin (S & C), Welsh National Opera, Andrei Serban.

The Umbrellas of Cherbourg, Phoenix Theatre, London, Andrei Serban.

The Magic Flute, Nancy, France, Andrei Serban.

Timon of Athens, Yale Repertory Theatre, Lloyd Richards.

Happy End, American Repertory Theatre, Lloyd Richards.

An Attempt at Flying, Yale Repertory Theatre, Mladen Kiselove.

1981

Has 'Washington' Legs?, American Repertory Theatre, Michael Kustow.

Uncle Vanya, Yale Repertory Theatre, Lloyd Richards.

The Resurrection of Lady Lester, Yale Repertory Theatre, James Simpson.

Heartbreak House, The Guthrie Theater, Christopher Markle.

Rodelinda (S & C), Welsh National Opera, Andrei Serban.

Cheaters*, Lunt-Fontanne Theatre, NYC, Robert Drivas.

Resident designer, Eugene O'Neill Theater Center.

1982

The Resurrection of Lady Lester, CBS Cable (television).

Playing in Local Bands, Yale Repertory Theatre, William Ludel.

Portrait of Jenny, New Federal Theatre, Dennis Rosa.

I Puritani (S & C), Welsh National Opera, Andrei Serban.

Tartuffe, The Acting Company, Brian Murray.

A Lesson from Aloes, Yale Repertory Theatre, Athol Fugard.

A Lesson from Aloes, Playhouse Theatre, NYC, Athol Fugard.

1983

Major Barbara, Yale Repertory Theatre, Lloyd Richards.

Astapovo, Yale Repertory Theatre, Lawrence Kornfeld.

Il trovatore (S & C), Opera North, Leeds, England, Andrei Serban.

The Lady and the Clarinet, Long Wharf Theatre, Gordon Davidson.

As You Like It, Hartford Stage Company, Mark Lamos.

Drama of Aida (S & C), Welsh National Opera, Andrei Serban.

Becoming Memories, Dennis Rosa.

Pal Joey, Indiana Repertory Theatre, Tom Haas.

1984

The Tempest, Hartford Stage Company, Mark Lamos.

Six Characters in Search of an Author, (S & C), American Repertory Theatre, Robert Brustein.

The Merry Widow, Welsh National Opera, Andrei Serban.

La Bohème (S & C), Welsh National Opera, Gördon Jarvafelt.

The King Stag, American Repertory Theatre, Andrei Serban.

The Homesteaders, Long Wharf Theatre, John Pasquin.

War Babies, La Jolla Playhouse, James Simpson.

The Man Who Came to Dinner, Indiana Repertory Theatre, Tom Haas.

It Had to Be You*, Robert Drivas.

1985

Tobacco Road, Long Wharf Theatre, Arvin Brown.

Stitchers and Starlight Talkers, Yale Repertory Theatre, William Partlan.

Twelfth Night, Hartford Stage Company, Mark Lamos.

Norma (S & C), Welsh National Opera, Andrei Serban.

Hay Fever, Music Box, NYC, Brian Murray.

Norma (S & C), New York City Opera, Andrei Serban.

The Changeling, American Repertory Theatre, Robert Brustein.

The Juniper Tree, American Repertory Theatre, Andrei Serban.

1986

The School for Wives, Center Stage, Irene Lewis.

Tonight We Improvise (S & C), American Repertory Theatre, Robert Brustein.

Carousel, The Kennedy Center, Washington, D.C., James Hammerstein.

End of the World with Symposium to Follow, American Repertory Theatre, Richard Foreman.

The Winter's Tale, Yale Repertory Theatre, Gitta Honegger.

Albert Herring, Long Wharf Theatre, Arvin Brown.

Lost in the Stars, Long Wharf Theatre, Arvin Brown.

1987

Carmen (S & C), Scottish Opera, Graham Vick.

Uncle Vanya (S & C), Center Stage, Irene Lewis.

Morocco (S & C), Hartford Stage Company, Mark Lamos.

The Stick Wife (S & C), Hartford Stage Company, Roberta Levitow.

The Matchmaker, La Jolla Playhouse, Des McAnuff.

Così fan tutte (S & C), Frankfurt Opera, Graham Vick.

Right You Are (If You Think You Are), American Repertory Theatre, Robert Brustein.

Our Town, Long Wharf Theatre, Arvin Brown.

The Tender Land, Long Wharf Theatre, Arvin Brown.

1988

Macbeth, The Shakespeare Theatre at the Folger, Michael Kahn.

Ah, Wilderness!, Yale Repertory Theatre, Arvin Brown.

Ah, Wilderness!, Morosco Theatre, NYC, Arvin Brown.

La Bohème, Scottish Opera, Elijah Moshinsky.

Regina, Long Wharf Theatre, Arvin Brown.

Kiss of the Spider Woman, Yale Repertory Theatre, David Chambers.

A Midsummer Night's Dream, Hartford Stage Company, Mark Lamos.

National Anthems, Long Wharf Theatre, Arvin Brown.

The Paper Gramophone, Hartford Stage Company, Yuri Yeremin.

1989

Werther, Australian Opera, Elijah Moshinsky.

Anna Bolena, Virginia Opera, Arvin Brown.

Ghosts, Portland Stage Company, Mel Marvin.

Nothing Sacred, Hartford Stage Company, James Simpson.

Playboy of the West Indies, Yale Repertory Theatre, Dennis Scott.

Some Sweet Day, Long Wharf Theatre, Seret Scott.

The Importance of Being Earnest, Hartford Stage Company, Mark Lamos.

Miss Julie, Yale Repertory Theatre, Dennis Scott.

The Crucible, Long Wharf Theatre, Arvin Brown.

1990

La forza del destino, Scottish Opera, Elijah Moshinsky.

Pygmalion, Yale Repertory Theatre, Douglas C. Wager.

Carousel, Houston Grand Opera, Gerald Gutierrez.

Attila (S & C), Royal Opera House, Covent Garden, London, Elijah Moshinsky.